The Polish Relatives of The Red Baron

Discovering the Forgotten Line of the von Richthofen Family

Ivona Tarko

ISBN: 978-0692846933
ISBN-13: 069284693X

To my children...
Adam and Natalia

Table of Contents

Table of Contents

Foreword

In this book the author chronicles the history of a German-Polish family covering seven generations over two centuries. The Polish nation's fate, division, resistance, world wars, occupation and oppression, and flight and exile imposed by its neighboring countries are the backdrop of this epic family history.

After Poland won its freedom and independence within Europe, the author sought her heritage roots, which she found in the Polish and German nobility.

The marriage of a member of the German family of the Barons v. Richthofen to a Polish lady of the Objezierski family founded a new branch of the Richthofens in Poland, which joined great Polish families in the course of its history. The pros and cons of German origin and patriotic attachment to Poland is a major topic of this family saga.

Extensive archival research and assessment of the carefully collected and archived family documents allowed the author to draw a family portrait of great authenticity and tangibility for the reader. With empathetic understanding of the strengths and weaknesses, successes and failures, and happiness and suffering of her ancestors, she entrusts the reader her family's history.

Stanislaus v. Richthofen is a classic example of the turbulent life between the nations of the author's family. Stanislaus was born in Kraków but was educated and influenced by the Cadet School of Wahlstatt and became a Prussian Major. He retired from his Prussian military career to protest against the German ban on children praying in the Polish language and lived thereafter a fulfilling life in Kraków. In 1945 he was expelled from Poland by the Communists and died later in Berlin.

The fate of Stanislaus unfortunately was not an isolated happening and was a reminder of another such person during the desperate uprising in Poland in 1830. The Poet August Count von Platen Hallermund – his family nowadays related to the family v. Richthofen - was highly committed to Poland and Polish emigrants after the uprising which is documented in his passionate, freedom-inspired Polish songs:

Wir ziehn von Weib und Kindern,   *We draw from wife and children*
Vermögen nicht zu hinder   *assets not to hinder*
Des Vaterlands Ruin.   *the father's homeland ruin*
Schon lechzt nach unserem Blute   *Already thirsting for our blood*
Die Petersburger Knute,   *The whip of Petersburg*
Die Fuchtel von Berlin.   *The rod of Berlin.*

(Aus: Nächtlicher Weichsel-Uebergang der flüchtigen Polen bei Krakau)

During a v. Richthofen family reunion, the author met for the first time the German extended family with whom she shares ancestors and encountered openess, tolerance, and curiosity. The free and modern Europe made understanding and reconciliation between the different nations possible.

For the whole family of the Barons v. Richthofen, this chronicle is a precious complement to its family history.

Karl-Friedrich v. Richthofen
Königsbrück, Summer 2016

Introduction

We write to heal our pain, to be useful to others, to remind those who would come after us what had happened ~ Leon Potocki

I felt the first spark of interest in my family history as a child when I learned that my Polish grandmother Antonina was the daughter of a baron and bore a German maiden name. Her parents were Bolesław von Richthofen and Bronisława Sędzimir, the family coat of arms Ostoja. But the young person I was then saw no significance in the von Richthofen surname nor that my grandmother's cousin was the famous World War I pilot, Manfred Freiherr von Richthofen aka the Red Baron. I was only puzzled by the German surname in our Polish family and that it belonged to noblemen.

Actually, this discovery of a German among my ancestors led me to doubt my Polish identity so I turned to my trusted family authority, my mother, to explain this confusing fact. She explained to me that we all are Poles. The German surname in our family line came about in the 19th century when Marynia Wielogłowska, my great-great-grandmother, married Henryk von Richthofen. It was difficult for me to fathom a family event that took place more than one hundred years ago. Frankly, I just knew it had to be a myth or family legend because it was impossible in the 1960s, only 20 years after World War II, when painful memories of the German occupation of Poland still haunted the generations of my parents and grandparents. I was attending a public school at the time in the Polish People's Republic, then under Communist rule, so I naturally thought that anything German must be connected to World War II and feared that telling anyone about our German family roots might expose my entire family to social ostracism. Still, it was an exciting departure from the harsh reality of my gloomy childhood in Communist Poland to ponder the fairy tale ideal of the distant past from the many stories my grandmother told me about my noble Polish and German ancestors.

3

It took me years to fully understand the consequences of the marriage between a German aristocrat and a Polish lady and to comprehend the events leading to Polonizing an entire branch of the von Richthofen family. In the 19th century, both families – the Wielogłowski on Polish land and the Richthofens in Germany – were strongly engaged in the politics and economic development of their countries. They were a part of the history of the region where they lived and contributed to its development by their work, diplomatic and military service, philanthropy, innovation, and pivotal involvement in establishing schools and public institutions. It still intrigues me to this day how it was even possible that the members of two families so different in their political views, interests, and even religious beliefs, could unite.

The Kraków line of the von Richthofen family was established in 1852 when Maria, the only daughter of Polish patriot Walery Wielogłowski, married Heinrich Freiherr von Richthofen. When my grandmother and mother talked about Maria, they always referred to her by her maiden name Wielogłowska. It seems that their memories of Maria as Baroness von Richthofen, the title she bore for 35 years, from her wedding day until her death, had faded in my family. I had so many questions that I wanted to answer. How did Maria and Heinrich meet? Why did they decide to marry? As their descendant and a historian by choice and education, as time went on, I started looking for an explanation in all the information I could find. After discovering a great deal about Maria and Heinrich, I continued studying the lives of their children and grandchildren, who lived in Kraków during the tumultuous years of the 20th century, including the horrors of World War II. I was curious about the impact of the German surname on their lives.

Bolesław and Stanisław von Richthofen from the Royn-Schutzendorf house, who were the sons of Heinrich and Maria, were the last male descendants of the Polish line of the von Richthofen family. Today, the only indications of the presence of the von Richthofen family in Kraków are inscriptions on the family tombs at Rakowice Cemetery. Bolesław was my great-grandfather, and he passed away in Kraków in 1924. His brother, Stanisław, who was 85 years old at the end of World War II, was exposed as a German citizen by Polish authorities in Kraków and was forced to leave the city and Poland in the autumn of 1945. He died in Berlin and was buried there. To my knowledge, nobody broke a sword or a shield with the family crest on his grave as the old Polish custom demanded when the last male descendant of a noble family passed away.

Although his surname was German, I believe that in his heart he remained Polish at the time of his death. I regret that I did not have the opportunity to ask Stanisław von Richthofen about his thoughts and convictions. Now, all that is left of him are his few letters from Germany, written in Polish, to his niece and my grandmother that told of the changes that World War II brought to him and to all those who lived to see the end of the war.

For centuries, the Richthofen family grew in number, power, and privilege in Germany. Today, they have a family web page, which includes essential facts from the family history. One of the most notable members of the family was Ferdinand Freiherr von Richthofen, a famous scientist and researcher of Asia, who coined the term the "Silk Road." Ferdinand was the nephew of my great-great-great-grandfather, Wilhelm Freiherr von Richthofen. The best known member of the von Richthofen family in the 20th century is Manfred Freiherr von Richthofen, aka the Red Baron, the World War I pilot whose courage and exceptional skills made him a legendary figure in the history of aviation. He was born in 1892 in Kleinburg (Borek) in the district of Breslau (Wrocław) in Silesia. Manfred belonged to the same generation as my grandmother who was born in Kraków in 1898.

Although I wrote this account of the Polish line of the von Richthofen family for my children and other family members, I believe that readers outside of my family circle, especially the residents of Silesia, Wielkopolska, and Kraków, whose lands changed hands for centuries, know of the people in my family line because they left a legacy in many places. As nations outside Europe grow more powerful, it is important to focus on what connects us in Europe, which oftentimes is the history of European families.

Thanks to the kindness of Dr. Karl-Friedrich Freiherr von Richthofen, the researcher and custodian of the Richthofen family archives, I had access to German documents that included information about my von Richthofen ancestors, particularly the members of the Royn-Schutzendorf line. Finding these family documents and information enriched my knowledge about our family's roots and provided important facts about my grandmother's ancestors. During this process, I also became aware of the loss of some family documents and of the importance of the ones I had. These documents survived turbulent years thanks to my grandmother who kept them safe.

This book includes stories about the Polish von Richthofen family told to me by my grandmother, mother, and aunt. They are as unique as the never-before published documents and photos from my private archives passed to me by my grandmother, Antonina née Freiin von Richthofen Strzelecka. A large collection of Wielogłowski family documents was given to the Polish Academy of Arts and Sciences (PAU) in Kraków by my great-grandfather Bolesław Freiherr von Richthofen before World War I. Thanks to Bolesław's wise decision, these files still exist and are available to researchers examining the history of 19th century Kraków, the November Uprising of 1830, and the Great Emigration. I accessed these records years ago as a student in the Catholic University of Lublin while writing my thesis about Walery Wielogłowski; and I searched them again years later in my pursuit of answers to my questions about Maria Wielogłowska and Heinrich Freiherr von Richthofen.

Thanks to the modern technology and digitalization of documents, I was able to access the records of various archives available on the Internet. For example, I contacted Teki Dworzaczka from The Kórnik Library of the Polish Academy of Sciences, the Digital Library of Wielkopolska, and the Pradziad database. I credit these and other sources in this book where it is due.

I deeply appreciate my husband, Andrew, for his encouragement and assistance during the process of writing this book.

Ivona Tarko
June 2016

The Polish Line of von Richthofen Family

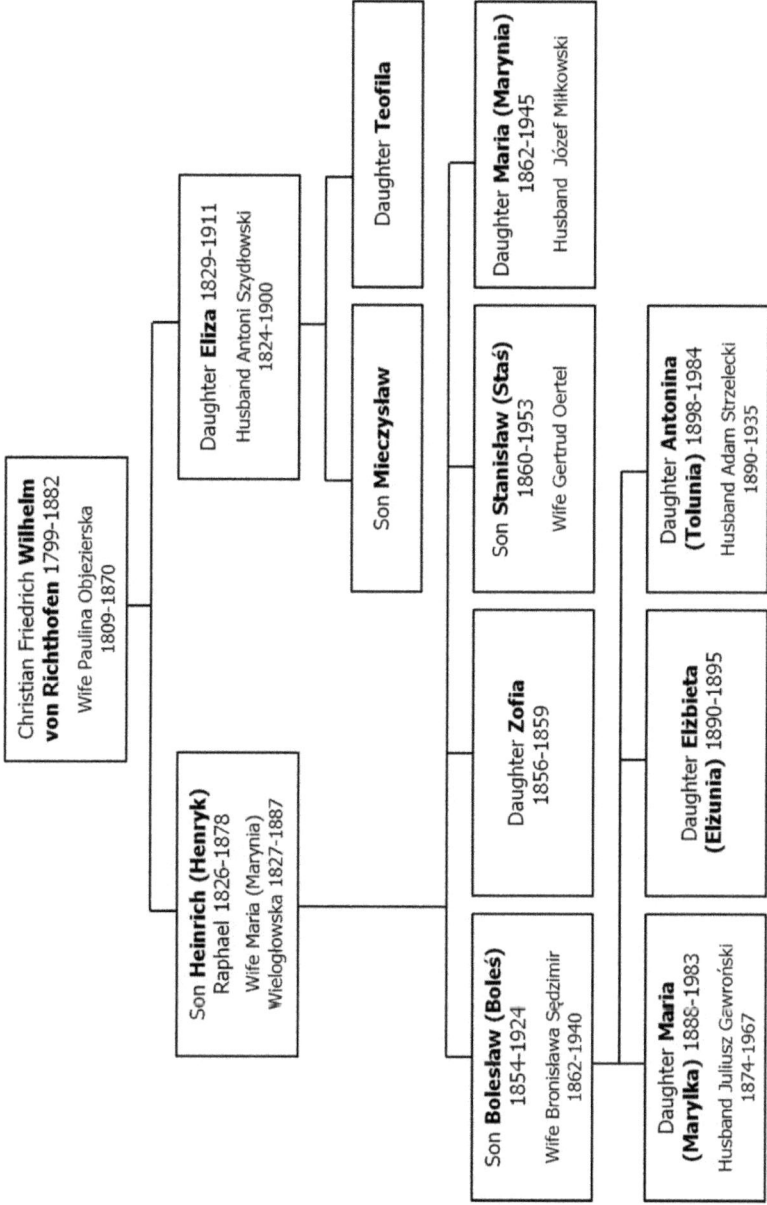

Christian Friedrich **Wilhelm von Richthofen** 1799-1882
Wife Paulina Objezierska 1809-1870

Son **Heinrich (Henryk)** Raphael 1826-1878
Wife Maria (Marynia) Wieloglowska 1827-1887

Daughter **Eliza** 1829-1911
Husband Antoni Szydłowski 1824-1900

Daughter **Teofila**

Son **Mieczysław**

Daughter **Maria (Marynia)** 1862-1945
Husband Józef Miłkowski

Son **Stanisław (Staś)** 1860-1953
Wife Gertrud Oertel

Daughter **Zofia** 1856-1859

Son **Bolesław (Boleś)** 1854-1924
Wife Bronisława Sędzimir 1862-1940

Daughter **Antonina (Tolunia)** 1898-1984
Husband Adam Strzelecki 1890-1935

Daughter **Elżbieta (Elżunia)** 1890-1895

Daughter **Maria (Marylka)** 1888-1983
Husband Juliusz Gawroński 1874-1967

CHAPTER 1 The Beginnings: The Ancestors of Wilhelm Freiherr von Richthofen and His Life Story

How they're all around us, these gentlemen in chamberlain's dress and jabots, like a night growing ever darker around its Order Star, implacably, and these ladies, slight and fragile, yet made large by their dresses. How they're around us all: around the reader, around the peruser of these bibelots, of which several remain their property

~ Rainer Maria Rilke

Curiosity drove me to learn about my ancestors. Before I knew how to find documented information about the marriage of Wilhelm Freiherr von Richthofen and Paulina Objezierska, I had heard only Grandma Antonina's wonderful anecdotal stories about their lives. I looked forward to visiting Grandma and perusing the belongings of my ancestors in her apartment, who came to life in the stories she told about them. One of my favorite discoveries was two large gold ash wardrobes in her bedroom that transformed to "treasure chests" in my young vivid imagination. Many a lively conversation took place when a bibelot from one of the chests piqued my curiosity, like the von Richthofen family seal. I immediately had to know which of my relatives owned the item and how I was related to them. Truth be told, Grandma's whole bedroom was a giant treasure chest. I was enticed every visit by the old books scattered everywhere; the boxes in her nightstand full of old postcards, 19th century prayer books written in French, and an 1868 German calendar; and family-crested photo albums that contained a huge collection of time-worn fragile images of my ancestors. Against one wall was an old black credenza with wine glasses, pieces of old German china, and old glass vases with the monogram PR. Perched on top of one of the wardrobes were a round medallion with the sculpted head of Wilhelm Freiherr von Richthofen and the antlers of an antelope, which according to a family legend, Wilhelm killed on safari in Africa.

As a child I spent many hours among grown-ups and senior citizens not because of a lack of children my age in my house or in my neighborhood, but because I was fascinated with stories about the past. My favorite bedtime stories were books about time travel, and I dreamed of living in the 19th century. Grandma was always eager to share her family stories and always careful to tell stories that were suitable for my young age. Her stories were not only about her relatives and friends, but also about pets and other assorted animals that were part of the family, such as Grandma's beloved terrier, Pikuś, and an unnamed piglet raised by the housekeeper in Paulina Freifrau von Richthofen's palace in Lusowo near Poznań in Wielkopolska. Pikuś appears in the picture of Grandma and her sister that graces the cover of this book. It was taken a few years before World War

I in the Polish mountains in the village of Zakopane. Only 10 years old at the time, Grandma wore a folk vest decorated with embroidery from the Tatra Mountains region, folk style leather Mary Jane shoes, and a Tatra mountaineer's stick with a decorative axe-like handle, and Pikuś is at her right side with his back turned to the camera. In contrast, Grandma's older sister, Marylka Freiin von Richthofen, who was nearly an adult, was dressed in the white lace blouse and long dark skirt that were appropriate fashion for her age at that time.

The sisters were not only physically different - Antonina was a blonde with blue eyes while Marylka was a brunette with dark eyes - but their personalities were different as well. They were the last persons to bear the von Richthofen surname in Poland. At the time this picture was taken, Grandma and her family were enjoying a summer vacation in Zakopane, a mountain resort in Poland, the climate of which was recommended by their physician to strengthen their immune systems. Knowing Grandma had such love for her family and the stories she would tell, I sometimes wonder whether Antonina and Marylka would be happy to know that I wrote this family history.

My ancestors' names and important dates in their lives were available to me from the von Richthofen family tree that my grandmother kept and I inherited; but I learned essential facts about their education, professions, and names of the estates they owned from Karl-Friedrich Freiherr von Richthofen, who made German documents accessible to me. I was able to trace the documented history of the von Richthofen family back to the beginning of the 16th century to Paulus Praetorius (1521-1565), who was born the son of a brewer and the grandson of a city mayor in Bernau, near Berlin. Paulus Praetorius finished law school at the Viadrina University in Frankfurt by the Oder River and became the headmaster of a school in Bernau. Thereafter, he was an advisor to the Archbishop of Magdeburg, a counselor in the diocesan administration, and a representative in the diplomatic missions of Sigismund of Brandenburg. He also was the author of historical works that were printed in Frankfurt by the Oder River. I think it is safe to say that Paulus Praetorius was an influential and prosperous man. In his will he established a foundation to support

11

talented children of poor financial means from his hometown. The foundation continued into the 20th century until it fell prey to severe economic inflation.

Paulus Praetorius' one regret in life was that he did not have a son to succeed him and so decided to adopt the son of his best friend, who passed away at a young age. Officially adopting Samuel Schmidt meant that Paulus was able to pass on to him the Praetorius family coat of arms, received from Emperor Ferdinand the First as a sign of his nobility. The Richthofen family acknowledged Paulus and Samuel Praetorius as their progenitors. Both were Protestants and lawyers. Samuel Praetorius studied law at the Universities of Wittenberg and Viadrina, where he served as dean and syndic of the law department. In his later years he served as a municipal judge and a mayor. I obtained this information about the beginning of the von Richthofen lineage from the website created by the family members *www.richthofen.de*.

At the beginning of the 17th century, the Richthofen family put down roots in Silesia. For centuries this region had different rulers and gradually was losing its independence. As a result of the Silesian Wars in the 17th century, the majority of this land became part of Prussia, and later, the German Imperium. Silesia, a province in Prussia, was divided into three districts: Legnica, Wrocław, and Opole. Samuel's son, Tobias Praetorius, also studied law at Viadrina University; and by marriage he became connected to the Silesian family of Böhm von Böhmfeld. Tobias was appointed the estate manager of Schmiedeberg and became the first member of the family to become a landowner. He purchased property in Silesia, which enabled the next generation of the family to rise to Bohemian knighthood. Tobias' son, Johann Praetorius (1611-1664) was knighted in 1661 and received the "von Richthofen" title. Thereafter, the full family name was announced as "Praetorius von Richthofen."

The Praetorius von Richthofen estate steadily grew over the years with the addition of more land and villages; and the family grew as well. The two sons of Johann Praetorius von Richthofen, Samuel (1656-1721) and Johann (1661-1739)) fathered two main branches of the von Richthofen family tree. The next Samuel (1700-1754) in the family, son of the second Johann, received the Prussian title of baron in 1741.

One of Samuel's sons was my ancestor in a straight line. His name was Carl Ludwig Freiherr von Richthofen (1733-1795) and he was the director of landscaping in the Kingdom of Schweinitz (Świdnica) and Jauer (Jawor), and the headmaster of the Striegau (Strzegom) District in Silesia. He also became a patron of a local church in Gross Rosen (Rogoźnica) after taking over the Gross Rosen estate from his older brother in 1767; and Carl Ludwig von Richthofen founded a timber-framed prayer-house there for local Protestants. Carl married Erdmuthe Edle von Waltmann, and they were blessed with several children, among them sons Wilhelm Ludwig (1761-1838), Carl Andreas Samuel (1762-1836), Andreas Ludwig (1764-1818), and Gottlob Samuel (1769-1808). These sons became the heads of the four main houses and lines of the von Richthofen family in Lower Silesia.

A photo of the portrait of Carl Ludvig Freiherr von Richthofen (1733-1795), director of landscaping in the Kingdom of Schweinitz (Świdnica) and Jauer (Jawor), and the headmaster of the Striegau (Strzegom) District in Silesia the grandfather of Wilhelm Freiherr von Richthofen.[1]

---

[1] Ivona Tarko's archives.

Die Hertwigswaldauer Pastell-Portraits[*]

von Franz Joseph Veronelli (1811)

Christian Benjamin Pertke v. Pertkenau
(1746-1820)

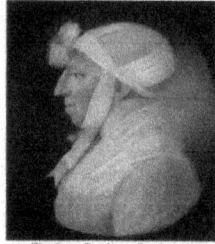

Charlotte Pertke v. Pertkenau,
geb. v. Warnery (1752-1811)

Wilhelm Ludwig Frhr. v. Richthofen
(1761-1838)

Henriette Frfr. v. Richthofen,
geb. Pertke v. Pertkenau (1777-1846)

Wilhelm Frhr. v. Richthofen
(1799-1882)

Karl Frhr. v. Richthofen
(1801-1874)

The family portraits by Joseph Franz Veroneli from 1811. **Left top**: *Christian von Pertkenau, maternal grandfather of Wilhelm and Karl Heinrich Freiherr von Richthofen.* **Left center**: *Wilhelm Ludwig Freiherr von Richthofen, father of Wilhelm and Karl Heinrich Freiherr von Richthofen.* **Left bottom**: *Wilhelm (Christian Friedrich Wilhelm) Freiherr von Richthofen.* **Right top**: *Charlotte von Pertkenau, maternal grandmother of Wilhelm and Karl Heinrich Freiherr von Richthofen.* **Right Center**: *Henriette née Pertkenau Freifrau von Richthofen, mother of Wilhelm and Karl Heinrich.* **Right bottom**: *Karl Heinrich Freiherr von Richthofen.*[2]

---

[2] Courtesy of Dr. Karl-Friedrich Freiherr von Richthofen.

Wilhelm Ludwig (1761-1838) Freiherr von Richthofen,[3] great-grandfather of Bolesław, my great-grandfather, was the founder of the Royn-Schutzendorf house. Wilhelm was not only the owner of several villages: Royn (Ruja), Schützendorf (Strzałkowa), Kummernick (Komorniki), Thiergarten (Zwierzyniec), Reppersdorf (Godziszowa), and Hertwigswaldau (Snowidza) in Lower Silesia, but also was an army officer who had planned a military career. During his military service in Breslau (Wrocław), however, he sustained a serious injury to his right arm in a duel. It seems that the physician who dressed his wound decided, perhaps too hastily, to amputate his right hand, leaving 25-year-old Wilhelm handicapped and no longer able to serve in the army. This story was passed on by our ancestor Emil Freiherr von Richthofen in his book about the family, *Der Familie Praetorius von Richthofen*, published in Magdeburg in 1884. The brother of Wilhelm, Andreas Ludwig (1764-1818) from the house of Gäbersdorf (Polish name Udanin) was the great-great- grandfather of legendary pilot Manfred Freiherr von Richthofen, aka the Red Baron.

Many members of the von Richthofen family were involved in diplomacy or state administration and believed that landlords should strengthen their positions by working as public officials or being present in a monarch court. The marriage of Gottlob Samuel Freiherr von Richthofen (1769-1808) to Friederike, the princess of Schleswig-Sonderburg-Holstein-Beck (1780-1862) linked the von Richthofen family to the royal family of Denmark. In 1863, the nephew of the princess of Schleswig-Sonderburg-Holstein-Beck became the king of Denmark under the name of Christian IX, and was given the nickname of "the father-in-law of Europe," when his descendants became the rulers of Great Britain, Russia, Sweden, Greece, and Hanover. Some of the von Richthofen family members devoted their lives to military service or the sciences, but the majority of them owned land and were in agriculture. Early in the 19th century, 31 villages in the districts of Schweinitz (Świdnica), Jauer (Jawor), Liegnitz (Legnica), and Reichenbach (Dzierzoniów) in Silesia were in the hands

---

[3] W. v. Hueck, Genealogisches Handbuch Der Freiherrlichen Hauser, B Band VII, 1978, p.316-317.

of the von Richthofen family. The most notable von Richthofens in agriculture then were brothers Karl, Ulrich, Bolko, and Ernest, who founded one of the first sugar mills in Lower Silesia. It was the largest sugar mill in this region before World War II and exported its sugar outside Germany. The sugar mill was in operation until Russians soldiers began coming into the region in 1945. They disassembled the mill and took it out of Silesia. Only the living quarters for the mill's laborers were left standing.

The Polish line of the von Richthofen family came to be in the middle of the 19th century when Baron Christian Friedrich Wilhelm Freiherr von Richthofen (1799-1882), son of Wilhelm Ludwig (1761-1838) married Lady Paulina Objezierska (1809-1870) from the Polish family bearing the coat of arms Nałęcz. According to the custom of nobility at that time in history, children received many names when they were born in honor of deceased or living relatives. For example, an ancestor of the Polish line of the von Richthofen family was named Christian in honor of his maternal grandfather Christian Benjamin von Pertkenau, but he did not use it as his first nor his second name. He was always called Wilhelm in our family, like his father, Wilhelm Ludwig Freiherr von Richthofen (1761-1838).

Wilhelm Ludwig Freiherr von Richthofen married Charlotte Ernestine v. Luttwitz (1761-1795) and they had three sons who died in infancy. Charlotte passed away four years after their wedding. Wilhelm married his second wife, Henriette Eleonora von Pertkenau (1777–1846) in 1797, and they had four children. Two of them died in early childhood, and only my great-great-great-grandfather Wilhelm (1799-1882) and his brother Karl Heinrich Ludwig (1801-1874) lived beyond childhood and started their own families.

There was a high rate of infant deaths during the 18th and 19th centuries, and privileged families were not exempt from this tragedy so Wilhelm and his wives were not unique in their painful experience and suffering. Recently I found a birth announcement in my archives announcing the birth of the son of Eduard Freiherr von Richthofen on May 2, 1835. Out of curiosity I asked Karl-Friedrich Freiherr von Richthofen, the archivist of von Richthofen family, about the life story of this child and found that he died in infancy, like two more of the ten other children born to Eduard Freiherr von Richthofen and his wife Amalie from Cammerau (Polish Komorów, the village by Świdnica). Finding the line of the von Richthofens from Cammerau caught my attention because it was connected to Lothar Freiherr von Richthofen, the younger brother of Manfred Freiherr von Richthofen, aka the Red Baron. Knowing this information clarified the family connections between the ancestors of my grandmother and the Red Baron, who lived in the same region.

The father of Manfred Freiherr von Richthofen, aka the Red Baron, and Manfred's two brothers, Lothar and Bolko, was Albrecht Julius Freiherr von Richthofen (1859-1920). Kunigunde Freifrau von Richthofen née von Schickuss und Neudorf (1868-1962) was their mother. Andreas Ludwig Freiherr von Richthofen (1764-1818), the brother of my ancestor Wilhelm Ludwig (1761-1838), was the great-great-grandfather of Manfred, Lothar, and Bolko. I came to the conclusion that the Red Baron and my grandmother Antonina Freiin von Richthofen were in the same generation of children born in the late 1800s and were cousins; and their great-great-grandfathers were brothers who lived during the late 1700s and early 1800s.

Since the main focus of this book is the Polonization of one branch of the von Richthofen family initiated by the marriage of Wilhelm Freiherr von Richthofen to Paulina Objezierska and continued in the lives of their son Heinrich, and Heinrich's descendants, I must talk about Karl Heinrich Freiherr von Richthofen (1801-1874), a German and the brother of my great-great-grandfather. Karl was the father of a few children, but only one of them became famous - his son Ferdinand Freiherr von Richthofen (1833-1905), who was born in Bad Karlsruhe (Pokój) in Silesia. Ferdinand was a renowned geographer, cartographer, traveler and geologist, researcher of China and Japan, and professor at Berlin University. He is credited with naming the well-known route between China and Europe used for transporting merchandise as the "Silk Road." Ferdinand Freiherr von Richthofen is pictured on the home page of the Richthofen family website. His tomb, which was renovated a few years ago thanks to family efforts, is located in Südwestkirchhof Stahndorf near Berlin. In 2012 in the town of Pokój in Poland, where Ferdinand Freiherr von Richthofen was born, a monument was erected to recognize him as its most renowned citizen.

While attending the von Richthofen family reunion in Bamberg, Germany, on September 26, 2014, I learned from the family archivist, Karl-Friedrich Freiherr von Richthofen that I was the closest relative of Ferdinand Freiherr von Richthofen among the family members who were at the reunion. I was surprised and fascinated at the same time and wanted to know more about this ancestor I had somewhat forgotten. I found not only encyclopedic notes about this legendary scholar at Wikipedia and other similar websites, but an article as well that was written in remembrance of Ferdinand Freiherr von Richthofen by another well-known Polish geographer, Eugeniusz Romer. The article was published in 1906 in *Kosmos,* the journal of the Polish Copernicus Society of Naturalists, issued under its editor-in-chief, Professor Bronisław Radziszewski in Lwów, of which I quote an excerpt.

> On October 6, 1905, Professor Ferdynand Richthofen of Berlin University, who was the best disciple of Humbold and Ritter in this renowned school, passed away. If his two noble predecessors are, not without a reason, the fathers of the new geography, Richthofen is the father of morphology, a new and most vital branch of geography. Following in the footsteps of Lyell, the initiator of the new geology, Richthofen created morphology using ontology engineering in rigorous extensive field study. The death of Richthofen is a huge loss for science, but the seeds of his work were extremely fruitful; and his students are working all over the world under his methodology and are an immortal monument to him (Romer, 1906).[4]

I cannot say that I am following Ferdinand's steps in this book, but I was in Shanghai while writing it and visited The Bund, the area of Shanghai

---

[4] E. Romer, Ferdynand Richthofen wspomnienie pośmiertne, 1906, Kosmos, Rok XXXI, p. 21.

connected to Germans, which my cousin Karl Friedrich Freiherr von Richthofen recommended I see because Ferdinand Freiherr von Richthofen spent a lot of time there more than a century ago. I now brag about Ferdinand to my Chinese acquaintances, telling them that my ancestor was responsible for the "Silk Road" name.

Today, when I think about the family resemblances of character, tastes, and talents that are passed in genes, I conclude, that in many ways Ferdinand, nephew of Wilhelm Freiherr von Richthofen (1799-1882) was more similar to Wilhelm than his own son, Heinrich. Wilhelm and Ferdinand had the same passion for travel and were eager to explore the world, while Heinrich liked seclusion and his greatest passion appears to have been music.

The main difference between Wilhelm and Ferdinand Freiherr von Richthofen, though, was the fact that Wilhelm was not a scientist. I like to think that my great-great-grandfather was the typical German nobility and the landlord of Silesia, but the word "typical" seems inappropriate for defining Wilhelm Freiherr von Richthofen. He reflected the virtues important in science like discipline, obedience, obligation, hard work put before recreation, etc., but only to a small extent, based on what I have read and heard about him.

Nobility was considered an obligation, according to Markus Bauer, particularly the skills of writing and reading, understanding the Bible and the directives of faith, and mastery of the seven liberal arts that were expected from nobility. Life in the monarch court, responsible tasks in administration, or service in the justice and military systems required knowledge of history, geography, law, and determined technical science (Bauer, 2014).[5]

Wilhelm, my great-great-great-grandfather was born on November 27, 1799 in his father Wlhelm Ludwig's estate by Frankenthal in the southeast part of Germany. Frankenthal was known for its china factory and advanced silk industry. Our family documents show that Wilhelm's brother, Karl Heinrich Ludwig (1801-1874) was also born there in 1801.

---

[5] M. Bauer, Edukacja i kultura: szlachta na Śląsku i Górnych Łużycach, 2014, p. 130.

19

Wilhelm Freiherr von Richthofen and Paulina née Objezierska Freifrau von Richthofen.[6]

Emil Freiherr von Richthofen, author of the von Richthofen family chronicle, indicated that Wilhelm Ludwig's sheep farm on one of his estates suffered heavy losses in 1801. This loss probably drove his decision to sell three estates in Frankenthal and then buy Hertwigswaldau (Snowidza) in Lower Silesia, where he moved his family. I assume that my ancestors led pretty typical lives as representatives of the noble class at that time in history. They were surrounded by beautiful possessions and enjoyed the comforts given to them and could afford to educate their children and travel as desired. Wilhelm Ludwig (1761-1838), despite the loss of his right hand, played piano and flute and was able to write and even draw. The family portraits of Wilhelm Ludwig, Henriette Freifrau von Richthofen, and their two sons, which were painted in 1811 by Joseph Franz Veronelli from Lipsk, show a strong resemblance between my great-great-great-grandfather, Wilhelm (1799-1882) and his mother.

---

[6] Ivona Tarko's archives.

Henriette Freifrau von Richthofen, at the time her portrait was painted, was 30 years old. Her husband and Wilhelm's father, Wilhelm Ludwig, was close to 50.

Unfortunately, the autobiography of Wilhelm Freiherr von Richthofen (1799-1882) published in 1878 did not survive in the family archives. I learned about its existence, or rather origin, from Karl-Friedrich Freiherr von Richthofen, the family archivist. After years of unsuccessful searching for this book, however, in August 2015, Karl- Friedrich found, by coincidence he said, the second volume of Wilhelm's autobiography in Germany and purchased it for the family archives collection. The autobiography of Wilhelm Freiherr von Richthofen was a source of information about the history of the family for his cousin Emil, who published a book about the von Richthofen family at the end of the 19th century, which I often cite in my text.

Wilhelm Freiherr von Richthofen's autobiography was based on his own diary, which he had been keeping most of his life. I only have one volume of his diary (1817/1818) with Wilhelm's handwritten notes. Wilhelm, only 18 years old at the time, wrote in his diary a few times per week with a pen in tiny, ornamental letters that slanted to the right. There was very little I could distinguish on the yellowed and faded pages written in Gothic German other than some numbers and dates. Karl-Friedrich suggested that I find a student of linguistics in Germany who might be able to decipher Wilhelm's diary entries.

Keeping a diary was a very popular practice in Wilhelm's time. Not only important events and social activities were described there, but the thoughts and feelings of the owner as well. Women often kept albums with diary entries made by those who were close to their hearts. In my family archives, I have a small album that belonged to Wilhelm's mother, Henriette Freifrau von Richthofen, whose maiden name was von Pertkenau. I have mixed feelings when I look at her diary entries because I recognize the names and dates in German that immediately remind me of important events in Poland's history. The year 1794 written below a friend's name in Henriette's album reminds me of the Kościuszko

Resurrection when the Poles attempted to save the independence of the Polish state, which makes me wonder if Henriette, 17 years old at the time, was interested in politics and knew about that event. Most likely, she did not, or knew very little, unless it had a direct impact on her life. Henriette was likely very interested in social gatherings, engagements, and weddings. In 1797, the year when Fredrick III of Prussia became King, Henriette became the wife of widower Wilhelm Ludwig Freiherr von Richthofen. She gave birth to four children; and one of her sons, Wilhelm, was my great-great-great-grandfather.

Wilhelm was a restless being. His parents planned a career for Wilhelm in diplomacy so he studied in universities in Berlin and Heildelberg. Wilhelm's cousin, Emil Freiherr von Richthofen, mentioned in his writings, however, that Wilhelm, since his youth, had loved traveling and frequently interrupted his university studies to travel. It is not documented why Wilhelm did not receive his diploma and did not start a career in diplomacy or administration. His last place of study was the university in Lipsk; and again, according to Cousin Emil, in 1822 Wilhelm left the university to travel to Switzerland and Italy and spent the next two years there. Perhaps I would know much more about this period of Wilhelm's life if I had found his missing diary. After Wilhelm's return from abroad to his Hertwigswaldau (Snowidza) family estate, his parents no longer pressed him for a career in diplomacy, and in 1825 they gave him the Schützendorf (Strzałkowa) estate in Lower Silesia to manage. According to Emil Freiherr von Richthofen's book, Wilhelm lived there alone on the estate; but after only eight days, he realized that he hated living by himself and started looking for a proper young lady with whom to start a family. It was not very long, in the summer of 1825, that he met Paulina Objezierska, who was vacationing in Bad Salzbrunn (Szczawno-Zdrój) with her mother Apolonia née Zaremba Objezierska. Paulina's mother was a very energetic, adventurous, and strongly opinioned lady.

Szczawno-Zdrój is one of the oldest spas in Lower Silesia, and the healing power of its water was mentioned as early as the 16th century. The spa grounds where Wilhelm Freiherr von Richthofen and Paulina Objezierska walked together still exist today. The most beautiful time of the year there is said to be spring, when the trees and ornamental shrubs are in bloom. Even the buildings from the 1822-1895 periods are in use today. On the list of notable guests in the 19th century was Zygmunt Krasiński, one of the three Polish national bards. I do not know the actual dates he visited Szczawno-Zdrój; but when Paulina Objezierska was there, he would have been only 13 years old. However, I know that he was interested in Paulina 10 years later when they both stayed in Italy and Paulina was already Baroness von Richthofen.

Wilhelm Freiherr von Richthofen's momentous visit to the spa and his chance encounter with Paulina Objezierska, for whom he "quickly lost his head over," ended in an almost immediate wedding according to his diary. Paulina was the beautiful, 16-year-old daughter of Rafał Objezierski from Objezierza, with the family coat of arms Nałęcz, who was the owner of the Rusko and Lusowo estates in Wielkopolska, and Apolonia née Zaremba with the Zaremba coat of arms from Kalinowa. Paulina was well educated and fluent in Polish, French, and German.

Paulina and her daughter used to write the surname Obiezierska with an "i" instead of a "j," which could be the surname's original form as it is written in the same way in *Złota Księga Szlachty Polskiej* [The Golden Book of Polish Nobility] by Teodor Żychliński. Since the "Objezierska" version is frequently used in the family trees and documents, including Teki Dworzaczka, I decided to use that version in this book.

According to our family stories, the clan Objezierski began in the 15th century, and the first known family name of my ancestors was Niemierza Objczicrski. Rafał Objezierski, Paulina's father, was the son of Józef, and he was born in 1764, the year when Stanisław August Poniatowski became the king of Poland and Lithuania. My research did not uncover much about Rafał Objezierski; but Emil Freiherr von Richthofen's book indicated that Rafał Objezierski was a poor member of Polish nobility who married Apolonia, daughter of wealthy Chamberlain Zaremba from Kalinowa and Princess Ponińska.

The office of chamberlain was an honorable title which, during the reign of king Stanisław August Poniatowski in Poland, replaced the old, traditional Polish title and office of "podkomorzy." The sign of the chamberlain office was a gilded key given by the king to the official on the day they took office. The main duties of a chamberlain were to be available at all times to fulfill the king's commands and requests, announce visitors and guide them to the king's chambers at monarch court, and work as his aide-de-camp. A chamberlain pledged loyalty to the king and promised perfection in his work. He was also bound to secrecy about the monarchy, which likely was not always easy.

Apolonia Zaremba came from a prosperous family and brought to her marriage the Rusko estate as her dowry; and her wedding to Rafał Objezierski was held in Rusko in 1807. Their first child, Paulina Felicjana Augustyna, was born on June 26, 1809.[7] Later the couple was blessed with two more daughters, Franciszka (called Fanny) and Elżbieta, and one son Józef.

Paulina Objezierska, like her parents, was Catholic, and Wilhelm Freiherr von Richthofen was Protestant, coming from a family that was content with religious reforms and proud of her ancestors founding Protestant churches and schools. The progenitor of the family, Paulus Praetorius, during his study at the university, was the close friend of Sebastian Faber Schmidt, a student of Martin Luther. Paulus Praetorius adopted Sebastian's son, Samuel Schmidt, in 1543.[8] He became Samuel Praetorius and had Lutheran traditions and is remembered as an ancestor of all the members of the von Richthofen family. A descendant of Samuel Praetorius, the grandfather of Wilhelm Freiherr von Richthofen was a patron of the Lutheran Church in Gros Rosen (Rogoźnica), where he founded the house of prayer.

---

[7] Biblioteka Kórnicka PAN, Teki Dworzaczka:
http://teki.bkpan.poznan.pl/search.php?section=3&single=&fileno=1&page=719&expr=&highlight=0
Accessed 07-19-2013.
[8] B. Freiherr von Richthofen, My Brother Manfred: P. Kilduff, The Red Baron Manfred von Richthofen, London, 1980, p. 158.

In 1826, when Wilhelm Freiherr von Richthofen fell head over heels in love and decided to marry Catholic Paulina Objezierska, both of his parents were alive and belonged to the Protestant faith. Even if they were not enthusiastic about Wilhelm's marriage plans, because of the differences in their religions, they did not stop the marriage and left the decision to their son. Wilhelm, on one hand, knew how important the Protestant faith was to his father and decided not to leave it; but on the other hand, he did not consider that marrying a Polish Catholic would be a problem for him. It appears that they discussed the future education and religious affiliation of the children they hoped to have before their marriage. Despite their parents making the decision that their future children would be raised in the Protestant faith, they followed their mother's Catholic faith instead. I write more about this in the next chapter. The marriage to Paulina did not convert Wilhelm to the Catholic faith before the wedding nor even after their many years of marriage.

Wilhelm's younger brother, Karl, married Protestant Ferdinande von Kulish in 1828, but became Catholic himself ten years later,[9] soon after the death of his father, Wilhelm Ludwig Freiherr von Richthofen (1761-1838). Wilhelm Ludwig, who was a lifelong member of the Lutheran Church, became furious when he heard that Karl wanted to convert to the Catholic faith. The children of Karl Freiherr von Richthofen, including Professor Ferdinand Freiherr von Richthofen, the well-known researcher mentioned earlier, were raised in the Catholic faith but his daughter Mathilde converted to the Lutheran faith later in her life. Karl and Ferdinande von Richthofen, Wilhelm's brother and sister-in-law, passed away in Hohenfriedberg (Polish Dobromierz) in Lower Silesia and were buried there.

Wilhelm Freiherr von Richthofen, the handsome, charming, wealthy aristocrat and man of the world, was 10 years older than his bride but young enough to enjoy fun, leisure time and traveling; and to Paulina, he was the man of her teenage dreams. Wilhelm pushed for an immediate wedding, and Paulina's parents did not see a reason to wait very long.

---

[9] W. v. Hueck, Op. Cit., p. 318.

Before the wedding, Paulina took a two-month pilgrimage to Częstochowa with her mother to pay homage to the Blessed Virgin Mother, well-known for miracles, whose painting was located in the monastery of the Pauline monks on Jasna Góra Hill four hundred years earlier. Devotion to Mary, the mother of Jesus Christ, was alive in Poland, and Jasna Góra was the center of worship and place of pilgrimage since the 15th century. Registering pilgrims who went there started in the 17th century, which showed that the Pauline monastery was not only visited by the faithful from former Polish territories, but also by pilgrims from Silesia, Czech, Prussia, Saxony, and even faraway lands. Twice during his reign, in 1754 and 1764 year, Frederic II the Great prohibited the citizens of Silesia to take part in pilgrimages to Jasna Góra, which is puzzling to me because history depicts him as religion-tolerant ruler. In 1764 the Polish Parliament proclaimed that the Polish Republic had faith in the Holy Queen Virgin Mary and her painting of Częstochowa well known for miracles, in whom they sought shelter in need and received her protection (Kaczmarski, 1987).[10] I do not know if Paulina Objezierska went to see the painting of the Blessed Virgin to pray for specific intentions or to ask for protection and blessings for her future husband and for herself as the pilgrimage was planned before the marriage proposal.

On March 5, 1826, Paulina Objezierska and Wilhelm Freiherr von Richthofen exchanged marriage vows at Rusko, the estate of the bride's parents. There are a few villages in Poland named Rusko; and the estate of the Objezierski family was located in Wielkopolska. The existing Catholic church in Rusko, was erected in 1833 so it was built after the wedding of Wilhelm and Paulina, but it contains a few elements from the previous church that connected it to my ancestors' time, such as an altar, a baroque pulpit, a painting of St. Adalbert from the 17th century, and a baptismal font from the beginning of the 19th century.

---

[10] H. Kaczmarski, Kalendarium, Jasnogórska Bogurodzica 1382-1982,Warszawa, 1987, p. 298.

I have a few items from Paulina's trousseau: one piece of china, a couple of wine glasses and a goblet with her monogram, and gilded forks and knives with shafts made of agate of various shades of brown, grey, honey, and black that may have been made of agates extracted from mines located in Lower Silesia. The pieces of cutlery are decorated with the monogram PR and the crown of Baroness Paulina von Richthofen. A very special memento of Paulina that I treasure is her tiny amethyst heraldic seal she used to seal her correspondence which also has Paulina's monogram, the date 1863, and her crown. The seal of Wilhelm Freiherr von Richthofen with the coat of arms of the Richthofen family from the House of Royn-Schutzendorf is much larger, made of metal, and attached to a wooden, painted black handle. To my astonishment, the set of wine glasses, which are a beautiful, deep green color, are in good condition after almost 200 years. My grandmother called them "the glasses of Rhine," but I think that correctly they should be called "the glasses for the wine of the Rhine region." They were made for serving white, dry wine. I seldom use them, generally just for celebrating very special family occasions. Serving white wine in green glasses was not done on a whim; rather, it was a custom in the social circles of that time. I was amused to find this paragraph in the memoir of Baroness von Sell, who described a perfectly set table prepared for hosting important guests that she remembered from her childhood:

> An hour before the arrival of the guests, my father subjected his study, the parlor, my mother's salon, the hall, and particularly the dining room to one last, thorough inspection. The delicate white china with golden-green rims, also a gift from the Kaiser from his private porcelain manufacturer, gleamed. The mandatory four glasses stood in front of each plate: green glasses for the white wine; goblets of various sizes for red wine and port; and the tall, slender vessels for champagne (Niemoeller, 2012).[11]

---

[11] S. Niemoeller, Crowns, Crosses, and Stars, West Lafayette, 2012, p. 57.

Objects belonging to the von Richthofens. **Top left**: The 19th century European wine glasses and water goblets. **Top center**: The 19th century gold-plated silverware with handles made of agate. **Top right**: The 19th century German china sauceboat.
Bottom left: The sigil of the von Richthofen family from the Royn-Schutzendorf house, the 19th century razor, and a hoof-shaped box, a hunter accessory. **Bottom center**: The von Richthofen 19th century photo album with Paulina Freifrau von Richthofen's initials and the sigil of the von Richthofen family with the coat of arms. **Bottom right**: The sigil of Paulina Freifrau von Richthofen with her monogram "PR" and baroness crown; on the side of the sigil, unseen in photo, is the date of 1863. [12]

Left: The antlers of the antelope shot by Wilhelm Freiherr von Richthofen on African safari (according to my grandmother). **Right**: The 19th century medallion with the profile of Wilhelm Freiherr von Richthofen.[13]

---

[12] Ivona Tarko's collection.
[13] Ivona Tarko's collection.

I learned from Emil Freiherr von Richthofen's book that Wilhelm and Paulina spent their first years of marriage traveling, attending parties, playing, visiting friends, and family, and just generally enjoying life. The couple had two children: Heinrich Wilhelm Raphael Freiherr von Richthofen, who was born on December 7, 1826, and the future husband of Maria Wielogłowska; and Eliza Paulina Apolonia Freiin von Richthofen, who was born on January 20, 1829, and would become the wife of Antoni Lubicz Szydłowski.

Wilhelm and Paulina loved traveling and European art. Wilhelm was not only a connoisseur and collector of European paintings, but was a painter himself. Unfortunately, I have only a fragment of a Sorrento landscape, not even the entire picture, which Wilhelm painted during one of his trips to Italy. Leopold Meyet in his comments to the letters of Polish poet Juliusz Słowacki, which he published in 1899, wrote that both von Richthofens collected precious pieces of art and were known as experts.[14]

Wilhelm and Paulina spent more time in Italy, mainly in Rome and Florence, than in Lower Silesia or Wielkopolska. They were not unique in their preferences. Many Poles lived in Florence in the 1820s and 1830s. In their group of Polish immigrant friends were aristocrats like Prince Michał Kleofas Ogiński (he lived in Florence in 1808-1810 and then in 1822 until his death in 1833), Aleksander, Leon, and Seweryna Potocki, Władysław Sanguszko, and Władysław Zamoyski.

The home of Prince Ogiński was open to Poles coming to Florence. It is said that poet Adam Mickiewicz, who visited Florence in 1828 and 1829, not only played chess with the Prince but was read to by the Prince from the *Stories from Florence* by Machiavelli in its original Italian language. Living in Florence, Polish historian Bernard Zaydler, encouraged by Prince Ogiński, was writing papers and articles in Italian about Poles, such as Mikołaj Kopernik, Jędrzej Śniadecki, and others. In 1831 Bernard Zaydler, with the help of Prince Stanisław Poniatowski, published his

---

[14] J. Słowacki, L. Meyet, Listy Juliusza Słowackiego: z autografów poety, Lwów, Tom II, 1899, p. 3.

history of Poland, *Storia della Polonia,* written in Italian. Polish writers also lived in Florence, such as Stanisław Dunin-Borkowski, author of *Travel to Italy;* and Konstanty Gaszynski, author of *Letters from Travel*; Edward Antoni Odyniec (1804-1885), poet and translator of English, German, and Russian literature into Polish language; and poets Cyprian Kamil Norwid, Juliusz Słowacki, and Zygmunt Krasiński.

Juliusz Słowacki stayed in Florence (1837-1838) in the company of Zygmunt Krasiński. Juliusz Słowacki's visit to Florence was memorialized by a plaque bearing his name on the building where he lived, Della Scala 65, which was owned by Bernard Zaydler. At the same time Juliusz Słowacki was visiting Florence, a group of other Polish aristocrats lived there as well: Zdzisław Zamoyski, son of Stanisław, Józef and Herman Potocki; violinist Aleksander Potocki; Zenon Brzozowski; the Dzieduszycki family; Seweryna Potocka, and Karol Przeździecki.[15]

Wilhelm and Paulina von Richthofen were in Italy together on two occasions. The first time was to visit Florence and Modena at the beginning of the 1830s, and they visited the second time in 1835-1837 when they mainly stayed in Rome. The Richthofen children, Heinrich and Eliza, stayed with their maternal grandmother, Apolonia Objezierska, in Rusko during the first trip; but both children accompanied them on the second trip. Emil Freiherr von Richthofen wrote that Wilhelm found a tenant for his Schutzendorf (Polish name Strzałkowa) estate in 1830; and for the next two years, the Richthofen family lived in Dresden, Munich, and Stuttgart. Wilhelm also traveled with his wife to Italy and Switzerland during their two-year stay.

In Rome, Paulina Freifrau von Richthofen's home, a gathering place for aristocrats and writers, became the center of Polish elite society. Teodor Żychliński wrote that Baroness Richthofen was famous in the circles of Polish society and foreigners alike, and lived with her husband, a great art

---

[15] M. Kałuski, Polacy we Florencji, 2007 http://www.florencja.it accessed 02-16-2017.

enthusiast and expert, for a long time in Italy; she assembled in her home in Rome and Florence all the distinguished Poles and foreigners (Żychliński, 1884).[16]

Now is the perfect time to relate the content of a letter written by one of the most distinguished Poles in Paulina's circle in Rome, poet Juliusz Słowacki, to his mother on May 28, 1836 about his contacts with the Richthofen family during his stay in Rome:

> I don't know if I should leave Rome for some inhabited land or stay in my apartment. It will feel sad and lonely. I will have only one home where I can spend evenings. It belongs to the Richthofen couple. He is a German; she is a Pole, a very nice lady, chatty, typical of our ladies from Warsaw, adorable and bursting with life, if you, my dear, could imagine what charm Polish women have. They seem to belong to another world, like heavenly and better creatures. You would not be surprised to hear that Zygmunt and I were running like maniacs to Italian villas to perchance see her. The idea, created by my imagination, disappeared after I met her the first time in Borghezy Gardens. Now it is just a nice friendship since Aleksander Potocki recommended me to her, and my name is a little bit known now and she helped me to be nicely welcomed there (Słowacki, 1836).[17]

Aleksander Potocki, whose estate on Polish land was confiscated by the Russians as a punishment for his fighting in the Polish-Russian War in 1830-1831, left Poland for Germany and France, and finally settled in Italy, where he was helping Polish immigrants.

Konstanty Maria Górski commented that it was hard to imagine the 19th century social life without a "salon" as it was a gathering of influential,

---

[16] T. Żychliński, Złota Księga Szlachty Polskiej, T. II, 1884, p. 419.

[17] J. Słowacki, L. Meyet, Listy Juljusza Słowackiego z autografów poety, wydał po raz pierwszy nakładem Księgarni Polskiej Lwów, volume 1, 2, 1899, p. 2.

well-educated individuals with good manners (Gabryś, 2006).[18] The salon of Paulina Freifrau von Richthofen, regardless of its location – in Rome, Florence, Paris, or Wrocław - always brought together many Polish immigrants. Knowing this fact helped me understand the atmosphere in which the Richthofen children lived and how these surroundings influenced them in choosing their friends and even potential spouses.

Juliusz Słowacki, as mentioned previously became associated with Paulina Freifrau von Richthofen thanks to a recommendation from Aleksander Potocki. The young poet gained Paulina's attention with his published patriotic verses. His friendship perhaps contained an element of flirting. Jerzy Jankowski in his book *Unromantic Romantics,* in a chapter devoted to Juliusz Słowacki, wrote that in Italy he stayed in the circle of Polish immigrants where he met aristocrat Zygmunt Krasiński, with whom he chased like a freak beautiful Baroness Richthofen to snatch her attention (Jankowski, 1997).[19]

Juliusz Słowacki wrote the following poem in Rome in 1836 dedicated to Paulina Freifrau von Richthofen.

> In the Sketchbook of Lady B. R
> I was thinking what kind of nugget to choose
> To put an inscription
> The surface of a column or Cypress tree?
> But the tree was weeping when I cut its bark
> And when I punched the column
> The stone was whining like in a sleep and talked.
> I was frightened by the scream of Rome's ruins
> So I tried to escape to listen to the sea storm.
> When you said "write something on the petal of a rose
> And I will put the petal into my enormous collection of
> Keepsakes and names."
> So I did.
> But I would curse the cascade of time that would suck this petal!

---

[18] A. Gabryś, Salony Krakowskie, Kraków, 2006, p. 2.
[19] J. Jankowski, Nieromantyczni Romantycy, Wrocław, 1997, p. 185.

And the Cypress tree was shrieking when I cut the bark,
Believe me, lady, by bludgeoning the stone bust with a dagger,
As a vicious murderer,
I came to its feeling and heart.
But this shy petal on which the name is
Will disappear soon, and your memory will fade.
If a white dove with beating heart brought it to you
From sisters or brothers, from others, but simply not from me
You would keep it in your heart, before crumpling in your palm.

The poem was initially published in Polish in 1857 in a magazine *Świt* [Down] in Lvov[20], and to my knowledge it was never translated into other languages. In my above English translation, I tried to be as close as possible to the original version.

Jan Zieliński in his biography of Juliusz Słowacki called the poem written by Słowacki for Paulina Freifrau von Richthofen a poetic description of the Aqua Paolina fountain located on Gianicolo Hill in Rome.[21] In my opinion, this poem is more personal and figurative than it seems at first reading. The words of Słowacki that the rose petal would find its way to your heart if it was brought by a white dove, from sisters or brothers, or from anybody else, but not from him, was his attempt to show Paulina's disinterest in his adoration and displayed her connections to a religious congregation founded by Bohdan Jański in 1836.[22]

I do not believe that Zygmunt Krasiński and Juliusz Słowacki crossed any lines while chasing the beautiful Paulina to get her attention, rather that both poets needed this platonic feeling to inspire their writing.

In 1836 Paulina was 27 years old. She was at the peak of her beauty and was a happy wife, mother of two children, and in touch with her

---

[20] B. Zakrzewski, Słowacki w sztambuchu baronowej Richthofen, Pamiętnik Literacki 88/3, 1997, p. 157-163.
[21] J. Zieliński, SzatAnioł- Powikłane Życie Juliusza Słowackiego, Warszawa, 2000, p. 147.
[22] The diary of Bogdan Jański written in Polish is available on a website: http://www.zmartwychwstancy.sosnowiec.pl/doc/dziennik_janskiego.pdf Accessed 08-28-2014.

spirituality. She supported the Congregation of the Resurrection of Our Lord Jesus Christ (CR), founded by Bohdan Jański, "the Lay Apostle" of the Great Emigration, and had many friends among them, including the Wielogłowski family. Walery Wielogłowski, who would become the father-in-law of Heinrich von Richthofen, Paulina's son, was an "external brother" of the congregation. Paulina Freifrau von Richthofen personally knew Fr. Piotr Semenenko from the CR, and financially supported the CR gathering. Paulina would be called a fundraiser nowadays because she was using her social connections to help this new congregation.

Fr. Tadeusz Kaszuba described the CR in his introduction to the letters of Fr. Piotr Semenenko, which were published in 2001.[23] He said that the CR's purpose was to include not only priests and friars and nuns, but lay Catholics as well, who were called the "external brothers." Both groups needed to be organized. The first lay members to be known as external brothers were people from Bohdan Jański's circle, such as Stefan Witwicki, Jan Koźmian, Walery Wielogłowski, and Karol Królikowski. Fr. Semenenko was in personal contact with them or directed their activities through correspondence. They also wanted to start a congregation for women; and during his first trip to the Polish lands, Fr. Semenenko met a few ladies who agreed to begin organizing a new CR congregation for women. The first step after the CR was founded was to bring the new members to Paris, and then Rome, find lodging for them, organize a board, and begin preparing them to be nuns.

Paulina Freifrau von Richthofen and her mother were in the circle of women engaged in founding the new congregation. Fr. Semenenko wrote the following in a letter on April 20, 1844 to Hieronim Kajsiewicz:

> She has already written to ask about one girl, the orphan daughter of her friend. I am going to see Baroness Richthofen (remember Spoleto 1837?), she is in Rome with her husband right now. Her mother, Madame Objezierska, was here as well. She left a few days ago for Poznań. It is possible she would encourage her

[23] T. Kaszuba, P. Semenenko CR, Listy 1842-1845, 2001, p. III.

daughter to join and maybe a few girls before October (Semenenko, 1844).[24]

Paulina's mother, Apolonia Objezierska (maiden name Zaremba) was a very strong person, whose opinion was honored by her daughters and son-in-law Wilhelm Freiherr von Richthofen. She took care of the children of Wilhelm and Paulina and influenced their early childhood education. In the 1840s the Richthofen children were teenagers and stayed in boarding schools, which gave their Grandmother Apolonia the time and freedom to engage in new accomplishments. In 1839 Apolonia Objezierska became a widow; and soon after her husband Rafał's death, she lost her youngest daughter Elżbieta, wife of Count Aleksander Szembek. Elżbieta, the youngest sister of Paulina Freifrau von Richthofen, passed away at the young age of 21, leaving behind her husband and infant daughter Maria.

Apolonia Objezierska enjoyed a long and active life. She passed away at the age of 95, but not before facing the deaths of her three children: her daughters Paulina Freifrau von Richthofen and Franciszka primo voto Topińska, secundo voto Miłkowska, and son Józef Objezierski. I was surprised to discover that all three Objezierski siblings passed away in the same year, one year before Apolina's own death in 1871.

Paulina Freifrau von Richthofen mainly was engaged in helping the CR, and the attitude of her husband Wilhelm toward the members, her Polish circle of immigrants, and Catholicism in general appeared to be very welcoming. I remind my readers that Wilhelm was German and Protestant. Wilhelm's daughter Eliza wrote to the Wielogłowski family in 1846 that her mother and father were with her and were waiting impatiently for the promised letter from Sir Wielogłowski; and Paulina Freifrau von Richthofen added a few words herself at the end of this letter that she hoped the dear husband of the Countess would make them happy by sending his letter. She gave her regards and words of reassurance of

---

[24] P. Semenenko, Listy 1842-1845, Studia Zmartwychwstańcze; redaktor ks.Tadeusz Kaszuba, v. VII, 2001, p. 217.

their friendship to the beloved and benevolent couple (Richthofen, 1846).[25]

Some of the members of the congregation hoped that one of Paulina's children would join them in the future. Fr. Piotr Semenenko stated the following in an August 5, 1844 letter to another member of the congregation, Józef Huby.

> ...About the children of Baroness Richthofen, that is a completely different situation. Children are not pressured to join the congregation. I don't know if in writing this, you even have thought about Baroness Richthofen. If yes, your reproach would be strange to me. I wish all children a sitter like Sister Julia (Semenenko, 1844).[26]

"Sister Julia" was a person from the CR, who accompanied Eliza and Heinrich von Richthofen as a nanny or governess. The idea of increasing the congregation by creating the nuns gathering was not realized at that time.

The von Richthofen family spent the summer of 1845 in Paris within the circles of Polish immigrants. According to Wilhelm's diary, his son Heinrich fell in love with Walery Wielogłowski's daughter, Marynia, that summer. This young couple will be discussed in the next chapter.

As noted earlier in this chapter, Wilhelm's father, Baron Wilhelm Ludwig Freiherr von Richthofen, passed away in Hertwigswaldau (Polish Snowidza), Silesia, on April 13, 1838. Wilhelm's mother, Henriette Freifrau von Richthofen, maiden name Pertkenau, died on February 26, 1846, in Breslau (Polish Wrocław).[27] Upon his mother's death, Wilhelm's closest living relative from the von Richthofen family was his younger brother, Karl Heinrich Ludwig (1801-1874), who was the owner of Schimmelwitz (Polish name Wszełomice in the area of Kąty

---

[25] B PAU, Kraków, rkps 1844, E. Richthofen to K. Wielogłowska, Letter, 1846.
[26] P. Semenenko, Op. Cit.
[27] W. v. Hueck, Op. Cit., p. 316-317.

Wrocławskie) and lived there with his wife Ferdinande and their several children.

In 1847 Wilhelm and Paulina decided to build a Gothic style palace in Lusowo where they wanted to display the paintings and art pieces they collected during their frequent European trips. A tall tower characteristic of the Middle Ages was designed to rise above the palace, and a beautiful park surrounded the grounds. The village of Lusowo was located by Lusowski Lake near Tarnowo Podgórne, a little more than eight miles from Poznań (Posen) and dates back to the 12th century. The diocese of Poznań owned this land until its sale to private owners in the 15th century.

Lusowo became the Objezierski family estate at the beginning of the 19th century, and the palace Wilhelm and Paulina built belonged to the von Richthofen family until Paulina's death in 1870 year.[28]   After Paulina's death, it was owned by the von Palm family in the late 19th century into the 20th century. Herman von Palm, who was a banker from Bernburg, added a new wing to the palace, which changed its appearance. After World War I, the Lusowo estate was divided into smaller lots, but the palace itself with the park was purchased by Polish General Józef Dowbor-Muśnicki (1867-1937), the leader of the Wielkopolski Uprising and the organizer of the Wielkopolska Army. General Józef Dowbor-Muśnicki lived in Lusowo until his death and was buried in a local cemetery. After World War II, during the Communist era, the palace in Lusowo was confiscated by the Polish Treasury. When Communism collapsed in Poland, the laws were changed and the palace was once again under private ownership, and a renovation was undertaken.

Our family anecdote from the period when Paulina Freifrau von Richthofen lived in Lusowo described an event involving the domestics working in the Lusowo palace and a piglet on the estate farm. Paulina told this story to her grandchildren, and they passed it to their children. It happened that a sow died during delivery, and a newborn piglet was left

---

[28] http://regionwielkopolska.pl/katalog-obiektow/palac-w-lusowie.html accessed 11-07- 2013.

behind. A servant woman decided to save the piglet and it survived. The story goes that as it grew, it behaved like a dog, following the servant everywhere, even to the rooms of the palace, which was amusing at first to everyone, including Wilhelm and Paulina. But once the piglet became full-grown, Paulina would not allow it to come to the palace and told the servant the pig must be kept in the pigsty. After a few days in the pigsty, sadly, the pig died. The servants of the palace told Paulina that the pig died of a broken heart because she missed her caretaker.

The strangest of all books, wrote Johann Wolfgang von Goethe, is the book of love. I found Goethe's photo in one of the old photo albums I inherited that belonged to Wilhelm and Paulina von Richthofen. Unfortunately, I do not know which one of them was fond of this romantic bard's poetry, but the above line from Goethe's poem, seemed to me the perfect introduction to the new chapter of the story of lives of Wilhelm and Paulina von Richthofen. They lived together 25 years and probably would have been a married couple until they died if fate had not put Miss Maria Carolina Kruger on Wilhelm's path of life. According to Emil Freiherr von Richthofen, it happened during a lonely journey to Breslau (Wrocław) for Wilhelm while the palace was being built in Lusowo. On a train in Frankfort, Wilhelm met Madame and Miss Kruger, mother and daughter from Rostock who were travelling together to a spa. Wilhelm was delighted in the company of the women, especially the lovely young daughter, who was named Maria, and he asked them to visit his house in Breslau (Wrocław). The ladies accepted the invitation, and that fateful one day they spent together in the Richthofen house in Breslau (Wrocław) changed the future of Wilhelm and Paulina's marriage and their entire family.

Wilhelm fell madly in love with Maria Carolina Kruger, who was a gifted young artist and wanted to see her more frequently. In the months after meeting Maria, Wilhelm's time was spent travelling back and forth to Breslau (Wrocław) and Posen (Poznań) to Rostock and Berlin, juggling his time among his family duties, supervising the building of Lusowo palace, and visiting Maria's residence. Wilhelm's passion for fine art and his own artistic penchant no doubt pushed him closer to Maria. It also is quite possible that he was going through a "midlife crisis" and was looking for new experiences. Very likely, every time he saw Maria, his heart would become more and more impatient, and eventually he realized he could not live without her.

On April 9, 1851, Wilhelm Freiherr von Richthofen divorced Paulina.[29] I was told that they divorced without spite, focusing rather on the happy moments they experienced together during their 25 years of marriage. After the divorce, Wilhelm wanted to put his family business in order and purchased an estate in Koninko in Wielkopolska for his son Heinrich (currently a village in Kurnik district near Poznań) and an estate in Kupientyn in central Poland for his daughter Eliza (now the region of Mazovia).

Paulina Freifrau von Richthofen kept the palace in Lusowo and lived there after her divorce. By that time, she was a stout matron, and a family anecdote about Paulina's "gluttony" was passed on from one generation of von Richthofen women to the next. My grandmother shared it with me. It seems that Paulina, awakened one night by the smell of fresh roasted piglet, went to the palace kitchen and ate half of the piglet. The facts and anecdotes I collected about my family, such as the one above, at times were like puzzle pieces without a guide; but I started to deduce a clearer picture of my family through my own experiences. I found myself looking at Paulina and her problems through different eyes. Was it not possible that Paulina's overeating was not "gluttony" necessarily, but rather her response to the stress she faced after her divorce from a husband who left her for a much younger woman and was now all alone in her empty palace?

The wedding of Wilhelm Freiherr von Richthofen and Maria Carolina Kruger, born on September 2, 1824, took place in Rostock on June 23, 1851.[30] The bride was young enough to be Wilhelm's daughter as she was only two years older than his son Heinrich. After the wedding, Wilhelm

---

[29] W. v. Hueck, Op. Cit., p. 317.
[30] Ibid.

and his young wife started a new life together with endless luxuries and leisure time, travelling, and fun. They visited not only the southern parts of Europe, but Norway and Sweden as well. According to family lore, Wilhelm Freiherr von Richthofen also went on an African safari in the 1860s. I have the antlers of the antelope he shot during the safari; and inside the antlers were pieces of a local newspaper printed in Dresden on May 21, 1869.

One of the 19th century photos from my collection was taken at one of the most well-known tourist points of interest in Saxon Switzerland, the Bastei Bridge, from where the stronghold of Konigstain and Mardertelle Canyon can be seen. This stone bridge was built in 1851 to replace the original wooden bridge built in 1826. The picture is from a collection that belonged to the von Richthofen family, and I believe the man in the left foreground is Wilhelm Freiherr von Richthofen.

*Left: The 19th century photo of Bastei Bridge in Saxon Switzerland from the von Richthofen family collection. **Right**: Wilhelm Freiherr von Richthofen and his second wife Maria Carolina née Kruger Freifrau von Richthofen.*[31]

---

[31] Ivona Tarko's archives.

Wilhelm stayed in touch with his grown children after he divorced their mother. He attended Heinrich's wedding to Maria Wielogłowska in Kraków in 1852 and paid a visit to Rybna, the estate of Heinrich's father-in-law, located near Kraków, where it appears that all the family also met at the end of the summer of 1858. Earlier, he visited his son and daughter in-law in Ostrowieczko in Wielkopolska. In 1855 at the Ostrowieczko estate, he saw the firstborn child to Heinrich, his grandson, Bolesław Freiherr von Richthofen, who was my great-grandfather. In 1861 Wilhelm traveled east to the Werbkowice estate, by Lublin, to visit his daughter, Eliza Szydłowska. There were also get-togethers arranged by Wilhelm Freiherr von Richthofen with his children in Breslau (Wrocław) and Dresden. In his autobiography, Wilhelm described how he celebrated his daughter's birthday in 1868 in Dresden with Eliza and her Polish friends by going to dinner and attending a concert.

The grandchildren of Wilhelm Freiherr von Richthofen, Heinrich's children, would vacation in Silesia when they reached school age. Wilhelm financially supported the education of the second son of Heinrich and Maria, Stanisław Wilhelm Freiherr von Richthofen, who was born in Kraków in 1860.[32]

1874 did not start well for Wilhelm Freiherr von Richthofen and his family. On February 8, 1874, in Hohenfriedeberg (Polish Dobromierz), the only brother of Wilhelm, Karl Heinrich Ludwig, passed away. The stress of losing his brother perhaps precipitated Wilhelm's health to begin to fail shortly after his death, culminating in Wilhelm having a stroke that left him partially paralyzed. Wilhelm's illness drastically changed the busy lifestyle of Wilhelm and Maria. Before the illness, Wilhelm was a very active 74-year-old. After the stroke he travelled less and spent most of his time in Dresden painting for pleasure.

His greatest achievement for the von Richthofen family, as the senior family member, was preparing the von Richthofen family tree, which included all the members of our family from Paulus Praetorius (the 16th

---

[32] W. v. Hueck, Op. Cit., p. 318.

century) to the generation of Wilhelm Freiherr von Richthofen's grandchildren (the second half of the 19th century). The Richthofen family tree, based on Wilhelm's manuscript, was published in 1878. I am very grateful that the documents preserved by my grandmother survived all the turbulent years of our family history and that the family tree I have is the oldest of the original, undamaged, available von Richthofen family trees. Wilhelm's family history work ended the different spelling of the surname by his decision to use only "Richthofen" in the family archives.

It is often said that bad luck strikes twice. So it was again for Wilhelm four years after his brother's death and his stroke. On May 12, 1878, in Kupientyn his only son Heinrich passed away, and 11 days later on May 23, 1878, Wilhelm's wife, Maria Carolina, died in Dresden. She was in her early fifties, just like Wilhelm's son. Wilhelm was 77 years old by then.

Devastated by his heartbreaks and illness, Wilhelm stayed at home for the next four years and was tended by Martha Studnitz, a nurse. Wilhelm unexpectedly married Martha, his third wife, on August 17, 1882.[33] Martha was born in Schweidnitz (Świdnica) in 1852, which made her 53 years his junior. I am not sure what motivated Wilhelm to marry a third time and to a much younger woman. Emil Freiherr von Richthofen believed that Wilhelm wanted to reward Martha for the four years she was so dedicated to him, a paralyzed, old man. The wedding of Wilhelm Freiherr von Richthofen and Martha Studnitz took place in Dresden. They were married only five weeks, however, as Wilhelm passed away in his sleep, in Dresden on September 24, 1882 at the age of 83. The third wife of Wilhelm Freiherr von Richthofen, Martha Studnitz married Dr. Eduard Klamroth in 1886.[34]

I learned recently about Martha Studnitz, the third wife of Wilhelm Freiherr von Richthofen from a correspondence with Dr. Karl-Friedrich Freiherr von Richthofen and German documents he sent to me. I could not hide my bewilderment.

---

[33] W. v. Hueck, Op. Cit., p. 317.
[34] Ibid.

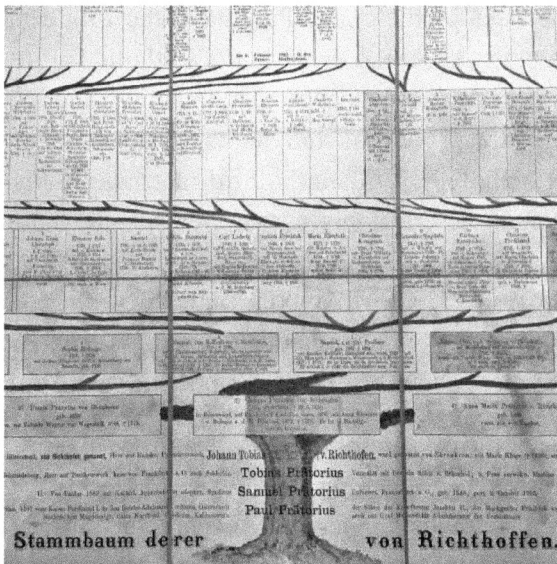

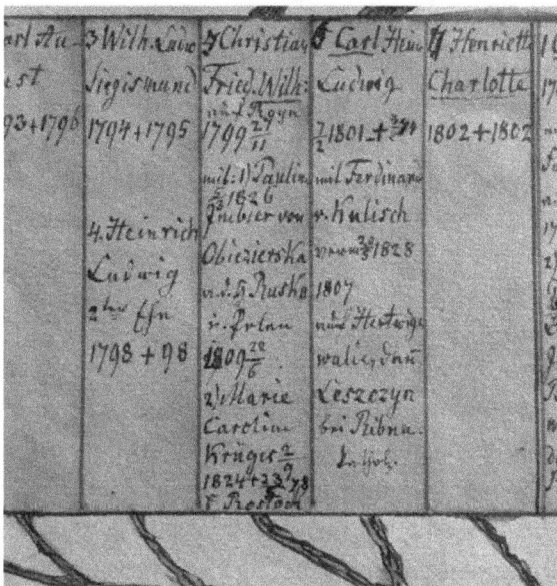

Top: The von Richthofen family tree printed in 1878 (fragment). **Bottom**: The fragment of the handwritten von Richthofen family tree, based on the Wilhelm's manuscript, showing the name of Wilhelm Freiherr von Richthofen and the names of his wives: Paulina Objezierska and Maria Kruger in the third field.[35]

---

[35] Ivona Tarko's archives.

The divorce between Wilhelm and Paulina in the 19th century appeared to have been a pretty shocking event in my Catholic family, but with the passing years I learned to accept this unanticipated event, which I confirmed during the process of studying the relationship of Wilhelm and Paulina von Richthofen. Wilhelm's third marriage in his eighties to a very young woman was not only unexpected for me, but also made me think about the wisdom of one Polish proverb that says that an apple does not fall far from the apple tree. Stanisław Freiherr von Richthofen, Wilhelm's grandson was in his nineties when he said his marriage vows. I will be writing more about Wilhelm's grandchildren in the next chapters.

The long process of examining the life of Wilhelm Freiherr von Richthofen was an eye-opening experience for me. I discovered an extraordinary person with a passion for life, art, and music, who loved his family and beautiful women. Wilhelm had a zest for life and his affirmation of life had an impact on the people surrounding him. Wilhelm enjoyed life almost to the end despite his limited mobility from his stroke and the heartbreaking tragedy of losing his only son and beloved wife. He no doubt left behind good memories for many people. Wilhelm's kindheartedness for Paulina's family and her circle of Polish immigrants, his compassion for the Wielogłowski family by opening his home to Polish patriots, and his plan to find a husband for his only daughter among the Poles, attest that he was friendly and open to other cultures.

Wilhelm's passion for art urged him not only to collect pieces of art, but to reach for a paintbrush and a palette himself. His sensitive nature also moved him to write poems which survive even now on yellowish and crinkled sheets of paper. I now imagine Wilhelm Freiherr von Richthofen as a charming and fascinating man. I should be angry with him that he did not want or could not fight his feelings for Maria Carolina and decided to divorce Paulina; but even Paulina forgave him his weakness and after their divorce they remained friends. Wilhelm became a real person to me during my family search, not just an image from an old photo. I no longer look impassively at his sculpted profile on the medallion family heirloom, which once was just a relic from the past that belonged to an unknown ancestor. I now look fondly at pictures of Wilhelm and see the features of my beloved grandmother. It astonishes me how some features are randomly repeated in different generations of the same large family. When I met briefly with Dieprand Freiherr von Richthofen, he reminded me of my grandmother so much in his features, gestures, smile, and kind demeanor that I felt like I had been in the company of a close relative I already knew.

As I came to the end of this chapter, I realized that Wilhelm's passing closed the Silesian period in the history of my line of the von Richthofen family. After being indifferent to Silesia past and present all my life and never visiting this region, now I look forward to seeing it. Krzysztof Fedorowicz named Silesia "the world from a certain height" and described its beauty in his book as follows.

> The landscape looks exactly like the drawings and engravings of the panorama of the city. Below are trees, fields, and a road, above them church towers, and then again fields and lonely trees. In the whole landscape, there is a predominance of land to sky, hills to clouds. In nearby Wrocław, there are more forests parallel to the horizon that looks like cumulus clouds (Fedorowicz, 2000).[36]

The obituary of Wilhelm Freiherr von Richthofen, the beloved husband, father, and grandfather, contained the names of three cities where his mourning relatives resided: Dresden where Wilhelm's wife Martha resided; Werbkowice – the estate of Eliza née von Richthofen Szydłowska and Antoni Szydłowski – daughter and son-in-law of Wilhelm; and Kraków, where Wilhelm's daughter-in-law Maria née Wielogłowska Freifrau von Richthofen and Wilhelm's grandson Bolesław, my great-grandfather, lived.

Paulina Freifrau von Richthofen, Wilhelm's first wife and my great-great-great-grandmother, did not remarry. After the divorce from Wilhelm, she devoted herself to her family and grandchildren, dividing her time in Lusowo, Ostrowieczko, and Breslau (Wrocław). She passed away in

---

[36] K. Fedorowicz, Imiona Własne, Kraków, 2000, p. 5.

Ostrowieczko in 1870 on the estate of her son Heinrich and was buried in Dolsk.[37]

Paulina's obituary was published in the 1863-1876 Chronicle of Obituaries of the Families from Wielkopolska and reads as follows.

> Richthofen Baroness Paulina née Obiezierska died on August 29, 1870 in her son's house in Ostrowieczko. The late Baroness Richthofen was well-known in the circles of Polish society as well as those educated in and passionate about the fine arts. Living with her husband, a great connoisseur of painting, in Italy, she gathered in her home the social elites of Rome and Florence. Then, her house in Wrocław was visited by many Poles. She had a museum of sorts with precious pieces of art in her home. She is survived by her son Henryk, who is married to Wielogłowska, and her daughter Eliza, wife of Szydłowski, a recognized citizen of the Polish Kingdom (Żychliński, 1877).[38]

About the time of Paulina's passing, the nephew of Wilhelm Freiherr von Richthofen, Catholic priest Karl Freiherr von Richthofen (1832-1876), who was the son of Ferdinande and Karl, was appointed a canon in Breslau (Wrocław) by the King of Prussia. Karl left the mainstream Catholic Church in 1875 year and joined the Old Catholic Church, which did not recognize papal supremacy and dogma about papal infallibility. Karl Freiherr von Richthofen passed away in 1876 in Berlin.[39]

---

[37] B PAU Kórnik, Teki Dworzaczka:
http://teki.bkpan.poznan.pl/search.php?section=3&single=&fileno=1&page=719& expr=&highlight=0 accessed 06-06-2015.
[38] T. Żychliński, Kronika Żałobna Rodzin Wielkopolskich od 1863-1876 z Uwzględnieniem Ważniejszych Osobistości Zmarłych w Tym Przeciągu Czasu w Innych Dzielnicach Polski i na Obczyźnie, Poznań, 1877, p. 376.
[39] W. v. Hueck, Op. Cit., p. 319.

CHAPTER 2 Children of Wilhelm Freiherr von Richthofen and Paulina Objezierska: Eliza and Heinrich (Henryk)

We are linked by blood, and blood is memory without language

~ Joyce Carol Oates

Searching for sources can be the most difficult task in research such as mine; but when a very good source is found, it is exciting! Such it was for me when I discovered that Wilhelm Freiherr von Richthofen's daughter, Eliza, was a driving force in connecting the von Richthofen and Wielogłowski families. Eliza met and befriended Maria Wielogłowska in Europe. Maria was the daughter of Polish immigrants and was two years her senior. Their friendship, which began during their school years, opened cordial relations between the families and made Heinrich Freiherr von Richthofen the acquaintance of Maria Wielogłowska. Eliza adored Maria and Maria's mother, Konstancja Wielogłowska.

I was fortunate to find young Eliza's letters written to the Wielogłowski family in the archives of the Polish Academy of Arts and Sciences in Kraków. Eliza's cordiality, empathy, and compassion in her letters confirmed the stories of my grandmother. Today, Eliza's feelings would be perceived as very passionate, but Eliza lived in a different culture and bygone era. Eliza had a heart of gold and warm personality so her compassion for family and friends was fondly remembered by the generations of my family who knew her. When she was a young girl, close family members and friends used to call her diminutively "Lisiątko."

Below are excerpts from a letter 18-year-old Eliza Freiin von Richthofen wrote in April 1846 to Maria's mother, Konstancja Wielogłowska:

> My angelic mother, I kiss your hands and feet for these few words which you, my beautiful mom, wrote to me in the letter coming from Marynia. Oh! How these words made me happy! I kissed the letters that your hand put on the paper…I enjoyed this letter so much, like a little child. I was carrying it to stores and wherever we went, reading it again, or at least looking at it... Now I am going to finish my note, dear mother, because I want to write a few words to Marynia. Don't forget about me…I assure you

about my appreciation and attachment... kissing your hands ...your daughter, Lisiątko (Richthofen, 1846). [40]

Young Eliza Freiin von Richthofen lived in a time in history when Poland did not exist as an independent country. Nevertheless, Polish families continued to cherish their roots, spoke the Polish language, and proudly taught their children the history of Poland. A few times during Eliza's life, Poles fought against their invaders for the independence of Poland. However, being a child of Polish German parents likely was a challenge for Eliza. In her heart, even if political events did not have instant and direct impact on her life, Eliza realized that the lives of people she loved were affected. On April 15, 1846, she wrote from Rusko to Konstancja Wielogłowska:

> I don't have much news from here. It is quiet and depressing... One more, sad message I have to deliver to you – Sir Lipowski, our relative, was killed. His wife still has been hiding in forests, she was severely wounded... Oh my God, my God, what's happening now? (Richthofen, 1846).[41]

Apparently, Eliza wrote about her Polish relatives repressed by Prussian authorities in the Grand Duchy of Posen. In the same letter, Eliza asked Konstancja about Kacper Wielogłowski, the great uncle of Marynia Wielogłowska and the Chairman of the Senate of the Independent City of Kraków. Kacper was engaged in the Kraków Uprising of 1846; and after the revolution failed, he was expelled from Kraków and sent to prison in Warsaw, which was occupied by Russians. Eliza wrote:

> I just learned from Konstanty Miłkowski the saddest news that the man about whom the newspapers write is Sir Kacper. Is it true? How much I have already cried and worried thinking about the grief you had to feel when you heard the news. What heartbreak you must go through when you do not know what is his destiny. I beg you, my dear mom, to let me know if you, I hope, have any

---

[40] B PAU Kraków, rkps 1844, E. Richthofen to K. Wielogłowska, Letter, 1846.
[41] Ibid.

better news. You know that I not only love you, but also all your relatives and friends (Richthofen, 1846).[42]

Unfortunately, Kacper Wielogłowski (1770-1846) was older and in poor health and could not survive a long imprisonment in the very poor conditions of the Warsaw prison, which was well-known to Poles as Warsaw Citadel. He died there on August 13, 1846.[43]

I wrote briefly about Eliza's childhood within the framework of her parents' lives in Chapter 1. She spent her early years under the care of her maternal grandmother in the Grand Duchy of Posen (nowadays Wielkopolska) while her parents traveled. At some point, she began to travel with her parents and brother Heinrich to Europe often and lived in different cities, including Paris, where Heinrich fell in love with Maria Wielogłowska, Eliza's beloved friend. Eliza spent a lot of time with the Wielogłowski family, who sometimes took care of her in the absence of her parents, and the knowledge of their engagement helped me to understand why Eliza called Konstancja Wielogłowska "my dear mom." I am confident that Eliza, as the child of nobility, received the traditional education of the time; and as a member of the German and Polish elite society, she spoke Polish, German, and French. I found no information that she had any artistic or musical talents.

She was raised in the Catholic faith, which was decided by her parents even before her birth. Her father also planned that she would marry a Pole. My grandmother did not tell me about the circumstances of Eliza meeting a young, childless widower, Antoni Szydłowski (1824-1900), a nobleman with the family coat of arms Lubicz and the owner of the Werbkowice estate, near Lublin in the eastern part of Poland. Eliza was 20 years old and Antoni was five years older; and they married on September 19, 1849. [44]

---

[42] B PAU Kraków, rkps 1844, E. Richthofen to K. Wielogłowska, Letter, 1846.
[43] J. Kuzicki, Orężem i pracą – Życie i działalność Walerego Wielogłowskiego (1805-1865), Rzeszów, 2005, p. 140.
[44] W. v. Hueck, Op. Cit., p. 318.

Eliza and Antoni were happily married for 51 years. They seemed to be well-matched and a loving couple, but unfortunately, they had their share of heartbreaks and tragedies in their lives. They lost two children: daughter Teofilka, who died as a child, and son Mieczysław Szydłowski, who passed away when he was only 20 years old. I learned the names of Eliza's children from Eliza's will, which I found in the archives I inherited, but the causes of their deaths were not available. One of the old photos from my family albums shows two children, a boy and a girl. The girl so closely resembles Eliza Freiin von Richthofen that it is easy to conjecture that the girl was her daughter, Teofilka Szydłowska. Unfortunately, the photo was not labeled with the family names and the date. Only the photographer's name was imprinted, Gerbruder Siebe, from Breslau (Wrocław).

Upon their son Mieczysław's death, Eliza and Antoni were childless. Eliza's deep faith strengthened her through all the heartbreak of losing both of her children, and she decided to pour her overflowing love on her brother Heinrich's children and then his grandchildren. She also was very close to her mother's family, the sisters of Paulina née Objezierska Freifrau von Richthofen and their children. In 1859, she became the godmother of Leonja Maria Franciszka, the daughter of Konstanty Miłkowski and Franciszka "Fanny" Objezierska (Paulina von Richthofen's sister). The godfather of little Leonja was Leon Smitkowski, who was the owner of Łęg in the Province of Posen (Prowincja Poznańska) and was among the 149 Poles accused of treason by the Prussian authory in 1864.[45] Some of the defendants, along with Count Jan Kanty Działyński as their leader, were convicted of fighting in the January Uprising of 1863, while others were found guilty of helping Polish revolutionaries break away from Prussia in an attempt to restore Poland within its former borders of 1771 before the Polish lands were seized by Prussia, Austria, and Russia in 1772. The treason trial, which was also called the Berlin Process, lasted from July 7 to December 23 of

---

[45] B PAU Kórnik, Teki Dworzaczka, Metrykalia katolickie część 5 nr. 34610 (Wieszczyczyn); N. Sulerzyski, Pamietniki Natalisa Sulerzeskiego b. posła ziemi pruskiej na sejm berliński, tom III, Kraków, 1871, p. 63.

1864, and Leon Smitkowski was sentenced to one year in prison. To my knowledge, Eliza Szydłowska and her husband were not involved in the uprising.

Eliza did not call her husband by his given name of Antoni, but rather a nickname, "Depciunio," so he was remembered as Depciunio by generations of my family. The nickname was formed from a Polish word "deputowany" which means "deputy" and referred to Antoni's title in the Parliament. The honor of Antoni's public service sometimes was extended to his wife; and people who adored titles called Eliza Szydłowska "Madame Deputatowa," which I learned from my great-grandmother's correspondence. Józef, an acquaintance from the circle of my great-great aunt Eliza, wrote to my great-grandmother that he learned from Madame Deputatowa that Bronia felt in a new house in Kraków like in heaven! [46]

Antoni Szydłowski started a sheep farm on the family estate he inherited from his father Adam in Werbkowice, which is near Hrubieszów in eastern Poland. The villages of Werbkowice, Konopne, and Wilków were owned by Antoni's grandfather, General Teodor Szydłowski, which then were passed on to Antoni's father, who built a palace in Webkowice in the middle of the 19th century. In 1827, when Antoni Szydłowski was a child, only 326 inhabitants lived in the 60 houses in the village of Werbkowice and the Werbkowice estate was in poor condition when Antoni inherited it.

Antoni's estate was very profitable; and his farm of 2,267 head of sheep was the largest sheep farm in the Polish Kingdom and one of the first to specialize in breeding lambs at the time. While sheep breeding was Antoni's domain, Eliza was fond of gardening. The Szydłowskis were members of the Association of Farmers and Artisans, and Eliza's gardening successes, such as growing a pineapple in a greenhouse on the Werbkowice estate, were heralded in the Warsaw Newspaper in 1874.[47]

---

[46] Ivona Tarko's archives: B. Richthofen, Correspondence.
[47] Gazeta Warszawska, 1874, Numer 209.

The lack of information about Antoni's childhood and youth is understandable because he joined the von Richthofen family as the husband of Eliza. I was able to confirm that his mother, Teofila Szydłowska, maiden name Kamieniecka, passed away in the year Antoni was born, probably in childbirth. Antoni named his daughter after his mother. I also was able to find few details about Antoni's activities in Werbkowice, such as a note in the Grabowiecki Biographical Dictionary which said that Antoni Szydłowski supplied horses from his estate for the visit of the Russian Tsar Nicholas in 1846. Antoni received three rubles and eight kopecks for his service. Antoni also was remembered by his descendants as the founder of the Uniate Church in Werbkowice, erected in 1864, which later was changed to the Orthodox Church, and much later, in 1918, the Catholic Church. The erection of the Uniate church during the year when the persecution of its members started was not only a generous gesture but also a testament of his support for the oppressed. The founding of the Uniate Church on Polish land was proclaimed by the Pact of 1596 and it continued to grow for the next 150 years. The members of the Uniate Church believed in Catholic dogma and agreed with papal supremacy but kept the Julian calendar and the organization and rites of the Orthodox Church. Both of Antoni's estates, Werbkowice and Kupientyn, were located within the borders of the Polish Kingdom and the region where many peasants belonged to the Uniate Church. Unfortunately, after the failure of the January 1863 Uprising, cruel oppression was inflicted on the members of the Uniate Church by Russian officials acting on the orders of the Tsar.

Kupientyn, which also was owned by Antoni and Eliza Szydłowski, was the estate Eliza Freiin von Richthofen brought in her dowry. This village was located north of Sokołów Podlaski in the central part of Poland. The first records about Kupientyn are from the 15th century. Throughout the years, it changed ownership frequently and shifted between glory and negligence for many years. The Kupientyn estate was in its worst condition during the Swedish invasion and occupation of Poland in the 17th century. In the 19th century, when it belonged to the Szydłowski family, its territory included 2,244 acres, of which 1,500 acres were dedicated to the palace located on a hill 100 meters from the Cetynia River and the palace grounds. When Antoni became the owner of Kupientyn, he decided to replace its old wooden mansion with a new Italian Renaissance style structure. In 1891, the Szydłowski family sold the Kupientyn estate, and it had various owners thereafter until the end of World War II. When the Communist regime came into power at the end of World War II, the estate was divided into small lots and a few families lived in the old, rundown palace. The palace with its surrounding park has been under private ownership since 1998.[48]

At the time of my great-great-grandparents, significant wedding anniversaries were important events for which families gathered to celebrate with the couple. The below photo celebrating the 50th wedding anniversary of Eliza and Antoni, still preserved today, is a perfect illustration of the customs from their special moment in time. According to Maria Estreicherówna, writer and translator, well-known in Kraków, Poland, for her book describing Polish society in the 19th century, the golden anniversaries of weddings were celebrated with precise rules of ritual. The spouses who celebrated the golden jubilee were expected to walk in a procession holding canes with golden crosses; and in front of them, their children and grandchildren should march with candles and flowers (Estreicherówna, 1968).[49]

Antoni died of natural causes in 1900 on the Werbkowice estate. Grandmother Antonina told me the following anecdote about Antoni's death. When Antoni was on his death bed, all at once, he felt the presence of the deceased members of his family and friends in his room, and loudly, but tenderly, he began reciting their names. The ladies tending him were sitting by his bed and heard the names of Antoni's grandfather, Teodor; Antoni's son, Mieczysław; and Antoni's mother and daughter, Teofila. Suddenly, Antoni at the top of his voice asked with bewilderment…is that you, Jasiu Rulikowski? Upon hearing that name, the ladies, terribly frightened, ran away in panic from Antoni's room.

---

[48] http://www.dwory.net/Sokolow%20Podlaski,%20powiat/kupientyn.html accessed 03-01-2016.
[49] M. Esteicherówna, Życie Towarzyskie i Obyczajowe w Krakowie w Latach 1848-1863, Kraków, 1868, v 1, p. 107.

Jubilaci

Eliza i Antoni Szydłowscy

serdecznie dziękują za łaskawie

przysłane życzenia.

Werbkowice d. 24 Września 1898 r.

Top: *Eliza née Freiin von Richthofen Szydłowska photos taken during her life.*
Bottom left: *Photo of Eliza and Antoni Szydłowski, who are in the middle of the first row, celebrating their 50th wedding anniversary with family and friends at the Werbkowice estate, and standing on either side of them are Eliza's cousin Liza Ślaska and husband Edward.* **Bottom right**: *Szydłowski's thank you note, which read as follows: The celebrators of the jubilee, Eliza and Antoni Szydłowscy, cordially thank you for the received kind wishes. Werbkowice, September 24, 1898.[50]*

---

[50] Ivona Tarko's archives.

Why were they so terrified? Jasiu Rulikowski, the owner of one of the nearby estates in the Hrubieszów region and Antoni's neighbor, was believed to be alive and in a perfect health when Antoni named him as one of the deceased in his room. The event caused even more amazement later that night in the Szydłowski household when a messenger from the Rulikowski estate came to Werbkowice to announce the sudden death of Jasiu Rulikowski that night.

Even though the Rulikowski family was not part of my research, out of curiosity I decided to check whether any Rulikowski family members actually lived at the time of Antoni. I learned from the website of the Oszczów and Honiatyn villages in the Hrubieszów region of Poland that these estates belonged to the Rulikowski family in the 19th century, and one of the owners was named Jan Rulikowski (the nickname of Jan is Jasiu). Was Grandmother Antonia's anecdote factual?

After her husband's death, tourism was a panacea for Eliza's loneliness. I think she inherited her love for travelling from her parents and enjoyed visiting elegant European spas and cities. Lizia Ślaska, Eliza's much younger cousin from Eliza's mother's family, usually accompanied her. The postcards written by them and sent to my great-grandparents show the places of their journeys and destinations. Every year Eliza also traveled from the Webkowice estate to Kraków and spent a few months in the city living in the Hotel Saski, which today still exists and even the name has not changed since the 19th century. The hotel is situated on Sławkowska Street number 3, close to the intersection with St. Thomas Street, in the center of Kraków, Poland.

Gradually, Eliza's health started to decline. She stopped travelling and stayed in the Werbkowice estate in the care of her cousin, Lizia Ślaska. Eliza's niece, nephews, and the nephews' children usually visited her in summer. They all tried to stay in touch by writing letters and sending postcards and photos. Eliza felt close to death several times so in 1904 she prepared her will, and below are excerpts of the will which were Eliza's farewell.

At the moment when I lost my best and dearest husband, the state of my ownership was changed because, besides my own assets (I have my dowry and an inheritance from my parents as well as what I earned myself), I own the estate that was left to me by my dear husband, Antoni Szydłowski. According to the wishes of my dear parents and my late husband, my goal is to divide in a fair way and with caring kindness the legacy among mine and my husband's relatives, those who offered us solace, kindness, and help in the time of our difficulties. Not only the family and friends, but also the servants, proved their true affection and dedication, so I say to all of you, on behalf my late husband and from the bottom of my heart, God Bless You! (Szydłowska, 1904).[51]

After Eliza's sincere introduction, the detailed list of her heirs and assets followed, from which I learned the names of relatives' unknown to me and never mentioned in our family stories. I also learned the magnitude of Eliza's wealth. Eliza née Freiin von Richthofen Szydłowska, my great-great-great-aunt, was not only the owner of the prosperous Werbkowice estate, but also, among other things, had shares in the profit of Radom Steel Glass in the Polish Kingdom, the Factory "Syrena," and the Hotel "Bristol" in Warsaw. She passed the ownership of the Werbkowice estate to her younger cousin Lizia, the daughter of Franciszka Objezierska.

In the closing statement of her will, Eliza said the following:

When I say goodbye to all of you, dear to my heart, I ask all of you for whom our memory would remain genial, for a gracious prayer for the souls of my husband and me, the souls of our children, and our dear deceased, and also for genuine harmony and love in the family and among friends (Szydłowska, 1904).[52]

---

[51] Ivona Tarko's archives: E. Szydłowska, Mój Testament, 1904.
[52] Ibid.

Her wishes came true and she was remembered by the members of my family as the candid Grandma Szydłowska.

In addition to the copy of Eliza's will and her few pictures, I have a booklet that belonged to her, which was published in Warsaw by Ludwik Biernacki i S-KI in 1909 entitled *Kiedy się urodził Juljusz Słowacki? Kilka uwag historyczno-prawnych o dacie urodzin poety* [When Was Juliusz Słowacki Born? A Few Historical and Legal Comments about the Date of the Poet's Birth], written by Leopold Meyet. The booklet was issued on the 100th anniversary of the birth of the Polish bard, who personally knew the parents of Eliza, Paulina, and Wilhelm von Richthofen and visited them in Rome in 1836. It is hard to say if Eliza, seven years old at the time of her parents' acquaintance with Juliusz Słowacki, could remember him, but perhaps she had an opportunity to meet Juliusz again in 1848 in Breslau (Wrocław) when he came to the city for a short visit.

The copy of the booklet written by Leopold Meyet is precious to me because it is signed by the author and dedicated to Eliza Szydłowska. Leopold Meyet (1850-1912) also published Juliusz Słowacki's letters to his mother in 1909, which I cited in Chapter 1. Meyet's writing was not valued much at the time, but rather was known as a researcher of the Romantic period in Poland and a collector of memorabilia from the era, including the signatures of well-known writers. Leopold Meyet came from a French Jewish family that assimilated in Poland. He was a lawyer by education and profession but a writer by passion. He gave his collection of the Słowacki archives to the Krasiński Library in Warsaw, which was lost in a fire that destroyed the library during the Warsaw Uprising of 1944. Leopold Meyet is buried in the Jewish Cemetery in Warsaw, Poland.

The heart has reasons that the mind knows not...Pascal

I had so many dots to connect and some mysteries to solve during my research, especially when I tried to find more than the date of birth and death of Eliza Szydłowska's only sibling, her older brother Heinrich von

Richthofen. I believe that Eliza introduced Heinrich to her best friend, Maria Wielogłowska, and that acquaintance flourished into love. As I wrote in the introduction, Heinrich and Maria seemed to belong to different worlds; and it was easier for me to find out what could divide them than what could connect them, except their feelings. Chapter 3 is mainly devoted to Maria Wielogłowska and her background, but now I will share some facts about Heinrich's youth and upbringing.

Heinrich Wilhelm Raphael von Richthofen, the son of Wilhelm, born on December 7, 1826, in Schutzendorf (Polish Strzałkowa)[53] in Lower Silesia, was not only my great-great-grandfather but also the most mysterious character among my von Richthofen ancestors because I found very little information about him. My grandmother and mother knew only the basic facts of his life and when I pressed them with questions, they responded, "Well, you know, Henryk (they used only the Polish form of his name Heinrich), he was Marynia Wielogłowska's husband, a melancholic young man who played the violin…but Maria was such a good person, etc., etc." So, I knew little when I started to write the book, but thanks to Karl-Friedrich Freiherr von Richthofen and the documents he sent me, gradually, I discovered more about the life of my great-great-grandfather.

First of all, I learned that Heinrich, in accordance with his father's wishes, was raised Protestant while Eliza, Heinrich's sister, was raised in the Catholic faith. This religious division between the von Richthofen siblings was the result of a compromise their parents made. I believe it was almost impossible to achieve because their Grandmother Apolonia Objezierska, a devout Catholic, cared for them almost exclusively in their early years. Later, when schools were chosen for them, especially when the schools were managed by religious orders, the religious division between Eliza and Heinrich became more pronounced.

I am sure that the arrival of their first child, Heinrich, was a happy event for Paulina and Wilhelm von Richthofen because Heinrich was the heir

---

[53] W. v. Hueck, Op. Cit., p. 317.

to whom the family title and estate would be passed and who would uphold the family name through his hoped for children to continue the Royn-Schutzendorf line of the von Richthofen family. Despite the significance of Heinrich's birth, Paulina and Wilhelm were minimally involved in his early childhood. Paulina and Wilhelm traveled extensively and Heinrich spent most of the time they were away at the Rusko estate, the Grand Duchy of Posen (Wielkopolska), which was owned by his Objezierski maternal grandparents, and at the Hertwigswaldau (Polish Snowidza) estate in Lower Silesia, the village located more or less 35 miles from Breslau (Wrocław) owned by the von Richthofen fraternal grandparents. The Hertwigswaldau estate manor, built in the 17th century and remodeled in the 19th century, was surrounded by a moat; and this medieval feature surely stimulated the children's imaginations. Besides Heinrich's grandparents, his uncle, Karl Heinrich Ludwig Freiherr von Richthofen, and his family also lived at Hertwigswaldau (Snowidza). In 1829, Karl's oldest son and Heinrich's first cousin, Hermann Freiherr von Richthofen, was born there. Throughout the years, four more children came into the world and eventually Heinrich lived and played with five first cousins from the von Richthofen family: Mathilda, Hermann, Karl, Ferdinand, and Eugen. There were no children close to Heinrich's age in the immediate Objezierski family of Heinrich's mother however. Heinrich lost both grandfathers when he was of school age. Wilhelm Ludwig Freiherr von Richthofen passed away at the Hertwigswaldau (Snowidza) estate on April 13, 1838; and one year later, Heinrich's maternal grandfather, Rafał Objezierski, died in Rusko.

According to Emil Freiherr von Richthofen, Wilhelm and Paulina returned from southern Europe to live with their children in 1834 when Heinrich was already eight years old. It is quite possible that his parents' long periods of recurrent and extended absences during Heinrich's early life induced his future problem with melancholy (depression). Although the von Richthofen family was finally united in 1834, Paulina and Wilhelm were restless staying in one place so they spent that first year going back and forth from Rusko to Hertwigswaldau (Snowidza) and

Marienbad and had already started planning their next trip to Italy. However, Wilhelm and Paulina's second stay in Italy from 1835 to 1837 was very different from the first as they took Heinrich and Eliza along as well as their governess and teachers because both children were in school by then. According to Emil Freiherr von Richthofen, one of Heinrich's teachers was a Polish Catholic chosen by Grandmother Apolonia Objezierska. Apparently, the children were homeschooled abroad for a few years, and then at the appropriate age were sent to boarding schools in Switzerland which had a good reputation. Emil Freiherr von Richthofen mentioned that Heinrich attended the Protestant school, which was managed by a Prussian mathematician.

Heinrich spent the summer of 1845 with his parents and sister in Paris, where they met many Polish immigrants who arrived in France and lived there after the November 1830 Uprising in the Polish Kingdom. Among them was the Wielogłowski family. Heinrich's father noted in his diary that his son fell in love with Maria Wielogłowska that summer. Jerzy Kuzicki wrote in his biography of Walery Wielogłowski that Heinrich wanted to marry Maria in 1845, but his parents disagreed; they thought that Heinrich was too young to start a family. This statement seems appropriate since Heinrich was only 19 years old, and his parents also wanted him to continue his education. On the other hand, I believe that Maria's parents considered their daughter, who celebrated her 18th birthday on February 14, 1845, was already at the suitable age for marriage. Maria's mother, Konstancja Wielogłowska, was 16 when she walked down the aisle as was Heinrich's mother, Paulina Objezierska, when she said "I do" to Wilhelm Freiherr von Richthofen. With every passing day, Maria Wielogłowska was closer to that moment when she could be called a spinster, which appeared to be the worst nightmare for 19th century young women and their parents.

Completing his education was a priority for Heinrich but more important for Heinrich at that time was returning to Germany to fulfill his aristocratic family's expectation that he would serve in Germany's military. His marriage plans thus receded into the background. I learned from the book by Emil Freiherr von Richthofen that Heinrich served in the military in Berlin during 1846 and 1847; and after he finished his service, he went to the Hohenheim Institute in Stuttgart to study agriculture because Heinrich, as Wilhelm's only son and his heir, had to be prepared to manage the family estate. The Hohenheim Institute was founded in 1818 and was a place where sons of notable landlords or wealthy citizens who wanted to devote their life to a farm household could learn theory and practical skills (Krynicki, 1824).[54] The institute offered classes in mathematics, physics, chemistry, botany, zoology, mineralogy, forestry, and veterinary. The schools of agriculture and forestry received good reviews, especially forestry, so the institute was upgraded to the level of academy in 1847. When Heinrich attended the academy, there were seven permanent positions for professors, of which two taught agriculture, two forestry, and the others mathematics, physics, and technology. Other subjects like apiculture, gardening, fruit-growing, veterinary, and accounting were taught by temporary, sometimes part-time, professors depending on the demand of students for the courses. The Hohenheim Academy provided its graduates with solid training in operating and managing farms and properties and also provided scholarships to the underprivileged sons of farmers.

There is no way to know if studying agriculture interested Heinrich. Most certainly, it was a practical education and was probably suggested by Heinrich's father. Heinrich did not give any indication of having an interest in academia because he did not go to study at the University of Breslau (Wrocław) or Berlin like his cousin Ferdinand Freiherr von Richthofen, who devoted his life to science and became a well-known geographer and expert in geology. I wonder when Heinrich's passion for the violin began and why he did not pursue this interest as his career. Whatever was decided about Heinrich's education, it most certainly was in agreement with his father. The subordination of children was expected at that time, as Walery Wielogłowski wrote in one of his books.

---

[54] J. Krynicki, Opisanie Instytutu Gospodarstwa Wieyskiego w Hohenheim Podług Najnowszego Urzędzenia, Wilno, 1824, p. 4.

In a family which consists of a father, a mother, and children, the father holds power, wife ministry, and children are subordinate to them because hierarchy is necessary; and it is not oppressive for any of them since it comes from love and is kept according to their mutual goal (Wielogłowski, 1849).[55]

I believe that, in general, Heinrich tried to be a subordinate and good son, but he was stubborn in one thing: he wanted to be a Catholic. He confessed to his father when he came of age that he felt close to Catholicism in his heart and conscience for years, and he wanted to convert. Apparently, the influence of Protestant schools was not strong in the face of the guidance of the Catholic Objezierski family; the circle of the CR congregation; Heinrich's uncle, Karl Heinrich von Richthofen; and Maria Wielogłowska, a devout Catholic.

In 1846 Heinrich lost his fraternal grandmother after whom he was named; Henriette Freifrau von Richthofen died in Wrocław, where she lived with her younger son, Karl Freiherr von Richthofen, and his family after the death of her husband, Wilhelm Ludwig Freiherr von Richthofen. The family decided to sell the Hertwigswaldau (Snowidza) estate when Wilhelm Ludwig passed away and they moved to Breslau (Wrocław). Henriette's older son, Wilhelm, already had a house there, full of life and frequent guests invited by his wife Paulina and him to discuss literature, art, music, and current social and political events. In 1847 the Wilhelm family, except Heinrich, who spent most of his time in Berlin and Stuttgart, was engaged in supervising the building of the Lusowo palace, about which I wrote in Chapter 1.

I was extremely happy when I found a letter dated March 1, 1847, written from Breslau (Wrocław) to the parents of Maria Wielogłowska by the Wielogłowski family's friend, Adam Rokossowski, in which he described his visit to the von Richthofens. The letter gave insight into what was happening between both families at the time when their children were in love.

---

[55] W. Wielogłowski, Godła Rewolucyjne Wobec Prawdy, Wrocław, 1849, p. 19.

Dear Kosia and Walery,

As your friend, I tried, as fast as I could to meet Paulina von Richthofen, and I have seen her a few times already before her departure. Our evenings became splendid, even when this worldly joy, instead of making me merry, increased my sorrow. At the beginning, I was with my grief alone but now I think about our mutual heartbreaks.

Baroness von Richthofen and her daughter (I did not meet him (Baron von Richthofen) nor their son) are very nice, cheerful, kind, polite persons, whom everybody would like, not only me, especially when they seem to love you and Marynia truthfully. They admire Marynia, and they seem to be very attached to you. We talked about you a lot, but never in a way that could suggest that they would like to be more related to you. I know from Zuzia, that they asked her a lot about your assets and your prospects in the future so I hold myself aloof to avoid similar investigation. They have style and their children's happiness honestly seems to be important for them. It gives hope that their son's constancy will decide. If you believe that waiting for him means happiness for Marynia, maybe you would consider meeting them and their children somewhere next summer, just to stay in touch, because you are far away (Rokossowski, 1847).[56]

The sorrow about which Adam Rokossowski wrote was caused by the family members and friends lost during the 1846 uprising. It was a difficult time for many Polish families in the Grand Duchy of Posen (Wielkopolska) and in the region of Kraków. In 1847, Maria Wielogłowska, the daughter of a political emigrant, whose assets and the Zborów estate in the Polish Kingdom were confiscated by the Russians as punishment to Walery Wielogłowski for fighting against the Russians in the November Uprising in 1830, lived in Western Europe. The financial situation of the Wielogłowski family was complicated so they

---

[56] B PAU, Kraków, rkps 1844: A. Rokossowski to the Wielogłowski family, 1847.

could not guarantee a big dowry for their daughter. I believe that feelings, not financial speculation, perhaps decided the future of their relationship. When Maria fell in love and was sure about Heinrich's feelings, she was willing to wait for an official engagement for a few years. Maria also knew the importance of love in a relationship from observing her parents for years, for which I provide more details in Chapter 3.

Maria Estreicherówna, in her book about social life in Kraków during 1848-1863, wrote the following:

> Marriage was often the result of common sense or conventional rules, and young girls decided about getting married quickly because they most feared being a spinster. The spinster life, which was not a desirable state, offered two options: the humiliating life of a resident in a family member's house or the life of a disrespected governess in somebody's residence (Estreicherówna, 1968).[57]

What would have happened if Maria Wielogłowska, after the years of waiting for Heinrich, did not become his wife? I believe that Maria would have considered entering a convent. What would have happened to Heinrich if he had not married Maria? We will never know, but it is obvious that if he had married a German girl, there would not be a Polish branch of the von Richthofen family.

In the first half of 1848, the political and social movement called the Spring of Nations that took place in Europe brought changes which gave the Wielogłowski family, as political refugees, the opportunity to return to their hometown of Kraków which they left 12 years earlier. In the summer of 1848, Maria Wielogłowska went with her parents to Breslau (Wrocław) in Silesia, where they waited for the permission of the Austrian authorities to return to Kraków. The few months which the Wielogłowski family spent in Breslau (Wrocław) was the perfect time to get closer to the von Richthofen family, who were focused at that time on preparing for the wedding of Eliza Freiin von Richthofen and Antoni

---

[57] M. Estreicherówna, Op.Cit., T 1, p. 101.

Szydłowski. I am sure that Maria Wielogłowska, a close friend of Eliza, was involved, perhaps not hands-on but emotionally, in the arrangements, and both young women were able to spend time together before moving the future Lady Antoni Szydłowski to her husband's estate in Webkowice near Lublin in eastern Poland.

I assume that Heinrich (Henryk) Freiherr von Richthofen and Maria Wielogłowska were officially engaged in the summer or autumn of 1851 when the Wielogłowski family settled in Kraków. Heinrich's family situation became complicated in 1851 with the announcement of the divorce of his parents in April and then his father's marriage to Maria Carolina Kruger in June. I conjecture that Heinrich's father's second marriage resulted in estrangement between father and son and accelerated Heinrich's decision to marry. There also may have been a positive impact on his decision by the contented marriage of Heinrich's sister, Eliza, who was the happy wife of Antoni Szydłowski and mother of Mieczysław.

The portrait of Heinrich as a young man, preserved by my grandmother, was a watercolor painted by an unknown artist but may have been Wilhelm Freiherr von Richthofen. Heinrich inherited the blonde hair and blue eyes of his father. My mother stated that Heinrich was a delicate, not physically strong melancholic, who spent most of his life playing the violin. Of course, my mother did not know her great-grandfather personally, but the family opinion about him, passed from one generation to another, could be one-sided and very iniquitous, and likely may have applied to Heinrich when he was already an older man.

The next chapter is devoted to Maria Wielogłowska, her family, her upbringing, and the period before her marriage to Heinrich (Henryk) Freiherr von Richthofen. Knowing the Wielogłowski family story helped me understand how the descendants of Heinrich (Henryk) Freiherr von Richthofen from the Schutzendorf House became more Polish than German.

The portrait of Heinrich (Henryk) Freiherr von Richthofen (1826-1878.).[58]

[58] Ivona Tarko's collection.

CHAPTER 3 The Wielogłowski and Wessel Families: the Ancestors of Maria Freifrau von Richthofen

For a man to achieve all what is demanded of him he must regard himself as greater than he is

~ Johann Wolfgang von Goethe

Heinrich (Henryk) Freiherr von Richthofen fell in love with Maria Wielogłowska in the summer of 1845 in Paris when he spent some time at the Wielogłowski home, which had become legendary for its welcoming atmosphere and hospitality in the circle of Poles visiting or living in exile in Paris. Maria's mother, Konstancja, was a kind person who took care of all those in need and was known by her friends as a wonderful example of what a mother, wife, and Christian woman should be. She lived up to that image through her philanthropy and volunteer work with poor immigrants in the Society of Polish Ladies. Maria's father, Walery Wielogłowski, tried to bring together the conflicting circles of Polish immigrants; but he mainly devoted himself to pastoral work within the Congregation of the Resurrection of Our Lord Jesus Christ and started different businesses to support his family. One of Walery's acquaintances, Stanisław Mieroszewski, remembered him as a noble, kind, warm gentleman, who was well educated and talented, but for whom immigrant life was a challenge because he was born into a wealthy family but lost his fortune during an uprising and was unprepared to work to support his family.

This chapter is devoted to the life of the Wielogłowski family. I think it would be helpful to review first some of the facts about Maria's parents, whose extraordinary lives deserved retelling in a book for centuries, but was not accomplished until Jerzy Kuzicki published his biography of Walery Wielogłowski in Poland in 2005, which was a very helpful information and reference source for me.

Maria's father, Walery Mikołaj Napoleon Wielogłowski, was born on December 6, 1805 on the Proszówki estate near Kraków, which was owned by his maternal grandmother, Józefa née Badeni Wielogłowska. Walery was the only son of Ignacy Wielogłowski, a Polish nobleman and the owner of many villages and farms located in the Polish Kingdom. Zborów was the largest manor in the Stopnica district in the Polish Kingdom, which the Wielogłowski family had owned since the 18th century. The beautiful classical-styled palace built by the Wielogłowski family in the 19th century and a beautiful park with linden and chestnut trees still exist. In 1799 Walery's mother, Marianna, married his first cousin Ignacy, which was perhaps the reason that the couple could not have more children.

The lineage of the Wielogłowski family, with the coat of arms Starykoń, has been traced back to medieval times; and Otto Topór, who was living in Kraków in 1260, is the oldest documented member of the Wielogłowski family.[59] Ignacy Wielogłowski, Walery's father and Maria's paternal grandfather, studied law at the Academy of Kraków and was a novice in the office of the court of the last Polish King, Stanisław August Poniatowski. Walery's grandfather and Maria's great-grandfather, Józef Wielogłowski, was a member of the Polish Parliament, called the Great Diet, from 1788 to 1792.

Walery Wielogłowski spent his childhood on the Proszówki estate in the care of his grandmother, which appeared to be a common practice at the time. It was in her home where he was introduced to the Catholic faith, Polish tradition and hospitality, and patriotism. Growing up during one of the times in history when Poland lost its independence, he learned about Polish history and politics by listening to the conversations of many guests who visited his grandmother's mansion. The atmosphere of the Proszówki estate is described in the memoir *Dom mojej babki* [My Grandmother's Home],[60] he wrote as an adult. Walery's early formal education when he lived with his grandmother was in the hands of two tutors, a Pole and a Frenchman.

Walery's parents spent most of their time on the Zborów estate; but in the winter during the carnival season, they visited Kraków where they owned a house in the center of the city. When Walery reached school age, he attended the best private school for young noblemen in Kraków, which was owned by Professor Józef Sołtykowicz where, although his favorite subject was chemistry, he showed a gift for writing. After finishing the six-year program at the Sołtykowicz School, Walery entered the Jagiellonian University and began classes in philosophy, history,

---

[59] J. Kuzicki, Uproszczona Tablica Genealogiczna Rodu Wielogłowskich, Op. Cit.
[60] W. Wielogłowski, Dom mojej babki, Kraków, 1856.

mathematics, and physics. However, 17-year-old Walery's education was halted in 1822 when Russian Tsar Alexander the First declared that students from the Polish Kingdom were banned from studying in Kraków. At that time, Poland was a semi-independent state and Tsar Alexander the First was the King of Poland, but Kraków was a "free city" in Austrian-held Galicia.

Between 1823 and 1830 Walery learned to manage the Zborów estate, which included 12 villages. He also made plans to create a spa in Solec, a village he owned, where saline springs were used in homeopathy. He became an active member of the Credit Association of Landowners and later its assessor of honor. He was also the marshal of the regional council of the gathered nobility of the Stopnica region.

In 1825, Walery married Countess Konstancja Wessel (1808-1863), the daughter of Count Karol Wessel, a nobleman with the coat of arms Rogala, and Lady Matylda Gostkowska. The Wessel family has a very interesting history. Their ancestors came from Hungary to Poland in the 16th century with Stefan Batory, who was Hungarian by birth but was chosen by Polish nobility to be the Polish King. The Wessel family settled in the region of Płock and became prominent citizens of the 17th century when a few members of the Wessel family became senators in Warsaw, the capital of Poland. In 1647, Adalbert Wessel founded the Church and Convent of Carmelites in Warsaw. Adalbert's son, Stanisław Wessel, accompanied Polish King Jan Sobieski on his war expedition to Vienna to save Christianity and to fight against the Turks, whom he defeated in 1683. While in Vienna, Stanisław Wessel met the niece of Count Ernst Rudiger Stahrenberg, the commander of Vienna; and they married and started their family in Vienna. The couple was blessed with many children, of whom one daughter, Maria, later became the daughter-in-law of King Jan Sobieski.

The website of the Wilanów Museum in Poland contains a chapter called "Personalities and Biographies," where there is information about the boisterous marriage of King Jan Sobieski's son, Konstanty Sobieski, and Maria Wessel.

I remember my mother's excitement when she read about young Maria Wessel in a book written by Hanna Muszyńska-Hoffmanowa, *Panie na Wilanowie* [The Ladies of Wilanów] where the author described the engagement party organized for the King's daughter, Kunegunda Sobieska. It was a joyful event that ended with drinking and dancing in the circle of the royal family; and among the royal sons, Konstanty Sobieski, who resembled his father in appearance, danced all the time with the daughter of the forewoman, Lady Wessel, who they called at that time a little Marysia. The girl was jumping like a small bird, and this image melted the heart of Konstanty Sobieski.

The wedding of Maria Wessel and Konstanty Sobieski took place in Gdańsk on November 18, 1708. The couple did not have children; and Maria née Wessel Sobieska, in her last will, in 1753, therefore bequeathed to her nephew, Teodor Wessel who was the Treasurer of the Crown, the town of Pilica with a castle, which was rebuilt in Baroque style on her demand. Theodor was the grandfather of Konstancja née Wessel Wielogłowska and great-grandfather of Maria Wielogłowska, Heinrich Freiherr von Richthofen's wife.

In remembrance of his aunt, Maria née Wessel Sobieska, Teodor Wessel placed a marble tombstone in St. Casimir Church in Warsaw, but the tombstone unfortunately did not survive the devastation of World War II. The photo of the tombstone, as well as images of Maria née Wessel Sobieska, her signature, and the story of her life are available on the website of the town of Pilica.

My mother remembered King Sobieski's bedspreads, which were inherited by my family in Kraków. My Grandmother Antonina used these bedspreads during the last winter of World War II in Poland (1944-1945) during the severely cold months to block a draft coming from a broken window. I was told that the Sobieski's bedspreads were rags of a gray color by that time and did not look special in any way, which could be expected from bedspreads that were used more than 300 years ago. The story about the bedspreads was passed to me with the following moral: *nothing lasts forever and measurable things were not important in the face of war or disaster.* I have never seen the Sobieski's bedspreads as they were lost in the winds of war and the dust of history before I was born.

But one piece of textile that belonged to the Wessel family in the 18th century survived all the wars and changes in ownership, a silk handmade sachet decorated with embroidery, which is now a part of my collection. According to my mother, the sachet was used to store a handkerchief. Embroidery on the front and the back of the sachet included the prominent coat of arms Rogala, which was the sign of the nobility of the Wessel family. The date of October 4, 1787 and the name of the town of Pilica, which was owned by Karol (Charles) Wessel at the time, also appear. Besides the date and the crest on the sachet, Josephe Wessel stitched in French the name of the owner, Charles Wessel, and a dedication "Pour le your naisance" (for your birthday). I could not determine the identity of Josephe Wessel, which could be one of the subjects of my next research project.

A few years ago, in the Polish town of Gdańsk, an exhibition of paintings by Jacob Wessel (1710-1780), the 18th century gifted artist from Gdańsk specializing in portraits, was organized. I regret that I could not visit the exhibition and see his works as he most likely was related to my great-great-great-grandmother, Konstancja née Wessel Wielogłowska. I feel that I missed an occasion which could have helped me define the author of the painting I inherited from the Wessel family. Was it perhaps painted by Jacob?

Konstancja Wessel and Walery Wielogłowski started their life together in a childish and funny way. They met for the first time in the Decjusz palace in Wola Justowska near Kraków when they were children and where Walery came with his grandmother one day to pay a visit to their friends. Walery was ten years old and Konstancja was only seven. My family story relates that Walery, who was playing in the garden with other children, suddenly left his playmates, ran to his grandmother, and told her with joy that he had just met his future wife. There were a lot of jokes and laughing among the grownups, but the boy was persistent in his feelings for years and the juvenile sentiment intensified to love. He looked for every occasion to meet Konstancja, who lived with her parents in Kraków.

Walery's prediction came true when he walked down the aisle at 19 with his 16-year-old bride with the approval of both families. They were married on September 29, 1825 in the Catholic parish of Żarnowiec in a lavish wedding common for distinguished families like the Wessels and Wielogłowskis. The whole affair lasted three days. According to Jerzy Kuzicki in his biography of Walery, their wedding was one of the last weddings that incorporated an old Polish tradition: it started and ended with the Polonez, the old-fashioned Polish dance. It is difficult for me to imagine the line of people dancing the Polonez that day because of the great number of wedding guests, which included members of the Wessel and Wielogłowski families in addition to the Wielopolski, Gostkowski, Badeni, and Popiel families and many friends of the families. The chain of carriages in the wedding retinue was said to have been so long that it extended from the town of Wola Libertowska to the town of Żarnowiec, a distance of about three miles.

In my family archives, I found a blue sheet of stationery from the 19th century decorated with a coat of arms I could not recognize, which caught my attention because along with a description of old Polish wedding customs, there was a verse written on the sheet titled *Oracja* [Oration]. The verse described the joyous atmosphere of family gatherings and large weddings with grand orchestra music and dancing, maids of honor, and many guests. The following blessing also was offered for the young couple:

> The Polish heart is pure and transparent like a jewel, without hypocrisy and falsehood. May the Blessed Virgin Mother of Częstochowa, who hears our petitions, bless this young couple with prosperity today and throughout their entire lives (author unknown).[61]

---

[61] Ivona Tarko's archives: Author and year unknown, Manuscript.

Top left: The fragment of the sachet heirloom from the Wessel family with the dedication to Charles Wessel from Josephe Wessel, dated October 4, 1787 in the town of Pilica, which was owned by Karol (Charles) Wessel at the time. Top center: Konstancja née Wessel Wielogłowska (1808-1863) mother of Maria née Wielogłowska Freifrau von Richthofen. Top right: Fragment of the Wessel family sachet heirloom with the coat of arms Rogala, a sign of their nobility. Bottom left: The painting of The Blessed Virgin Mother of Częstochowa owned by Walery Wielogłowski. Bottom center: Walery Wielogłowski (1805-1865) father of Maria née Wielogłowska Freifrau von Richthofen. Bottom right: The button heirloom which includes the coat of arms of the Wielogłowski and the Wessel families.[62]

After I read those words, I realized that they could have been written by the Dutkiewicz family from Kraków and may have accompanied their wedding gift to Walery and Konstancja, which was the above painting of the Blessed Virgin Mother of Częstochowa with their dedication and 1825 written on the back of the painting. Walery always kept the painting with him; and according to Jerzy Kuzicki, a copy of the painting was made at Walery's request and given to the church of St. Roch in Paris in 1847.

---

[62] Ivona Tarko's collection.

Upon Walery's death, the original painting was passed down through the family as follows: Walery's daughter, Maria née Wielogłowska von Richthofen; Maria's son, Bolesław; Bolesław's daughter, Antonina; Antonina's daughter, Alicja; and Alicja (my mother) to me. The painting remains in my possession.

Walery and Konstancja were so young when they married that their families asked an old, devoted family servant to take care of them on their honeymoon journey. When they returned, they lived on the Zborów primary estate, and then in the village of Kikowa near Solec-Zdrój in the Polish Kingdom, where their daughter Maria, called Marynia, was born on February 14, 1827. Maria, as you may recall is one of the main characters in the story of the Polish line of the von Richthofen family.

A few years after the birth of Maria, Walery decided to lease a few of his villages, including the village of Kikowa, and moved back with his family to the Zborów estate, which was close to Solec-Zdrój where he planned to open a spa using the therapeutic quality of the local springs. In his 1830 descriptive booklet, *Plan do Towarzystwa Akcyionaryuszów w Celu założenia Kąpieli w Solcu* [A Plan for Shareholders, the Founders of Spa in Solec], he promoted the Solec springs and related their history. His story of the springs claimed that peasants discovered the healing powers of the springs; and poor farmers who did not have money to pay a doctor or a pharmacist looked for and usually found a cure in the Solec springs. People traveled miles to obtain water from the springs, which was thought to be helpful in liver and spleen problems and cured rheumatism if the water was used in a bath (Wielogłowski, 1830).[63]

Walery's spa plans in Solec had to wait, however, because he was called to fight for his homeland in the November Uprising of 1830 against the Russians in the Polish Kingdom. Walery organized a cavalry squadron by recruiting farmers from his village of Kikowa and equipped them with his own money. Maria was only three years old when he left the family

---

[63] W. Wielogłowski, Plan do Towarzystwa Akcyionaryuszów w celu założenia kąpieli w Solcu, 1830, p. 4.

to join the Krakusy Squadron. He fought the Russians during 1830-1831 alongside General Samuel Różycki, who, at the end of the war, chose Walery to be a member of a committee responsible for negotiating the conditions for the Polish Army to enter the Free City of Kraków. A few years after these events, Maria was old enough to understand her father's sacrifices and was proud of her father. For his fearless combat service during the war, Walery was awarded the War Order of Virtuti Military, the highest military decoration in Poland for heroism and courage in the face of the enemy. Walery left the Polish Army at the rank of captain.

Maria was too young at the time to understand how dramatically her family's financial situation changed after the war. Their entire estate in the Polish Kingdom was confiscated by the Russians as punishment to Walery for his engagement in the November Uprising of 1830 and the Polish-Russian War. The family decided to rent a farm and lived in three different places near Kraków during 1831-1836. Walery stayed engaged in the fight for Poland's independence, joined a conspiracy movement, and even founded two secret organizations, "Numa" and "Synowie Świata." In 1836, one of Walery's servants from the Dębno estate reported Walery's activities (organizing secret meetings and possessing conspiracy literature) to the Austrian authorities. This turn of events was unfortunate to me because Walery conducted Saturday schooling for farmers at the Dębno estate, where he taught them about the need for social changes. He believed that the next fight for the independence of Poland had to be preceded by educating the workers, whom he felt would be more involved in the fight for freedom of their homeland if they knew more about the issues.

Walery was aware that he might be arrested when he learned that his activities were uncovered. Therefore, facing detainment and being expelled from the Kraków region, he decided to leave on his own terms. Konstancja chose to go with him, and they decided not to leave behind their beloved only daughter Maria. In the spring of 1836, the Wielogłowski family left Kraków not knowing when, if ever, their return would be possible. Walery sold the Kraków house he inherited from his parents to Jan Nepomucen Walter, asking Jan and his wife, Agnieszka, to keep some of the Wielogłowski furniture, clothes, and other belongings for them. Konstancja wrote an eight-page list of the possessions she left with the Walters family. Among the many items on her list were: a piano, two tables for playing cards, a hutch, a black pine wardrobe, a blue sofa, six hanging mirrors, a portrait of Grandma, a vanity table with silver accessories, an oval mirror in a silver frame, two basins with two pitchers, containers for perfumes, two pink satin quilts, two big accent rugs, two red curtains with silk fringes, 42 large beautiful napkins, 12 small tea napkins, a silver sugar bowl with golden interior, 36 china dinner plates decorated with green leaves, six plain mugs, Walery's uniform with silver embroidery, servant's uniform, 11 pieces of needle-stitched decoration, a large cloak made of ermine, an ermine collar, a green hand-knitted robe, and a red hand-knitted coat [Wielogłowska, 1836].[64]

I own three items that remind me of the Wielogłowski family's stressful spring of 1836: the handwritten list of their belongings prepared by my great-great-great-grandmother Konstancja and two buttons with the coat of arms Starykoń and Rogala from the uniform of the Wielogłowski's servant.

The Wielogłowski family left Kraków under the cloak of darkness one night with the help of a friendly Jewish merchant, who transported them and two trunks with their personal belongings on his wagon. Jerzy Kuzicki stated that the Wielogłowski family traveled, without passports and very little cash, through the southern part of Germany to France. They moved through the countryside on the wagon, where they were hidden under the marquee of the Jewish trader's wagon with merchandise, according to Ludwik Dębicki's statement, who heard the story from Walery Wielogłowski. Their journey lasted a few weeks and was excruciating because of early spring cold weather and a need to elude the authorities, especially during their stops for the night, which precluded the comfort of hotels and boarding houses. The journey was particularly tiresome for their young daughter (Kuzicki, 2005).[65] I believe that nine-

---

[64] Ivona Tarko's archives: K.Wielogłowska, Lista Rzeczy, 1836.
[65] J. Kuzicki, Op. Cit., p. 87.

year-old Maria did not feel well, not only because of the obvious inconveniences but also the unusual conditions of her family's exodus. Even if Maria's parents did not explain why they had to leave Kraków, she was old enough to feel her parents' anxiety and stress.

The Wielogłowski family suffered during this period of their lives; but their love, trust, and belief in God's protection and the kindness of people helped them to face the difficulties thrust upon them. Jerzy Kuzicki, in his book, noted that the Wielogłowski family was able to survive their exile due to the cash they received from the sale of their house in Kraków as well as the money they began to receive on a regular basis from Konstancja's relative, Karol Godeffroy, who, with Walery's agreement, bought the Wielogłowski Zborów estate at a public auction in 1840.

The Wielogłowski family first headed for France because they would be able to join other Polish political refugees who went to France after defeat in the November Uprising of 1830. There were so many Poles leaving Polish lands at the time that historians named this movement of refugees "The Great Emigration." The Wielogłowski family spent 12 years in exile, living in France and Italy as nomads and continuously moving from one place to another. Sometimes they were able to stay in one place for as much as a couple years or as little as a few weeks. Their longest stay was finally in Paris where they lived from 1845 until 1848 and where the momentous event occurred with which this chapter began.

In 1837, the Wielogłowskis arrived in Versailles, where Maria received her First Communion in the Catholic faith on June 13, 1839. Maria's parents organized a party to celebrate this occasion and invited Polish immigrants living in Versailles, who were mostly political refugees from Kraków, such as Walenty Zwierkowski, Hipolit Terlecki, Reces Wątróbka, and Antoni Hłuszniewicz. Walery's cousin, Bolesław Wielogłowski, lived in Versailles at the time as well. Konstancja stayed in touch with the Polish ladies from the immigrant circle: Klementyna

Hoffmanowa, Franciszka and Karolina Giedroyc, Alma Łopacińska, and Karolina Mycielska.[66]

During their exile, apart from her parents, Maria had only one family member related to her by blood: her father's cousin, Bolesław Wielogłowski, to whom she was extremely attached. There was no face to face contact with other members of the family unless they visited the Wielogłowskis in Western Europe. Maria knew her distant family mainly from her parents' stories and correspondence. Although this isolation from family was very sad, the thought occurred to me that if the Wielogłowski family had not left Kraków for Western Europe, they likely would not have met the von Richthofen family and, more importantly as far as my family's story, Maria and Heinrich would not have married.

Maria Wielogłowska was fluent in French and Polish thanks to her parents. She was brought up to honor the Polish traditions and the Catholic faith and to be respectful to others, especially her elders. Her memoirs from Ischia Island, which she wrote later in life, not only described the time she spent with her mother and father there but also conveyed the close relationship she had with her parents. They stayed on the island for a few months in 1841, after traveling in Italy from one place to another, so Maria's memoirs were full of the joy of having an opportunity to live in the same home for a longer time. She wrote that their nomadic life brought many inconveniences, which she insisted were not a problem for her as a young girl; but for her parents, who were born into a comfortable lifestyle, it was true hardship. Her parents took care of themselves as far as staying healthy, but they knew little about taking care of a household. Maria helped her mother in their small household by keeping their clothes and other belongings tidy, and she learned all of this as her parents did. She remarked that in her free time, she would run outside, free and happy like a "little goat" (Richthofen, 1879).[67] She also wrote about becoming fascinated by lizards.

---

[66] J. Kuzicki, Op. Cit., p. 114.

[67] Ivona Tarko's archives: M. Richthofen, Wspomnienia z młodych lat – Pobyt na Wyspie Ischia w 1840 roku, przez córkę Walerego Wielogłowskiego, Kraków, 1879.

I was occupied with my beautiful, green lizards, which were coming every day and waited for their supper from me, which consisted of fresh figs peels. They looked at me with their black beady eyes and stretched out their little tongues. I sang them Polish songs from the Kraków region, which they seemed to like very much. I did not disturb my parents' conversations with Mr. Chevalier by singing loudly to the lizards because I respected adults (Richthofen, 1879).[68]

I read with interest an agreement between Maria and her parents, prepared on August 23, 1841 in which they wrote about their household tasks and Maria's learning schedule during their stay on Ischia. Breakfast was planned at 8:00 am after a bath and prayer. From 9:00 am until noon, Maria was left to learn and memorize the things they gave her the night before. At noon, they had a meal together and a scheduled break until 1:30 pm; and Maria then had a one-hour lesson at 1:30 pm with her mother, followed by free time. At the end of her learning day, from 4:00 to 5:00 pm, her father checked what she had learned and gave her an assignment for the following morning (Wielogłowski, 1841).[69]

The Wielogłowski family enjoyed swimming in the sea and taking long walks together. Apparently, there were no children Maria's age on the island so most of her time was spent with her parents or alone. Maria recounted in her memoirs her family encountering a very poor Italian family during one of their walks.

> What a terrible scene - a starving family was picking up wild figs growing on rocks and they fought for every fig to calm down their hunger and to prolong their waning lives. Corpses in Poland looked better than them. Father and Mother were picking up the figs with their weak hands and giving them to their children, who wolfed them down almost unpeeled. The man said in a frail voice that he was a shoemaker but lost his job because of illness and he

---

[68] Ibid.
[69] Ivona Tarko's archives: W. Wielogłowski, Umowa, [1841].

had nothing to feed his family. My father asked the poor where they lived and decided to help them in whatever way he was able. He went to Laggo to look for the mayor of Ischia, and my mother and I came home and put into baskets whatever we had and took them to the unfortunate. My father gave them some money, which was meager because he was a person in exile; and my parents bought a goat for this poor family. Thanks to my father's intervention at the mayor's office, the poor shoemaker received financial help and started working again (Richthofen, 1879).[70]

One day the Wielogłowski family came close to a tragedy that could have changed their lives forever. Maria was drowning and luckily her father's fast action saved her life. The sea was not friendly to them on another occasion as well. A few months earlier, before Maria's near drowning, they were on a boat coming from the mainland to Ischia Island. Maria recollected the scene as follows:

> The sea became a scary color and huge waves were throwing our boat up and down, and it felt like we were entering an abyss. Between the waves, in a fog, we saw rocks in the distance. My father exchanged looks with the helmsman and they were obviously thinking the same thing but did not say a word because they did not want to worry my mother and me. My mother was aware of the impending disaster but, trusting in God, she took my father's hands and mine, asked us to kneel by her side, and started to pray 'Who Is Trusting in God, Gives Himself in His Care'. We knelt for what seemed like a long time, ready for death if it was God's will. Standing was impossible even if we wanted to do so because the boat was swinging and rolling and could cause us to fall overboard. Suddenly, the helmsman joyously cried out, 'Ischia!' We struggled to our feet and saw the bay toward which the experienced helmsman steered the boat successfully after

---

[70] M. Richthofen, Op. Cit.

miraculously avoiding so many dangerous places (Richthofen, 1879).[71]

In spite of these dramatic experiences, Maria remembered her stay on Ischia with deep affection, which felt like a sweet fading dream, writing that they awaited with heavy hearts the day when they would leave the island and return to the problems and matters of the outside world. They became friends on Ischia with Dr. Ferdynand Dworzaczek, who before coming to Italy worked in Warsaw in the 1830s where he dedicated his life to treating people during the cholera outbreak, Lady Komar with daughter Natalia, a beautiful and charming young person, daughter of the late general and sister of Delfina née Komar Potocka, the legendary muse of renowned Polish poet, Zygmunt Krasiński. The Komar family was well-known in the circle of Polish immigrants and then Italian citizens when Natalia Komar married Lavinio de Medici Spada in Rome in 1848. The couple was childless and sadly they both died at a fairly young age.

The Wielogłowski family spent the autumn of 1841 in Rome in a rented apartment on Santa Maria dell Anima close to the Navona Square. This stay was a time of near tragedy too because Maria Wielogłowska was again close to death. Historian Jerzy Kuzicki, in documenting the sad chain of events that autumn, was unable to locate any details in the available sources about the cause of Maria's illness. Her "miraculous" recovery was also noted by Dębicki, the biographer of Walery Wielogłowski, who knew Walery personally. He wrote that Maria Wielogłowska was gravely ill and the five best physicians from Rome left Maria's deathbed informing her sorrowful father that there was no cure to be found in the art of medicine and that Maria was in agony. Walery refused to accept the news about the imminent death of his only child and ran in desperation to seek the intercession of the Blessed Virgin Mother, whose portrait, well-known for miracles, resided in the Augustinian Fathers Church in Rome. Praying for a cure for his beloved daughter, Walery made a promise to the Virgin Mother that he would introduce the

---

[71] Ibid.

May devotions to Catholics who lived in Polish lands, a promise he later kept.

A few months after Maria's serious illness and astounding recovery, the Wielogłowski family witnessed the taking of vows of the priests from the CR of Our Lord Jesus Christ. This ceremony took place on Easter Sunday in the St. Sebastian catacombs in Rome. The Wielogłowski family and Józef Zaleski were the only witnesses chosen from the large group of Poles who were living in Rome then.

In April 1842, the Wielogłowski family returned to France, starting their journey in Cassis, where they unfortunately could not stay long. Regrettably, the ensuing three years in France continued to be a time of almost constant change. They lived for varying lengths of time in places like Vernet, Tuluza, Chateau Guitand, Lucheon, Aix en Provenece, and Fontainebleau; and everywhere they stayed, they searched out other Polish immigrants and the CR members.

In 1842 Maria Wielogłowska was 15 years old, but she could not attend a formal school as they were traveling from one place to another. She continued to be educated at home by her parents and tutors. At 15 Maria was nearing the proper age to marry. During the family stay in Fontainebleau, Maria's father was making plans to arrange her marriage to Jan Koźmian, Polish writer and publicist, who was much older than her. The plan failed because Jan was already interested in another woman, Zofia, the daughter of legendary Polish General Dezydery Chłapowski.

After years of wandering from one place to another in Italy and France, the Wielogłowski family gained some stability and security in 1845 when the French Ministry of the Interior allowed them to permanently settle in Paris. Almost from the beginning, they were the center of Polish social life, opening their salon every Thursday, primarily in the apartment on rue de Sevres, later on St. Honore. The Wielogłowski salon gathered people of different political views, even antagonists, artists, writers, and musicians. Among the visitors were Polish poets Adam Mickiewicz and

Kornel Ujejski, well-known composer Frederic Chopin, and Prince Adam Czartoryski, the owner of the Hotel Lambert in Paris and the leader of a political party. Chopin's "La Polonaise" was composed exclusively for the Polish ball held in the Hotel Lambert every year.

In the summer of 1847, in partnership with his cousin Bolesław Wielogłowski, Walery opened the Polish Interests Office in Paris, which focused on mediating commission sales of various works of art and watches by Antoni Patek from Switzerland as well as publishing manuscripts. This office also served as an employment agency. The financial situation of the Wielogłowski family improved a great deal as they were now able to secure some of their money from the Zborów estate, some of which Walery used for his investment in the Polish Interests Office and to help poet Kornel Ujejski to print his book *Skargi Jeremiego* [The Grievances of Jeremy], which included a poem *Z Dymem Pożarów* [With the Smoke of Fires] that was later popularized in the Polish Kingdom as the anthem of the January Uprising of 1863. Walery also helped Polish immigrants who lived in poverty in Paris financially. Maria also received an inheritance at that time from her fraternal grandmother, Marianna Wielogłowska.

In spring 1848, the Wielogłowski family left France for Belgium, where they spent Easter at the home of Polish General Jan Skrzynecki.[72] They reached Breslau (Wrocław) in the summer of 1848, where they perhaps stayed in the popular inn there, "Under the Golden Goose," which was famous for its exquisite cuisine. In a manuscript from the 19th century by Józef Korzeniowski, I found a description of the inn:

> This is a place where all noblemen stay. Their coming is announced by ringing grand bells, and they are welcomed by the entire staff, who stand outside the entrance to the inn and bow to them (Korzeniowski, year unknown).[73]

---

[72] J. Kuzicki, Op. Cit., p. 155.
[73] Ivona Tarko's archives: J. Korzeniowski, Podróżomania, Manuscript.

The other place likely visited by the Wielogłowski family was a coffee shop by Pernini, which had the best coffee in the town and sold Polish, French, and Italian newspapers. Many Poles who lived in or visited Breslau (Wrocław) gathered at the coffee shop, including Polish poet Juliusz Słowacki and Fr. Hieronim Kajsiewicz from the CR.

The Wielogłowski family wanted to return to their hometown of Kraków, which they were forced to leave 12 years earlier, but they could not do so without a permit from the Austrian authorities. They waited for the needed documents in Breslau (Wrocław) while Walery's cousin, Paweł Popiel, watched over the bureaucracy in Kraków. Paweł was an alderman during 1848-1853 and the restorer of Kraków, and a well-known and influential person in the city. In 1848, he initiated the publishing of a conservative journal *Czas* [Time] in Kraków. He opened his salon for social gatherings every Thursday during the long period of 1835-1890, where conservative landlords, patricians, and intellectuals from Kraków gathered to discuss politics and religion, science, and social matters. Paweł Popiel was not only Walery's relative but also his best friend. In his last will, Walery requested:

> My dearest daughter, after my death, shall give my big bronze crucifix, which stands on an oak pedestal, to my beloved relative Paweł Popiel, one of the most honorable people I know, who through his entire life has given me true friendship (Wielogłowski, year unknown).[74]

According to Jerzy Kuzicki's book, the Wielogłowski family left Breslau (Wrocław) in mid-September of 1848, and their first stopover in Kraków was at the home of Count Moszyński on Bracka Street. The family applied for citizenship in the Free City of Kraków; but political tension and an impending uprising in the city, as well as fear that the Russians would occupy the city, forced the Wielogłowski family to leave Kraków again and spend uncertain times in Breslau (Wrocław). Why did they choose Breslau (Wrocław) again? They already knew a few friendly

---

[74] Ivona Tarko's archives: W. Wielogłowski, Ostatnia Wola.

families there: the Rokossowskis, Dembińskis, and von Richthofens. Maria's best friend Eliza was preparing for her wedding; and for Maria and her parents, the stay was another good occasion to be closer to Heinrich von Richthofen and his family. It appears that 1848 and 1849 were spent travelling again, between Kraków and Breslau (Wrocław) this time. Walery devoted himself to writing; and in 1849 he published in Breslau (Wrocław) two books: *Emigracya Polska Wobec Boga i Narodu* [The Polish Emigration to God and Nation] and *Godła Rewolucyjne Wobec Prawdy* [The Emblem of Revolution and Truth]. The copy of the book *Emigracya Polska Wobec Boga i Narodu*, which I own, includes a dedication from the author to his daughter Maria.

As I previously mentioned, Maria was fluent in Polish and French. She used these skills to translate a religious book devoted to Catholic doctrine, written by an Italian priest, Fr. Zamma Mellini, which was published

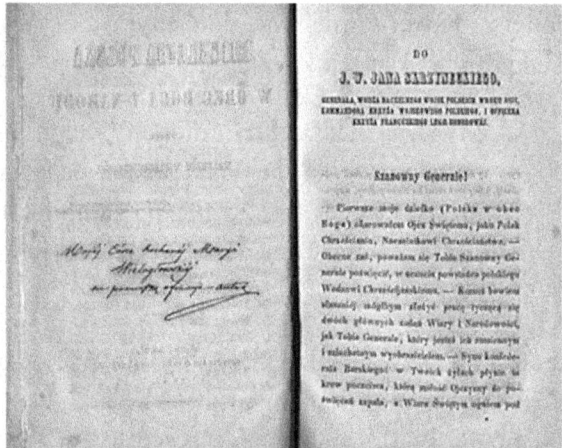

The 19th century photo of young Maria Wielogłowska and the book by Walery Wielogłowski, written in Polish, with handwritten dedication to his daughter Maria.[75]

---

[75] Ivona Tarko's archives.

several times in Italy. The title of the book was *Chrystus Pan Mówiący Do Serca Młodzieńca* [Christ, the Lord, Speaking to the Heart of a Young Man]. In her introduction, Maria dedicated the Polish version of the book to the children of Paweł Popiel, her dearest uncle. She wrote:

> If this book arouses passion for spiritual growth, desire for virtues, or any other spiritual good, we shall thank God from Whom all good and every perfection come (Wielogłowska, 1852).[76]

---

[76] M. Wielogłowska, Chrystus Pan Mówiący Do Serca Młodzieńca, Dziełko Z Francuskiego Na Polski Przetłumaczone Przez Marya Wielogł., Kraków, 1852.

CHAPTER 4 The Engagement and Marriage of Heinrich Freiherr von Richthofen and Maria Wielogłowska

The joys of parents are secret, and so are their griefs and fears

~ Sir Francis Bacon

I wonder what Maria's first impressions were when she arrived in Kraków in September 1848 after 12 years of exile with her parents. Those years were painfully long for her parents because they missed the life they left behind in Kraków, which were a lifetime for Maria as she only knew of Kraków from the stories of her parents and other Kraków refugees. What an amazing story she had to tell of spending her formative years as a nomad across Europe. It is entirely possible that Kraków at first was just another place to live to Maria and only became her home gradually. Now she was in Kraków with her parents and they longed for stability. But was that even possible in Kraków in the middle of the 19th century?

I discussed earlier the unsettled future of Kraków after the partitions of Poland at the end of the 18th century, but here is a quick review. Kraków, which was located in Galicia in the southern part of Polish land, was occupied by Austria in 1772. Then, for a short period of time, 1810-1813, Kraków belonged to the Duchy of Warsaw, an independent Polish state created by Napoleon in 1807, but the freedom of Kraków's citizens vanished again under Russian occupation in 1813. In 1815, by declaration of the Congress of Vienna, the Republic of Kraków was established and Kraków became the only Polish territory to enjoy relative freedom. After the Kraków Revolution in 1846, the city came under Austrian rule yet again. The citizens of Kraków attempted to overthrow the Austrian occupiers by a new uprising in the spring of 1848, which ended when the Austrian artillery attacked Kraków. In January 1849 martial law was declared in Galicia, and the city located closest to the Russian border, Kraków, was established by the Austrian authorities as a military camp. In 1850 the decision was made to build fortifications around Kraków. During the next few years, the Polish language was gradually eliminated in schools and administration, and in 1852 the Polish language was replaced by German as the official language.

Despite the uncertain circumstances, Kraków families organized balls (mainly in the period of the winter carnival), concerts, and special events and opened their salons to social gatherings. Maria Estreicherówna wrote in her book that every carnival ended with many engagements and weddings; and that some of the salons were open almost nonstop. Just turning on the lights in a home signaled that the owner was ready to receive guests. The members of Kraków high society usually had plenty of free time so an unexpected visit was no inconvenience at all; on the contrary, visitors likely broke up the monotony of a long day for them. The Wielogłowski family kept their salon open for social gatherings on Thursdays, the same day as their dear relatives, the family of Paweł Popiel. This information made me wonder how Walery was able to visit Paweł and vice versa. Perhaps their salons were open during specific parts of the day that did not overlap so there was no disadvantage, but knowing Polish customs and hospitality, their salon gatherings had no frame time.

Maria barely remembered or even knew the people who welcomed her family back to Kraków and made the effort to include them in the social circles to which they belonged. I was glad to find in the archives of the Polish Academy of Arts and Sciences (PAU) in Kraków a few letters from this period in time. One of the letters was from Countess Jadwiga Tarnowska to the Wielogłowski family, on New Year's Day, 1849, which read as follows:

> Deprived of the pleasure of finding you at your home a few times, I dare to ask you to pay me a visit. If already somebody lucky did not do it before me, I would be honored to invite Mr. and Mrs. Walery Wielogłowski with their daughter for tea at 6 o'clock. My carriage will be at your disposal. January 1st, 1849. J. Tarnowska (Tarnowska, 1849).[77]

In another letter, Countess Potocka wrote:

> I spent the entire morning looking for a lady or a girl who would like to sing at a concert, and when I did not find and doubted already if it would be possible, Mr. Krzyżanowski came up with a suggestion that his sister could sing. She is a well-mannered young girl, who is well-known here. Would it be enough to encourage Miss Maria? Will she allow us to recognize her beautiful voice? She could not refuse to participate in such a good

---

[77] B PAU, Kraków, rkps. 1844: J. Tarnowska to K. Wielogłowska, Letter, 1849.

purpose. Those who have already bought tickets count on the pleasure of hearing Miss Wielogłowska's singing. Sokalski will serve tonight. Please accept the expression of my gratitude and respect. Julia Potocka (Potocka, 1848?).[78]

This letter was followed by the next one, written again by Julia Potocka:

> I am so sorry to bother you again with the same request. Mr. Krzyżanowski begs, as we all do, your lady daughter to contribute in our concert that is planned for Friday. I only dare to ask you and your daughter to come tonight because of the object of the concert. There will be artists glad to arrange a program. If your daughter agrees to sing, she could choose an accompanist. Maybe Sokolski or Mirecki? Each of them would be ready for her orders. I send you my deepest respect and esteem, asking you for a generous answer – Julia Potocka, Kraków, December 20th (Potocka, 1848?)[79]

Obviously, the ladies did not know that the Wielogłowskis had left Kraków for a couple of months. I believe that both letters from Countess Potocka were written at the end of 1848 (there is only a day and a month on the manuscript) when the Wielogłowski family was absent in Kraków, and her letters did not get to their hands in time. I guess that the concert was organized at Christmastime, possibly in the palace belonging to the Potocki family in Kraków. The palace, which the Potocki family had owned since 1822, was called *Pod Baranami* [the Palace of the Rams]. One of the most magnificent palaces in the city, the Palace of the Rams was located in the center of Kraków on the Main Square. It became the center of high society in the 19th century when Artur Potocki opened his salon for social meetings, which included the most prominent individuals from Kraków. An invitation to the Palace of the Rams was considered a high honor in Kraków social circles.

---

[78] B PAU, Kraków, rkps. 1844: J. Potocka to K. Wielogłowska, Letter, [1848].
[79] Ibid.

The Wielogłowski family finally made their home again in Kraków. Maria Estreicherówna wrote in her book that:

> Any social gatherings could not be organized without the presence of Walery Wielogłowski, man full of initiative and entrepreneurship, who did not waste his time. He admitted that his businesses usually ended as fiascos and used to say that if he opened a funeral home people would stop dying; but his initiative in social issues brought permanent good, such as the introduction of the May devotion in churches and the founding of the Society of Friends of Fine Arts in Kraków (Estreicherówna, 1968).[80]

I found no evidence of whether Maria enjoyed the Kraków social life or how much she wanted to be involved at that time. She arrived in Kraków at the age when a young woman was perceived a spinster if she was not yet officially engaged. She was not interested in meeting young men and potential candidates for husband because her heart already belonged to Heinrich Freiherr von Richthofen Maria was accepted and recognized from the beginning by the members of her family in Kraków, even distant relatives, because family ties were strong at that time in history, and blood relatives wanted to be connected. However, making friends may have been a different matter. I believe it would have taken time for her to make friends, especially when most of the young women her age were already married and occupied with their own families. It is likely that Maria spent a lot of her time with her parents, especially her mother. The people Maria befriended before moving to Kraków belonged to a slightly different world in the cities of Breslau (Wrocław), Paris, and Rome where Maria spent her childhood and youth. Eliza Freiin von Richthofen became her closest friend and she met Eliza's brother, Heinrich, in Western Europe, the world more familiar to Maria than Galicia or the city of Kraków.

Maria lived in a world full of conventions for betrothed couples that nowadays seem unbelievable. Even after an engagement, a young couple was expected to minimize the contact between them.   Maria

---

[80] M. Estreicherówna, Op. Cit., p. 109.

Estreicherówna, whose book I cited earlier, described the engagement of her parents. It seems her mother was allowed to directly correspond with her fiancé who lived in another city at the end of the second year of their engagement. Before that period, the fiancée's father corresponded with the fiancé.

I am very disappointed that I could not find any letters written by Heinrich to Maria or at least to somebody from the family. When I try to picture Maria and Heinrich together, I imagine them as shy and quiet. I only know of a few statements about Heinrich from his father's diary and his characteristics from pictures and family stories. If Heinrich was depressed, he could look for support in Maria who seemed to be an understanding and caring person. I discovered that music could connect Maria and Heinrich very well as both of them played musical instruments, Heinrich violin and Maria piano. Maria also had a pleasant voice and liked singing. One of the letters written by Maria's friend, Klementyna Dembińska in March 1849 to Maria from Breslau (Wrocław) gave me additional information about Maria's character.

> I have never met a person who is more tender or calmer than you, my dear. Do not take this just as a casual compliment because we do not treat each other that way and we should never do that. I wish I had your sweetness because, just between us, I do not feel I have many admirable values. I do not have a good heart and I am not able to change it. I discover my impatience in handling the various and many problems of everyday life. Monotony is my nightmare. I love you from the bottom of my heart, my dear Marynieczko – your devoted Klementyna Dembińska (Dembińska, 1849).[81]

Undoubtedly, Maria's apparent natural serenity helped her face the troublesome life in Kraków, which was far from monotonous. In her first months there, a cholera epidemic struck Kraków, but no one from the Wielogłowski family contracted it; and martial law was declared in

---

[81] B PAU Kraków, rkps 1844: K. Dembińska to M. Wielogłowska, Letter, 1849.

Kraków in the middle of January 1849 and lasted until May 1854. Gradually, the politics of Aleksander Bach, the Austrian Minister of the Interior since 1849 brought centralized administration to Kraków and reduced freedom of the press; Minister Bach wanted to Germanize all non-German countries inside the Austrian Empire, including Kraków.

Families from the same social circles spent time together in joy and sadness. Not only ballrooms and salons gathered society but churches in Kraków as well, especially the Mariacki Church (St. Mary Church), located on the Main Square, which was a place that witnessed splendid weddings and magnificent funerals. Maria preserved the obituary of Princess Zofia Sapieżanka, who passed away in Kraków on February 24, 1850. Zofia, the daughter of Prince Leon Sapiecha, Galician politician and statesman, was 16 years old, and her death was tragic not only because of her young age but also because of the circumstances of her passing. The recognized chronicler of Kraków, Józef Wawel-Louis, wrote in his diary about the end of carnival in Kraków in 1850 and serious social March events, which followed the period of carefree time.

> After many days of joy and entertainment, the days of sadness and mourning came. Today three memorial services were held. The first one was in St. Mary's Church where nobody cried because it was the memorial service organized in the remembrance of the anniversary of Emperor Franz I death. One hour after this service, we took part in moving the body of Princess Zofia Sapieżanka from the Poller Hotel to the Capuchins Church. She caught smallpox while traveling from Lvov to Kraków. Her mother, the fanatic enthusiast of Pricssnitz methods, treated Zofia with cold water and wrapped her in cold sheets until she breathed her last gasp. She looked amazingly beautiful after her death (Wawel-Louis, 1962).[82]

The Priessnitz methods were water treatments and hydrotherapeutic techniques recommended by Wincenz Priessnitz (1799-1851), a farmer's

---

[82] J. Wawel-Louis, Pamiętnik Krakowskiej Rodziny Louisów, Kraków, 1962, p. 234.

son from Lower Silesia. Priessnitz treated people with cold water to cure various illnesses and opened a clinic in Graefenberg, near Freiwaldau in Silesia. He also believed in "nature cures" so when he became ill himself in 1851, he did not seek treatment from physicians, choosing instead to wait for nature's cure. Unfortunately, he passed away on the same day he fell ill. His methods were very popular in Europe and Priessnitz is recognized today as the father of hydrotherapy.

Walery Wielogłowski met Zofia's mother, Princess Jadwiga Sapieżyna, at the Graefenberg spa where he traveled in search of a cure for his sore throat during the summer of 1849. The spa's water treatments did not help him, but they were not detrimental to his health either, and the chance acquaintance with the Princess sadly reminded him of the death card of her daughter, Princess Zofia.

"Death cards are a feature of German funerary culture; from the 1840s it was a common occurrence for Catholic families to arrange for the printing of small card folders bearing religious observances, images of Christ or the Madonna, and religious tracts. The issuance of holy cards traditionally marked the passing of family members, alerting the local population to the loss of a loved one and asking them to partake in a religious observance, the act of praying for the deceased over a mourning period of, typically, 100 days" (Doyle, 2014).[83]

Zofia's death card included the date and place of her birth: September 2, 1834 in Wysock, and the date and place of her death: February 24, 1850 in Kraków; a prayer and lines from Scripture were also included. Her title of princess was not mentioned because it was not important in the face of death and God's judgment. Her life was short on Earth but her family believed that it was in accordance with God's will. Their prayer ended with these words: We loved her, let's not forget her! She loved us, she will not forget us!

I was surprised to learn that Zofia's death was caused by smallpox rather than cholera, which was the cause of death of several of her siblings.

---

[83] P. Doyle, World War I in 100 Objects, UK, 2014.

Zofia Sapieżanka is known in Poland as the "White Lady," whose ghost wanders the Krasiczyn castle in eastern Poland. The gorgeous marble tombstone with the sculpture of Zofia Sapieżanka is located in the tower of Baszta Boska in the castle. The story of the tombstone is interesting as well. It was sculpted in the 19th century by the recognized Kraków artist Henryk Stattler and was broken into many pieces by Russian soldiers during World War II when they plundered and demolished the Krasiczyn castle. The tombstone was reconstructed in 2010 by a student of the Kraków Academy of Art, Mariusz Wrona.

In the summer of 1850 a huge fire destroyed part of the Kraków center, including four churches, two convents, 160 houses including the Wielopolski palace, the Bishop's palace and its historical museum, and the Dominican convent and the priceless books in its library. Miraculously, two other buildings located on the Main Square, the Jabłonowski palace and the Wentzel house with the picture of the Blessed Mary on the façade, survived the fire. Walery Wielogłowski had become one of the most involved citizens of Kraków by this time and organized aid for the victims of the fire. He worked in the committee for the victims of the fire in Kraków and also collected money to rebuild Kraków's churches. To solicit donations for this purpose, he wrote and printed two pamphlets that were handed out, one showing *Kościół Świętej Katarzyny w Krakowie* [The Church of St. Catherine in Kraków] and the other, *Obraz Matki Boskiej na domu Jana Wentzla* [The Painting of the Blessed Mary on the Wentzel House].

Walery did not lose much in the Kraków fire in 1850 because, sadly, his businesses (the publishing house and the bookstore) did not generate much income even before the fire. Furthering his misfortune, however, in 1851, the concession that allowed him to run the bookstore was taken from him because he was accused of distributing the banned books written by the members of the CR.[84] Walery tried to survive all the misfortune. In 1852, he even rented his carriage to Kraków citizens to make money.

---

[84] J. Kuzicki, Op. Cit., p. 191.

The Wielogłowski family reached out to people in need by volunteering for the Philanthropic Society of Kraków. The purpose of the society was to help the poor by running orphanages and houses for the elderly and homeless. Maria's recognition certificate, issued on January 5, 1851, confirmed her membership in the society, "whose virtues and mercy were known openly or secretly" (Towarzystwo Dobroczynności, 1851).[85] Walery was a volunteer for another association that helped young beggars in Kraków, where he taught unprivileged youth to read and count and familiarized them with the basics of the Catholic faith.

The Wielogłowskis were a close-knit family. On Christmas Day 1850, Walery presented Maria with a notebook with her initials on its magenta cover, and inside the notebook were recipes for Polish dishes. This gift might be a surprising one from a father to a daughter, but it was actually a very thoughtful gift because it also contained a few of her father's drawings. I believe that the recipe notebook was given to Maria to prepare her to manage her own home in the near future.

Some of the Wielogłowski recipes are impossible to follow because of the needed amount of ingredients, such as half of a cow, six rabbits, etc. to prepare a pate. Also, the cooking terminology in the recipes was not always comparable to the terms used today. Some of the recipes are pretty simple: different soups and meat dishes, desserts and preserves, even liqueurs. I chose a few to translate from Polish and present here, which with some effort could be attempted in our modern kitchens.

Ratafia Dobrej Gospodyni [The Ratafee of a Good Housewife]
Start with the first available fruits like wild strawberries and gradually add different fruits, even if they are not perfect, including the peels and stones, and put them in a carboy with alcohol. Add one bitter orange and cinnamon and cloves (the amount you can buy for six pennies). At the end of summer, decant the alcohol and pour wine (1/2 pot) on the fruits. Then, keep the fruits for the next few days and after that period, pour out the liquid. Mix the liquid with the alcohol and add sugar dissolved in

---

[85] Ivona Tarko's archives: Dyplom Towarzystwa Dobroczynności, Kraków, 1851.

water. For one quart of liquid use one pound of sugar. After everything is mixed, filter the liquid through a felted hat.

Pasztet ze Skrzydeł Kapłonich [The Capon's Wings Pie]

Remove the bones and skin of 30 capon wings and put them in a pot with bullion to cook. Make pasta from flour and egg yolks only, cut into small pieces, not too thin, and cook the pasta in boiling water. Drain the pasta and put part of it with pieces of lean ham into a baked crust pie. Season it with pepper. Add pieces of fresh butter and part of the cooked capon wings. Continue putting the pasta and meat in layers. Bake.

How to make a pie crust:

Take six egg yolks, 1.5 quarts of flour, one pound of butter, and a little bit of water to make the dough.

Melszpeis Wypróbowany [The Tested Melszpeis]

Make pasta dough, as usual, but do not add water. Roll the dough and cut into pieces two fingers wide and the length you need. Pour one-half of a pot of sweet cream and add to it one-half pound of unsalted butter, a lot of sugar, and vanilla or orange water for aroma. Slowly boil the cream and add one piece of the dough at a time to the pot to cover it completely with the cream. When all the pieces are soaking in the pot, cover the pot with a lid, add coal to an oven, and cook the dough slowly until all the liquid evaporates. Take the cake out of the pot and put on a table. The cake will be moist.

Grzaneczki do Piwa [The Beer Croutons]

Cut a baguette in slices, smear with olive oil, and grill the slices until slightly brown; then sprinkle them with salt and caraway seeds. Put warm on a table. Serve with beer.

Karp [Carp]

Cut fish in fillets, sprinkle with salt, and put aside. Prepare vegetables: a couple of carrots, parsley, and celeriac roots, and a piece of Savoy cabbage; peel and cut the vegetables into pieces and put in a pot. Add peppercorns, nutmeg, allspice, two slices of rye bread, cold beer, and the fish fillets and cook slowly. Prepare sauce by adding a little bit of flour and fish bullion to brown honey, mix well. Pour the sauce into a pot and cook. Add raisins, almonds, lemon, and allspice to the sauce and boil. Pour the sauce over the boiled carp fillets. Serve.

Zrazy Modne [Fashionable Slips]
Mince the slices of beef and season them with pepper. In a pot, sauté chopped mushrooms and onions in butter. Put a spoonful of the mushroom mixture on every slice of beef and roll it. Put all of the rolled pieces of beef into a casserole dish and bake in an oven until ready to eat. Decorate with slices of lemon.

Pączki Krakowskie [The Kraków Doughnuts]
Take one quart of flour, one quart of sweet cream, one tablespoon of melted butter, nine egg yolks, three tablespoons of fresh yeast, and 50 grams of sugar grated on lemon peel. (The recipe indicates the original unit of measure as "4 Łuty." One łut was equivalent to 12.65625 grams, and this unit of measure was used in Europe from the Middle Ages until the end of the 19th century). Mix all the ingredients except the flour. When they are all well blended, pour the mixture into the flour. Make dough with your hands until it is no longer sticky. Place the dough in a warm place to rise. When dough has risen, take a portion of the dough with a small glass to make a doughnut. Make a small ball and put inside some jam or plum butter. When all the doughnuts are made, cover them with a linen towel and leave them to rise for 30 minutes. Heat butter or lard in a big pot until the pot is two-thirds full. When the butter or lard is hot enough, place the doughnuts in the pot using a wooden spoon and fry them. Remember to put the doughnuts into the pot on the side facing up on the board. Fry a few doughnuts at one time. Cover the pot, fry, and check if they are getting brown. If they are ready on one side, turn them and fry, but do not cover again so they do not absorb too much grease. Remove doughnuts one by one with slotted spoon from the pot, put on a tray and sprinkle them with confectioner sugar while they are still hot.

Although I do not know the length of Maria and Heinrich's engagement, I do know that at some point Maria's trousseau had to be prepared. In

Maria's social circle, preparing a house for the newlyweds was the obligation of the groom's family, but the family of the bride was expected to equip a kitchen and furnish a bedroom in the house. The basic provisions included a large amount of bedding, tablecloths, napkins, doilies, china, silver cutlery, and pots. Seamstresses were hired to prepare sheets, bed skirts, bedspreads, quilts, covers, nightgowns, etc. The monogram of the future bride was sewn on all the fabric items, and it was preferable that the bride perform some of the monogramming. Monograms were also put on the tableware. The bride's parents were also responsible for providing her wardrobe, which would be the apparel she would wear for several years because fashion then did not change as frequently as it does nowadays and most of the women from society were not eager to follow fashion news because too much attention put into a woman's clothing was seen as frivolous behavior.

I believe the atmosphere in Kraków in the 1850s was not ideal for nationally-mixed marriages. In September 1852, Count Adam Potocki was arrested in Kraków by the Austrian authorities and was accused of criticizing the Archduchess Sophia and supporting the National Guard in 1848 by suppling weapons to the guards who fought against the Austrians. A German fiancé for a girl from a Polish family that revered Polish traditions and fought for the independence of Poland was an unexpected choice in Polish social circles of that time when Poles were not allowed to use the Polish language at the university, schools, and businesses in Kraków. At the same time, a Polish fiancée in a traditional German family undoubtedly raised eyebrows in German social circles as well. Maria Estreicherówna reminded me of the story of Miss Drzewiecka from Kraków, who lived in the city in the middle of the 19th century under the watchful eye of her grandmother. The girl became acquainted with an Austrian officer, Wagner, unbeknownst to her grandmother. She knew that her family would not allow her to marry an Austrian or a German and arranged for Mr. Wagner to run away with her because she thought it was the only way to force her family to accept Mr. Wagner as her fiancé. The young couple's relationship was discovered by Miss Drzewicka's family and the girl was taken away from Kraków; but she was so unhappy that her family finally agreed to her marriage with Mr. Wagner. After the wedding, however, their relationship brought them so many disappointments that the couple was not content at all.

I wonder to what extent Heinrich was seen solely as German in Kraków Polish society. Even more important for me is knowing what Heinrich's feelings were as the child of a German father and a Polish mother and whether he considered himself a German or a Pole. His parents were cosmopolitans who enjoyed the beauty of southern Europe more than the loveliness of Silesia or Wielkopolska. Perhaps Heinrich considered himself a citizen of Silesia. Teodor Żychliński in *Złota Księga Polskiej Szlachty* [The Golden Book of Polish Nobility] included a note about Maria Wielogłowska's husband which read:

> Baron Henryk von Richthofen belonged to the outstanding Silesian family in which one branch bore the title of Count and the other the title of the Prussian Baron. His father, the heir of fidei commissum, married Paulina Obiezierska of the coat of arms Nałęcz (Żychliński, 1880).[86]

More than likely, I will not find answers to many of my questions, but I am certain that Maria knew Heinrich and his family long enough to believe that he was the one and only for her. Their decision to marry was not hasty and Heinrich was accepted by Maria's parents. Maria loved Heinrich and had enough faith in him to hope for a good marriage; and Maria's parents whole-heartedly embraced Heinrich and were confident that they could entrust him with their beloved only child.

I am sure that Heinrich's position in society assured Maria's parents that Maria would have a comfortable life married to Heinrich and they would not need to worry about her financial situation. One member of Maria's family, Paweł Popiel, provided 20,000 Polish zloty for Maria's dowry, which was the remaining money confiscated by the Russians from the estate of Walery Wielogłowski. [87] To grasp the value of this amount of

---

[86] T. Żychliński, Złota Księga Szlachty Polskiej, Poznań, 1880, v. II, p. 419.
[87] J. Kuzicki, Op. Cit., p. 242.

money, I reached again for Maria Estreicherówna's book where she wrote that a sumptuous wedding party organized as a late dinner or supper buffet could cost 1,000 Polish zloty (Estreicherówna, 1968).[88]

After their long engagement and endless wedding preparations, September 29, 1852 finally arrived and Maria Wielogłowska and Heinrich (Henryk) Freiherr von Richthofen walked down the aisle in St. Mary Church, which was the main Catholic parish in the city. Located on the Main Square, it was built in the 15th century in the Gothic style with a city watch-tower and an outstanding high altar by Wit Stwosz (Veit Stoss). The altar and the church were dedicated to the Assumption of the Virgin Mary. Today the church is one of the main tourist attractions in historic Kraków.

Left: The 19th century photo of the high altar in St. Mary Church in Kraków. *Center*: One side of a holy card memento of the wedding of Heinrich (Henryk) Freiherr von Richthofen and Maria Wielogłowska, courtesy of the father of the bride, which included the names, the date, and a prayer for the newlyweds in which the parents asked for God's protection and the friendship of the guests for the young couple. *Right*: The back side of the holy card.[89]

---

[88] M. Estreicherówna, Op. Cit., Tom I, p. 105.
[89] Ivona Tarko's archives.

The Wielogłowski family was attached to St. Mary Church in a special way, not only because it was their parish but also because it was the church where the very first May devotion was celebrated thanks to the efforts of Walery Wielogłowski. In the spring of 1849, Walery published a brochure *Nabożeństwo majowe poświęcone czci Najświętszej Panny Królowej Korony Polskiej* [The May Devotion Dedicated to the Worship of the Blessed Virgin Mother, the Queen of the Polish Kingdom] to prepare Catholic communities to participate in the observances, which were already known in France and Italy but were never practiced in Polish lands before 1849. Walery, by establishing the May devotions to Mary, fulfilled the promise he made a few years earlier in Rome when he begged the Holy Mother to save his dying daughter. Father Zygmunt Golian was the first priest to celebrate the May devotions in Kraków; and from there, the observance of May devotions spread to other parts of Galicia and then to all the Polish lands occupied by the three empires.

Maria was 25 years old when she married Heinrich, who was only two months older than her. The wedding of the daughter of Walery Wielogłowski, the recognized philanthropist, community organizer, publisher, and writer, as well as very active member in the Committee of the Kraków Fire Victims at that time, was a grand social event in the city. Maria Estreicherówna described the event in her book about life in Kraków in the 19th century. She wrote that the wedding was spectacular. She especially noted that the wedding guests looked with awe at Maria's maternal grandmother, Matylda née Gostkowska Wessel, who wore an impressive dress made of old, rich Persian fabric embroidered with gold, and a gold diadem studded with precious jewels rested on her head. I was not surprised to learn about the magnificent appearance of Matylda Wessel, who was related to the family of Polish King Jan Sobieski (I wrote about these connections in Chapter 3), but I was startled that the guests focused on the grandmother of the bride, not on the bride. I do not have any image or description of Maria's dress on her wedding day. I believe her wedding gown likely mirrored Maria's modesty, and I imagine her dressed in a white, long, empire waist wedding gown with a long veil as was the fashion in the 1850s.

Maria's father escorted her to the main altar where Heinrich waited. The wedding was performed by the Catholic Bishop, Ludwik Łętowski (1786-1868), a former officer in the Duchy of Warsaw. Bishop Łętowski's sermon was full of zest and humor to the delight of the families and wedding guests. The wedding guests received holy cards as a memento of this happy event courtesy of the father of the bride, who had 500 cards printed. Some of them were well preserved in my family archives and are shown above.

I must say that I was struck by a few things on the printed cards: Maria's fiancé's first name was in its Polish version, Henryk, the part of Heinrich's last name "von" and the title of baron were missing, and his last name was printed Rychthofen, not Richthofen. I think that Heinrich himself decided to use the Polish version of his name on the marriage certificate and the printed cards. I also suppose that his last name was written differently not as the result of a printing error but more likely was Henryk's choice of spelling to match the phonetics of the Polish language. In Kraków in the 19th century, it was common for families with German roots and surnames to become Polish in the second or third generation like Stehlik, Wencel, Kirchmeyer, Friedlein, Estreicher, Zoll, and Helcel, whose original name was Hölzel von Sternstein. For the Hölzel von Sternstein family, the decision to use the changed surname Helcel in accordance with the phonetics of the Polish language was the first step to assimilation into Polish society.

The wedding of Maria and Henryk was celebrated according to Polish tradition. The majority of guests belonged to the bride's side and usually celebrated through the night so at dawn it was the custom for the groom to provide a "sugar supper" (Estreicherówna, 1968).[90] It is possible that one of the wedding guests was Anna Różycka, the daughter of Polish General Samuel Różycki, whom Walery Wielogłowski knew personally and under whose command he served in the November Uprising of 1830. Anna Różycka was involved in the conspiracy movement in Kraków and collaborated with an emissary, Lesław Łukaszewicz, whom Walery knew

---

[90] M. Estreicherówna, Op. Cit., Tom I, p. 105.

personally as well. Lesław Łukaszewicz was her co-conspirator and the owner of a printing house in Kraków. Unfortunately, Anna Różycka was arrested in December 1852 because banned books containing Polish national poems were found in her house during an inspection ordered by the Austrian authorities in Kraków. Anna's life ended in tragedy. She was imprisoned in the Theresienstadt fortress handcuffed in chains in a damp cell. Anna died after four years of living in these conditions on the same day that an order for her release was granted.

I hope, despite all the difficulties in Kraków, which on September 29, 1852 included oppression under martial law and a measles outbreak, that the wedding day of Maria and Henryk was happy and memorable. Someone from the Polish social circle of the family wrote for the groom an acrostic, a poem in which the first letter of every verse reading down spells out Henryk's name.

> Hail to your buxom wife when you bring her for the first time,
> Elysium will be the name of your new happy home,
> Nothing more can be wished if you have your sweet wife
> Rejoicing you will find by her side.
> You receive from her what your heart desires,
> Knit together every happy moment as a floral wreath! (Author unknown, 1852).[91]

After the wedding and a short stay in Kraków, Maria and Henryk arrived at the Ostrowieczko estate in Greater Poland Voivodship (Wielkopolska). This area had been under Prussian occupation since the second partition of Poland in 1793 so Polish families there had to cope with the growing presence of the German language in institutions and schools and German colonization.

The Ostrowieczko estate was located in west central Poland where Henryk's previous estate, Koninko, was also located. I believe that Ostrowieczko was bought to replace Koninko because it had a mansion

---

[91] Ivona Tarko's archives: Author unknown, Manuscript, 1852.

more suitable for the newlywed couple to start a family. Polish readers and enthusiasts of memoirs may know Ostrowieczko from a book *Marianna i Róże* [Marianna and Roses] written by Marianna née Malinowska Jasiecka. The Jasiecki family bought the Ostrowieczko estate in 1904. Heinrich (Henryk) Freiherr von Richthofen, my great-great-grandfather, lived there fifty years earlier, but I learned that the Ostrowieczko mansion, garden, and grounds were almost the same at his time and the time described by Marianna Jasiecka in her diary, so I would like to cite her description of the place:

> Our new dwelling will be the Ostrowieczko estate. This is one of the most beautiful estates located in Wielkopolska I have ever seen. Aside from a main road which connects Śrem and Gostyń, near Dolsk, it is picturesquely set between two lakes, and a splendid alley lined with linden, oak, and ash trees goes to Ostrowieczko. A big mansion built on a hill, it is more than sixty years old but well-maintained and in perfect condition. The mansion is surrounded by a beautiful park that leads to a sizable lake with a clean and sandy bottom. The park is almost baronial, complete with diverse trees and marked lanes. At the front of the mansion, there are flower beds and a nice driveway for carriages. The mansion has huge windows and beautiful entrance stairs, and a porch with a railing. Outbuildings sufficiently large for assets are also in decent condition. Soil is good; fertile enough (Jasiecka, 1904).[92]

Everyday life in Ostrowieczko may have been rather mundane for Henryk and Maria and very different from their city lives, but I like to believe that the newlyweds spent their best years there because they were young and in love. Maria learned how to supervise servants and organize her new home, and Henryk learned how to manage the estate. In Maria's recipe notebook given to her by her father on Christmas Day in 1850, she added new recipes and notes by her hand. Besides her recipes for jams, she

---

[92] J. Fedorowicz, J. Konopińska, Marianna i Róże- życie codzienne w Wielkopolsce w latach 1890-1914 z tradycji rodzinnej, Poznań, 2008, p. 336.

wrote practical recommendations: how to cure rabies, how to bleach yellowish shirts, what to do with duck feathers, how to store and send apples, how to use potatoes as decorative plants, how to grow early potatoes in pots, and what to do with poultry after butchering. I wonder how many recipes from the notebook were used in Maria's kitchen in Ostrowieczko. She spent her early childhood and youth in France, where her taste for French cuisine was probably developed. One of her belongings was a French cookbook which I inherited. The book was written by Chef Destaminil from "Provençal Brothers," a restaurant in Paris and was published in 1854. It included old and "new" recipes, which referred to the traditional French cooking from different parts of France, with the richness of its flavors and smells. Destaminil lamented that the culinary art collapsed in his lifetime because customers' appetites were stimulated by absinth with water, which they drank before a meal, rather than the aroma of dishes that should lure their nostrils and stimulate digestive juices.

There were Polish families in Dolsk and the neighboring estates of Ostrowieczko if Maria and Henryk wanted to stay in touch with the Polish community; and Henryk's mother, Paulina Freifrau von Richthofen, lived nearby and visited her son and his growing family. Also, Paulina's sister and Henryk's aunt Fanny née Objezierska Topińska lived in Wielkopolska.

Maria and Henryk visited Maria's family in Kraków, usually in the summer. Walery, who continually tried his luck in various enterprises, opened a commission house in Kraków and worked as a mediator in the trade of wheat and agriculture produces, delicacies, and industrial products. He had associates and offered collaboration to Henryk, his son-in-law, as well. Henryk, with his agricultural background and estate in Wielkopolska, seemed to be a good candidate for such an endeavor, but I do not know how much he was motivated to undertake this work and if he had the business sense of Walery.

If Henryk and Maria visited Kraków in 1853, they may have attended the first public exhibition of western art and paintings created by the Polish artists who lived in three different parts of the Polish lands under Russian, Prussian, and Austrian rule. The exhibition was such a grand artistic and financial success that it inspired Walery to organize the Kraków Society of Friends of Fine Arts.[93] The society, which was founded in Kraków in 1854 and was the first organization of its kind in Polish lands, still exists today. Walery Wielogłowski was the secretary of the society for many years.

The first quarter of 1854 brought joyful news to the von Richthofen and Wielogłowski families; Maria was expecting her first child. The pregnancy was not an easy one. In the archives of the Polish Academy of Arts and Sciences, I found a letter written by Lady Plater to Konstancja Wielogłowska, Maria's mother, on August 8th, 1854.

> Dear Madam, I hope that after all the fear and anxiety today you are already a happy grandmother of a healthy grandson or granddaughter. From the bottom of my heart I desire news from your family. Son or daughter? What is the baby's name? Does mama nurse the baby? (Plater, 1854).[94]

The first child of Maria and Henryk Freiherr von Richthofen was born in Kraków on August 29, 1854 at 6:30 in the morning according to the baby's birth certificate, which stated the following.

> On August 30th, at 12 noon, in one thousand eight hundred fifty-four (1854), the Honorable Baron Henryk Rafał Richthofen, a citizen of the Prussian Kingdom, 28 years old, who lives in a house on the Main Square number fifteen in Kraków, came to me, a curate and the deputy civil of the Parish of Saint Mary registrar. He showed me a baby male, who was born in his house on August 29th the current year, at six thirty in the morning, and acknowledged that the baby was conceived by him and Marianna, maiden name Wielogłowska, and that his will is to give the baby the names of Bolesław, Jan, and Paweł. After this declaration and

---

[93] Rocznik Krakowski (1904) volume 6, p. 246.
[94] B PAU Kraków, rkps. 1843: Plater to K. Wielogłowska, Letter, 1854.

showing me the baby in the presence of the citizens: The Honorable Walery Wielogłowski, the baby's grandfather, 49 years old, living on the Main Square Number 15, and the Honorable Józef Żabiński, 48 years old, living on Grodzka Street Number 234, this birth certificate was read to all present and signed by all. (The signatures of priest Stanisław Anderski, Henryk Rafał Richthofen, Walery Wielogłowski, J. Żabiński).[95]

I discovered in my amazement that Bolesław, the firstborn son of Henryk, did not receive the name of his father or grandfather, which seemed to be the tradition in the von Richthofen family. Even the baby's second name did not honor the baby's grandfather or his great-grandfather from the Royn-Schützendorf house. I believe that it was caused by strained relations between Henryk and his father at the time. I know that Wilhelm came to Henryk's estate to see his grandson and earlier participated in his son's wedding, but those visits did not change my conviction that Henryk was not emotionally close to his father.

Bolesław, the name which Maria and Henryk chose for the baby, first appeared in Poland in the Middle Ages and means "one that would be famous," There were no saints in the Catholic Church who bore the name Bolesław, but a few Polish kings and knights did; and it became popular in the 19th century. In Silesia, the name was prevalent in a slightly different form, Bolko, and there were some members of the von Richthofen family who bore this name. I believe that my great-grandfather received the name Bolesław in honor of Bolesław Wielogłowski, the cousin of Walery and son of Kacper, who was not only a close member of Maria's family but also their companion in exile, in France, to whom Maria was very attached. It is possible that the two other names were given to the baby in honor of von Richthofen ancestors: Johann Praetorius (1611-1664) and Paulus Praetorius (1521-1565).

If Maria read patriotic poems like the one written by the Polish bard, Adam Mickiewicz, *Do Matki Polki* [To the Polish Mother] she could have been anxious to think about her baby's future. Could she foresee another

---

[95] The Archives of St. Mary Church in Kraków: The Certificate 181/46.

fight for the independence of Poland? Maria was practical but very spiritual at the same time. I wonder how she wanted to raise her son to prepare him to live in balance with his Polish and German heritage. How much was Henryk involved in his son's upbringing?

Left: Heinrich (Henryk) Freiherr von Richthofen with his firstborn son, Bolesław.
Right: Bolesław Freiherr von Richthofen, my great-grandfather.[96]

Bolesław was a frail and sickly child and a little spoiled by his parents. They raised Bolesław on children's books and verses by the Polish poet Stanisław Jachowicz, who is considered the founding father of children's literature in Poland and the author of the first European magazine for children. They also read the German tales by the Brothers Grimm to him. From his infancy, he heard both Polish and German spoken. He liked books, nature, and music. Maria dressed Bolesław in fancy clothes and kept his hair long for the first seven years of his life according to the old Polish tradition. When I saw the above picture for the first time in my grandmother's home, I saw young Bolesław with his blond hair falling to his shoulders, standing tall in a velvet suit with a lace collar and cuffs and

---

[96] Ivona Tarko's archives.

stockings, and holding a sword in his little hand as a curious character from a fairy tale, like a page in a king's court.

Not long ago, Karl-Friedrich Freiherr von Richthofen, our family historian, made me aware of two facts which connected the Brothers Grimm to the von Richthofen family. The first one was the visit of Wilhelm Grimm to one of the von Richthofen estates in Silesia in 1850. The second one was the influence of Jacob Grimm, not only the fairytale writer but the philologist, jurist, and mythologist, on Karl Freiherr von Richthofen, a professor of law at the University of Berlin at that time. Jacob's works inspired Karl to investigate Frisian rights. The inspiration was fruitful and Karl Freiherr von Richthofen wrote an impressive work about the investigations into Frisian legal sources. He made several contributions to the history of law for *The Monumenta Germaniae Historica.*

The visits of Maria and Henryk to Kraków were documented by the births of their children because all of them were born in Kraków. During these visits, they stayed with Maria's parents. Apparently, Maria felt more comfortable staying in Kraków, a city with good physicians and a maternity ward in St. Lazarus Hospital and then could recover in her parents' home in Kraków under the care of family members. As a side note, in 1851, Dr. Józef Dietl came to Kraków and brought new test methods and showed that patients with different symptoms should be put in separate rooms in a hospital. He also saw the great importance in hygiene, diet, and balneology.

On January 3, 1856, the first daughter of Maria and Henryk Freiherr von Richthofen came into the world, and they named her Zofia. Which family relative were they honoring this time? There were no women bearing this name in the closest relatives of Maria and Henryk. Did the baby girl receive her name in memory of the late Zofia Sapieżanka or Zofia, the Duchess of Austria? I believe that the connotation of the name was important to Maria and Henryk, which is based on the Greek word "Sophia," which means "wisdom." Unfortunately, no pictures of baby Zofia Freiin von Richthofen were preserved in my grandmother's archives.

With two little children in the house by now, life assuredly got busier for Maria. The Richthofen family usually visited Kraków in the summer so they probably did not take part in the sledging cavalcade organized during the winter carnival in Kraków, which was led by Maria's father, of which Maria Estreicherówna wrote.

> A historical sledging cavalcade went from the Palace of the Rams to the Prince Sanguszko's Palace on February 14, 1858. The participants were dressed in authentic Kraków costumes. Walery Wielogłowski gave an excellent speech and was followed boldly by Aleksandra née Deskur Florkiewiczowa, known for her wit (Estreicherówna, 1968).[97]

February 14th was Maria Freifrau von Richthofen's birthday, but in Poland, the "name day" customarily was more recognized for the celebration. Maria celebrated in May because her patroness was the Blessed Virgin Mother, whose major feast day fell on May 3rd.

1858 started merrily with winter fun but brought mourning to the Wielogłowski family in the summer when Matylda Wessel, Maria's maternal grandmother, passed away at the Owczary estate in the Polish Kingdom.[98] At the end of August, Maria, Henryk, and their two children vacationed at Rybna village, near Kraków, where the farm owned by Maria's parents was located. Henryk's father, Wilhelm Freiherr von Richthofen, paid them a visit in Rybna then as well. There are indications that Maria and her children were in Kraków every summer. Her stay in June 1859 was reported in a correspondence between Antonin Wysocki and Emma née Ogińska Wysocka, when Antonin wrote from Kraków to his absent wife on June 4, 1859.

> In the evening, Madam Wielogłowska with daughter and two grandchildren came to visit you and asked me to send you a bow (Wysocki, 1986).[99]

---

[97] M. Estreichrówna, Op. Cit., p. 71.
[98] J. Kuzicki, Op. Cit., p. 246.
[99] H. Wysocki, Przemówiły stare listy, Kraków, 1986, p. 96.

Madame Wielogłowska was Konstancja Wielogłowska with her daughter Maria née Wielogłowska Freifrau von Richthofen, and grandchildren Bolesław and Zofia. Antonin Wysocki was an artist, painter, and fighter for the independence of Poland. His wife Emma was the daughter of Michał Kleofas Ogiński, a diplomate and composer of polonaises, whom I mentioned in Chapter 1. Originally from Lithuania, they lived in Kraków in the middle of the 19th century and belonged to the Kraków circles of bourgeoisie and intelligentsia.

I imagine the stay of Maria Freifrau von Richthofen and her family in summer 1859 in Kraków included walking with the Wielogłowski family on the Main Square and around the Planty Park, taking part in Sunday services in the Kraków churches, paying visits to the friends and the relatives of the family, eating meals together, and planning another departure to the farm in Rybna village. At that time Maria's father was the owner of two estates, Rybna and Lipki, near Kraków. In Rybna, Walery was the patron of the Catholic parish and supporter of the local school. He came back to his roots by becoming a landlord again. Farming, especially the introduction of agricultural innovations, was a source of joy for him. He easily became connected to farmers, who liked and respected him. He wrote and published short stories and made calendars for them. The harvest festivals in Rybna were celebrated by the owner of the village and the peasants together. One person who remembered the Wielogłowski family, Stanisław Mieroszewski, wrote in his diary about one of those festivals in Rybna that at the end of the festival.

> The crowd saw his Kocia (Konstancja), his wife, who was a very short and plump person and the head of the county, standing on the hill in the Wielogłowski garden under the rain of the Bengal fireworks (Mieroszewski, 1964).[100]

In summer 1859 both families, the Wielogłowskis and the von Richthofens, with two little children, went to Rybna to escape from the

---

[100] S. Mieroszewski, Zapamietane osoby z dawnych czasów w Wspomnienia lat ubiegłych, Kraków, 1964.

summer heat in Kraków. How could it be that a tragedy occurred that summer that the many generations of my family never talked about? Perhaps the parents and grandparents wanted to forget about the death of three-year-old Zofia and did not pass down any memories about her short life. She literally was removed from the family recollection. Only two dates from the von Richthofen family tree and the other German document and a short note from the Antonin Wysocki letter I cited above, reminded me about the existence of the little girl.

Zofia (Sophie) Freiin von Richthofen was born on January 3, 1856 and died on August 19, 1859 in Rybna. Her death could have been due to an accident on the farm or an illness (a flu epidemic spread throughout Europe during 1859-1860). In general, the death rate of children in the 19th century was very high. I cannot even imagine the family's despair after losing little Zofia. I think this tragedy perhaps accelerated Walery Wielogłowski's decision to sell the Rybna estate and also weakened the health of Konstancja Wielogłowska, by that time not resilient.

How did the grieving family handle the situation? It is still heartbreaking when I think about their loss, but life had to go on for them. Thirteen months after Zofia's death, on September 19, 1860, Maria and Henryk were blessed with another son, Stanisław Wilhelm; and two years after the birth of Stanisław, on December 21, 1862, they welcomed a baby girl into the world, Maria Eliza.

Baby Stanisław, called Staś in my family, received his middle name in honor of his fraternal grandfather, Wilhelm Freiherr von Richthofen. This name would have a symbolic impact not only on his contacts with Grandfather Wilhelm, but on his life story. The names given him in his baptismal ceremony were an attempt by Maria and Henryk to join two cultures, two houses, and two traditions – Polish and German. Stanisław is an old Polish name with Slavic roots that means "the one who is from the famous home" and Wilhelm is a German name that means "the one who gives refuge."

Baby Maria, was called by her parents the diminutive name Marynia, which also was used for her mother, which caused some confusion. When there were two Maria von Richthofen women, mother and daughter, with exactly the same name and even the same diminutive name, their descendants had to look for a way to distinguish them by adding their surnames every time they talked about them. However, my grandmother ended the confusion with the names by referring to older Maria only with her maiden name Wielogłowska and to younger Maria with the surname Miłkowska, her husband's last name. Maria née Freiin von Richthofen Miłkowska received her middle name in honor of Aunt Eliza née Freiin von Richthofen Szydłowska, the only sister of Henryk Freiherr von Richthofen, Maria's father.

Stanisław and Maria von Richthofen were born when their Wielogłowski grandparents were still alive, but the children were not old enough at the time of their grandparents' deaths to remember them well. Bolesław Freiherr von Richthofen, the first and beloved grandson of the Wielogłowskis, on many occasions spent time with them during the period of ten years he knew them and was exposed to their traditions, patriotism, and faith. The influence of the Wielogłowski grandparents and the family was seen in Bolesław's attachment to Kraków in his return to study at the Jagiellonian University and to start his family and raise his own children there.

How difficult it must have been for Maria to learn that her mother was seriously ill when she had a baby in arms and was raising two older children. Maria also was worried about the fate of the January Uprising of 1863 and the lives of her relatives who took part in it. One of them was Maria's first cousin, young Jan Godeffroy, the owner of Ulanowice in the Polish Kingdom. Jan, born in 1838, was the son of Joanna Wessel, the sister of Konstancja née Wessel Wielogłowska, and Karol Godeffroy.

Konstancja Wielogłowska passed away on August 4, 1863 in Kraków. Family, friends, and acquaintances gathered for her funeral mass in the Church of the Reformed Franciscans on Reformacka Street in Kraków. This church had significance for the family because the mother of Walery, Marianna Wielogłowska, was buried there, and her table tombstone located on the left side in the church entrance still can be seen today. The church was built in the 17th century and is known in Kraków for its specific microclimate within a crypt beneath the main building, which causes the resting corpses to undergo mummification.

The mourners who attended the funeral of Konstancja Wielogłowska received death cards with holy pictures, some of which I still have in my archives. Konstancja Wielogłowska, as the first from my family, was buried in the Wielogłowski family tomb designed and built by the sculptor Edward Stahlik (1825-1888), which was commissioned by Walery Wielogłowski. The tomb is located in Rakowice Cemetery in Kraków.

Maria Freifrau von Richthofen prepared the following epitaph for her mother.

> Konstancja née Countess Wessel Wielogłowska, born in 1808, passed away in 1863. Pious, humble, peaceful, good mother and wife, faithful companion of her husband in the state and during their exile, the adornment and comfort of his life (Richthofen, 1863).[101]

The below picture of Maria Freifrau von Richthofen from that period of her life shows the young woman in her mourning attire: a dark dress and a chain bracelet made of steel with a black oxide finish on her wrist. The bracelet was a typical piece of jewelry worn by Polish women as the sign of the national mourning after the fall of the January 1863 Uprising. Below is the first verse of a poem, *Czarna Sukienka* [Black Dress] written by Konstanty Gaszyński that captures the mood of despondency in Polish society after suffering the loss of another hope for their independence.

> Mother, put away my dresses, pearls, garlands of roses
> Festive garb, magnificent apparel –
> These are not for me any longer.
> I liked them in the past when the spring of hope gushed,
> But when Poland entered a grave, am obliged to only one cloth –
> the black dress.[102]

---

[101] Ivona Tarko's archives: M. Richthofen, Manuscript, 1863.
[102] Author Konstanty Gaszyński, http://www.bibliotekapiosenki.pl/binaries/ teksty i nuty/009 czarna sukienka t.pdf accessed 08-03-2015.

Maria née Wielogłowska Freifrau von Richthofen.[103]

---

[103] Ivona Tarko's archives.

I have no doubt that Maria was going through a difficult period in her life in 1863. She not only mourned her beloved mother but was also worried about her aging father. She had to return to the Ostrowieczko estate, leaving him alone in his distress and poor health in Kraków. The death of his wife was a painful experience for Walery. He had lost his best friend, his love with whom he had spent two-thirds of his life. He used to say that the best decision of his life was marrying his beloved Konstancja at a young age. In addition to his grief, bitterness and disappointment associated with the fall of the January Uprising 1863 only added to his suffering. Walery fought against the Russians as a Polish army officer in the previous uprising of 1830 and the Polish-Russian War in 1830-1831, but was opposed to the new insurrection in 1863. His negative attitude toward the uprising came from his belief that Poles could recover their independence by hard work but not by a new fight with a much more powerful occupier. He believed it would bring many losses and had no chance for a success. This view put him in opposition to the ideas of even his friend and kin, Paweł Popiel, and many people from his conservative circle, but most of all Walery was criticized by the young Polish citizens who were eager to fight the Russians. They openly criticized Walery and even in public he was subjected to annoying and even humiliating comments. At the age of 60, Walery became an embittered and ailing old man. He succumbed to pneumonia on July 11, 1865 in Kraków. Maria, his beloved and only child, was by his side during his illness.

The biographer of Walery Wielogłowski, Jerzy Kuzicki, related an article from 1865 in the *Czas* [Time] newspaper number 158, which contained this description of Walery's funeral.

> On July 13, 1865, the funeral of Walery Wielogłowski took place. The day started with a service celebrated by Bishop Ludwik Łętowski and the Dean of the Cathedral, priest Antoni Rozwadowski in the Church of the Reformed Franciscans. Then, a funeral procession to Rakowice Cemetery took place, which was led by priest canon Alfred Sosnowski. The coffin containing the deceased was carried by the peasants of Rybna, who came in great number to the funeral of their former landlord, from his home on Gołębia Street to the church, and then to the cemetery. In his last

journey Wielogłowski was accompanied by a group of relatives, friends, and students from the Agriculture School in Czernichów. Worthy of note was the fact that peasants from villages other than Rybna, near Kraków, broadly participated in the funeral. Their presence gave tribute to the deceased, who devoted many years of his life to active work for the good of the villagers (Kuzicki, 2005).[104]

---

[104] J. Kuzicki, Op. Cit., p. 301.

CHAPTER 5 The Broken Home: Heinrich, Maria, Bolesław, Stanisław, and the Little Maria

What arises and arouses, it all comes to end, what happens – who exactly knows

~ Gotfried Benn

Although the death of Maria's parents weakened her ties with Kraków she apparently did not want to sever them completely as she kept the house in Kraków she inherited from them. In 1867, however, perhaps for financial reasons, she sold or leased the Mineral Water Workshop located in the Planty Park by Gołebia Street founded by her father shortly before his death.[105]

I believe that Maria spent the next few years mainly on the Ostrowieczko estate with Henryk and their children: Bolesław, who was almost twelve years old; Stanisław, who was five years old; and Maria, who was three years old. Bolesław was old enough to remember his grandfather Walery as a loving, cordial, and thoughtful man who was always eager to share an interesting story about the past, people, and customs with his grandson. The younger von Richthofen siblings, however, likely did not remember much about Grandfather Walery, but they were close to their paternal grandfather, Wilhelm Freiherr von Richthofen, as they grew into young adults. Stanisław had been very close to Wilhelm since his school years; and all the von Richthofen grandchildren spent some time with Wilhelm and his second wife during vacations when they were older. I am certain that their grandfathers were a positive influence on the von Richthofen children, and I now can understand some choices Bolesław, Stanisław, and Maria made when they became adults.

When I look at the below pictures of Bolesław, Stanisław, and Maria, the facial resemblance of the siblings is striking to me; but even though they resembled each other, it became obvious to me that they differed in physical prowess and disposition. Bolesław, my great-grandfather, was frail from birth and sickly all his life; Stanisław was always healthy, energetic, and balanced; and Maria was delicate physically and had a shy and nervous disposition. The siblings loved and supported each other and stayed in touch throughout their entire lives; but Maria seemed to be closer to Staś, probably because they were only two years apart in age and likely were playmates and confidantes. Maria did not remember Bolesław as a playmate but rather as the older and protective brother.

---

[105] J. Kuzicki, Op. Cit., p. 259.

As the years passed, Henryk unimaginably forgave his father for his second marriage and looked to him for support, perhaps financially. In 1869 Wilhelm Freiherr von Richthofen wrote in his diary that he had a serious discussion with Henryk about his poor financial state.

In 1870 Henryk lost his mother, Paulina Freifrau von Richthofen, about whom I wrote in Chapter 1. She passed away on her son's Ostrowieczko estate and was buried in nearby Dolsk. When I first learned about her death, the thought occurred to me that her death could have worsened Henryk's depression and augmented the tension between Henryk and Maria. The discovery of Henryk's father autobiography in 2015 revealed facts from Henryk's life that astonished me and changed my opinion about my great-great-grandfather. A note made by Wilhelm in 1870 about Paulina's death also said that Henryk lost his mother's assets, which led to a dispute with Henryk's brother-in-law Antoni Szydłowski. Wilhelm stated in 1871 that the dispute continued concerning the remaining assets of Paulina Freifrau von Richthofen and the possibility of buying back the Ostrowieczko estate! I could not believe what this note meant...Maria, Henryk, and their children lost their home!

All my life, before reading Wilhelm's notes, I thought that Henryk was a weak man who did not take good care of his estate and likely faced some financial problems because of his incompetence or neglect. I even suspected that the source of the problems perhaps was inept managers or farmers, crop losses due to bad weather, or downright bad luck. As Henryk's story unfolded through Wilhelm, though, I realized that something much worse was the source of his problems. In fact, losing his estate and his mother's enormous assets could have been caused by actions rather than inactions on his part. I believe unfortunately, that he may have been involved in reckless activities and suspect that Henryk could have lost everything because he was a gambler. In the 19th century card games were very popular in the circles of gentry and were an inseparable part of their leisure time.

Top left: Bolesław Freiherr von Richthofen. ***Top center***: Stanisław Freiherr von Richthofen. ***Top right***:Maria Freiin von Richthofen. ***Bottom left***: Heinrich (Henryk) Freiherr von Richthofen. ***Bottom right***: Maria née Wielogłowska Freifrau von Richthofen.[106]

Ownership of the Ostrowieczko estate never returned to the von Richthofen family, and Henryk and Maria's marriage was quickly falling apart. Maria moved to Kraków and lived in the house inherited from her parents; 16-year-old Bolesław, 10-year-old Stanisław, and 8-year-old Maria stayed in different boarding schools; and Henryk was offered a

---

[106] Ivona Tarko's archives.

place to live in Kupientyn, the estate of his sister and brother-in-law, the Szydłowskis. It was painful for me to discover that their marriage, which began in boundless patient love, ended after 18 years with broken hearts and home, destroyed trust, and painful separation. Walery Wielogłowski, Henryk's father-in-law, wrote shortly before his death about Henryk that he could not imagine a son-in-law better than Henryk and frankly loved him. No one could foresee the magnitude of their coming misery; maybe Maria worried when she saw signs of financial problems, but perhaps hoped that they were temporary. When the worst happened, she completely lost her trust in Henryk and there was no hope for his redemption in her mind.

Eliza née Freiin von Richthofen Szydłowska maintained her warm relationship with Maria and was close and supportive to Maria and Henryk's children. Wilhelm Freiherr von Richthofen financed the education of his grandson Stanisław, who attended the Kauffersche Institute in Dresden in 1872 and then in 1873 joined the Cadet School in Wahlstatt (Legnickie Pole). Work and duty were the foremost features of the Prussian education, and a military career was desirable for a young and healthy boy from an aristocratic German family at that time. Stanisław possessed all the qualities needed to be a good cadet: energy, zest for life, interior discipline, and strength of character. The Prussian Cadet School in Wahlstat (Legnickie Pole) had a good reputation and was attended by the members of von Richthofen family. One of the family alumni was Manfred Freiherr von Richthofen (1892-1918), aka the Red Baron, who graduated from Wahlstat in 1911.

The choice of school and career for Stanisław determined his future and a place in German society, while Stanisław's older brother Bolesław, on the other hand, was seeking Polish association as far as his preparatory school and university because the brothers were educated in different surroundings since they were young children. When the family's Ostrowieczko estate was lost, Bolesław was a student in the high school of the boarding school in Śrem (German name Schrimm), a little town in Wielkopolska, in Poznań province, which had Polish character at a time when Poland did not exist as an independent country. Many Poles lived there, and the school my great-grandfather attended was one of the oldest in the region and was built as a joint effort of the Polish and German communities. The teachers and students came from Polish and German families, and the school documents were prepared in both languages until the beginning of the 1870s. The bicultural, bilingual atmosphere of the school, which had a classic profile focusing on the Humanities, was a good match for Bolesław, who came from a German-Polish family and was interested in languages and history.

One of the alumni of the school was Fr. Piotr Wawrzyniak, recognized by Polish historians as an activist and pragmatist involved in the preservation of Polish culture in the area. He was known for his social work and struggle with peaceful methods, such as working and organizing the Union of the Earnings and Economic Societies to keep the presence of Polish families and landlords in the region of Wielkopolska. Piotr, who was much older than my great-grandfather, became a Catholic priest and the vicar of the Blessed Virgin Mother Church in Śrem in 1872, when my great-grandfather was still a student.

Maria Freifrau von Richthofen was 43 years old in 1870 when she lost her home in Ostrowieczko and moved to Kraków. I cannot imagine how lonely she must have felt there once the news about the family situation spread and her separation from Henryk became obvious. I do not have any information about Henryk's life during the period 1870-1878. Was he completely absent from the lives of his wife and children then? Wilhelm Freiherr von Richthofen noted in his diary that he met Maria with all three grandchildren on holiday in Silesia in 1872 and that his grandson Stanisław came to visit him in Dresden in that same year. He mentioned that Bolesław was ill for four weeks and lived with his mother - I guess only during his illness - and that little Maria became ill due to neglect in a boarding house in Dresden. In 1873, Wilhelm noted that Stanisław and Maria came to Bad Landeck (Lądek Zdrój) in Silesia for vacation, but there was not one word about Henryk.

In 1873, in Kraków Dr. Stanisław Krzyżanowski, an archeologist and a member of the Biographical and Historical Committee of the Polish Academy of Sciences in Kraków, contacted Maria Freifrau von Richthofen to ask her if she could make available to him all the materials and documents left by her late father because he wanted to write a biography of Walery Wielogłowski.

Dear Lady Baroness! My wish is to commemorate your venerable late father by writing an accurate biography of him, with his portrait, which is planned to be published by Władysław Jaworski in Kraków. I would like to ask you to send me all the materials left after the death of your venerable father, such as his memoirs, notes, letters, records, etc., which will be returned to you intact after their use in the literary work. I am honored to be, Your Lady Baroness, the greatest servant. With deep respect, Dr. Stanisław Krzyżanowski, Kraków, February 3rd, 1873. The Main Square number 57 (Krzyżanowski, 1873*).*[107]

I could not determine what happened between the request for materials and publication of the biography of Walery Wielogłowski – perhaps it was lack of cooperation by Maria or a change of plans by the publisher - but the planned book was never published. There were some short stories about the life of Walery Wielogłowski written by people who knew him personally, like Ludwik Dębicki and Franciszek Starowieyski, and biographical notes in the various encyclopedias and dictionaries of the 19th and 20th centuries. Ninety years after Dr. Krzyżanowski's request for materials, however, our family in Kraków received another letter written by a scientist, Dr. Franciszek German, from the town of Gliwice in Silesia, who informed us that he had many notes and materials about the impressive activities of Walery, but he was not able to write his biography. Finally, at Rzeszów University, the first comprehensive biography of Walery Wielogłowski was written by historian Jerzy Kuzicki and published in 2005. The book is an excellent chronicle of the life of Walery Wielogłowski and was a valuable source of information about my ancestor and his close family in the Polish language. This publication belongs to the series *Galicja i jej dziedzictwo* [Galicia and its Heritage].

---

[107] B PAU, Kraków rkps 1844: S. Krzyżanowski to M. Richthofen, Letter, 1873.

In 1874, my great-grandfather Bolesław graduated from high school. I deeply appreciate the thoughtfulness of the person who placed the list of graduates from this school on the site of the Genealogical Society of Wielkopolska *Gniazdo*, where I was able to find my great-grandfather's name. The list was short, only ten names for the graduation class in 1874, but it showed the different ethnicity of the students: Graduation 1874: 1. Baron Richthofen Bolesław, 2. Bartolomaus Richard, 3. Biefel Karl, 4.Brodowski Zbigniew, 5.Bruski Leo, 6. Goldmann Eduard, 7. Holec Michael, 8. Iffland Walter, 9. Kricke Oswald, 10. Pufke Kasimir.[108] After graduation Bolesław considered linguistic and theological study, which did not surprise me since he was a devout Catholic raised by a very religious mother and influenced by his maternal grandparents.

"Philosophiren ist dephlegmatisiren vivificiren" [to philosophize is to rid oneself of inertia, to come to life], said Georg Phillip Friedrich Freiherr von Hardenberg (1772-1801).[109] Bolesław Freiherr von Richthofen decided to study philosophy in Breslau (Wrocław) University which at the time was named the Universitas Litterarum Vratislaviensis. The university dates back to 1702 when the Leopoldina University was founded in Breslau with faculty members in the areas of Catholic theology and philosophy. In 1811, this university was joined with the Viadrina University, where the progenitor of the von Richthofen family, Paulus Praetorius, studied law in the 16th century. After the two long-standing universities were combined, a new modern one was founded which had five schools: Catholic Theology, Evangelic Theology, Law, Medicine, and Philosophy. The Philosophy School included the departments of geography, history, Sanskrit, philology, music, science, and agriculture. In 1841 the department of Slavic languages and literature was founded. Many years later, in 1911, the university changed its name to the University of Frederic Wilhelm. After World War II, in the fall of 1945, the Polish Uniwersytet Wrocławski was in operation again in a dilapidated building, and today it is the largest university in Lower Silesia.

---

[108] WTG GNIAZDO:
http://www.wtg-gniazdo.org/forum/viewtopic.php?p=22641 Accessed.02-17-16.
[109] B. Richards, The Greatest Books You'll Never Read, UK, 2015, p. 44.

A renovated, beautiful, baroque assembly hall called Aula Leopoldina[110] reminds us about the beginning of the school.

In the 19th century the University in Wrocław was the choice of many Polish families. Polish students founded their associations as Concordia and Polonia, and were active in the Slavic Association of Literature created in 1836. Bolesław Freiherr von Richthofen was a member of this association from 1875 to 1878. The purpose of the association was to learn the languages, literature, history, and laws of the Slavic nations through discussion of papers prepared by the students and books from the library of the association. During the summer semester of 1876 Bolesław presented a paper in which he analyzed a play *Irydion*, written by the Polish bard Zygmunt Krasiński. The association was open to every student in the university regardless of their nationality and the only condition required for membership was that the student had to speak Polish or other Slavic languages. The members met weekly but sometimes organized special meetings to celebrate important anniversaries; for example, in 1873 they celebrated the 400th birthday of Mikołaj Kopernik, the Polish astronomer, and the 50th anniversary of the writings of Józef Kraszewski.[111] Among the memorabilia from my great-grandfather's college years, I found a picture that contained images of the Polish poets: Sebastian Klonowicz and Jan Kochanowski of the Renaissance period in Poland; and Franciszek Kniaźnin, Franciszek Karpiński, Tomasz Kajetan Węgierski, Adam Naruszewicz, and Stanisław Trembecki of the Age of Enlightenment. Bolesław signed the back of the photo.

---

[110] Aula Leopoldyńska
https://www.youtube.com/watch?v=d8QC53dyk7kAccessed 02-18-2016.
[111] J. Szymański, Pamiętnik Towarzystwa Literacko-Słowiańskiego Przy Uniwersytecie Wrocławskim Wydany w Roku Złotego Jubileuszu Nakładem Drukarni Polskiej we Wrocławiu, Wrocław, 1886.

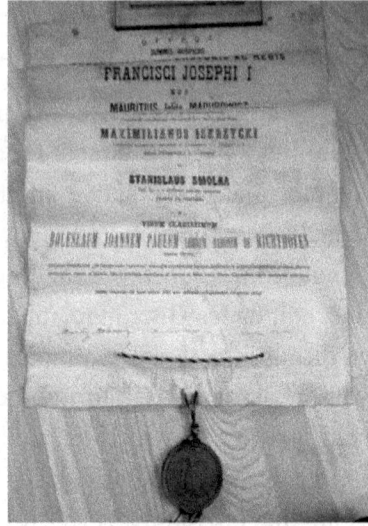

Top left: Bolesław Freiherr von Richthofen as a student. Top right: Bolesław Freiherr von Richthofen Ph.D. diploma. Bottom: Clipping from the Kraków newspaper from 1881 containing a note about Ph.D. graduates from the Jagiellonian University; among them my great-grandfather Bolesław von Richthofen.[112]

While Bolesław was studying philosophy in Wrocław, his brother Stanisław was completing the three steps of education required for becoming an officer in the Prussian Army. The first step was to graduate from the Cadet School; the second was to graduate from one of the seven existing Prussian military schools at that time; and the third was to graduate from the Military Academy in Berlin. From my family stories and a few German documents, I learned that Stanisław was assigned to

---

[112] Ivona Tarko's archives.

the Third Posenschen Infantry Regiment F58 after graduation from the Military Academy which was shortly after Fort Posen (Poznań) was built.

Maria Freiin von Richthofen, the youngest of the children of Henryk and Maria, was only eight years old when her family life fell into turmoil, their home was lost, her parents separated, and her life changed forever. Almost nothing was said to me by my grandmother about Maria's childhood or education. The little I determined about Maria was found in the short notes in the autobiography of Wilhelm Freiherr von Richthofen that told about her stay in Dresden and vacationing in Bad Landeck (Lądek Zdrój) in Lower Silesia with Stanisław and their mother. I learned from her few cards and letters I found in my grandmother's archives that Maria knew the German language, but expressing her thoughts in writing in German was somewhat difficult, which she confessed in her correspondence. She was fluent in Polish.

On May 12, 1878, Heinrich (Henryk) Freiherr von Richthofen passed away in Kupientyn at the age of 52. His father, Baron Wilhelm Freiherr von Richthofen, wrote in his diary that Henryk died totally alone, without support, and abandoned by his family. He left behind his debts. The oldest of Henryk's children, Bolesław, was 24 years old at that time. I still do not know the reason for the unfortunate turn in Henryk's life that ended in isolation. I know the date of his death from Wilhelm's notes and the von Richthofen family tree. I wanted to find his death certificate and grave, which I thought might be located in Kupientyn or a different place nearby. After educating myself about the administrative divisions in Poland then and now, I wrote a letter to the Catholic parish in the area Henryk passed away with no response. I finally called the Office of the Civil Status in Sokołów Podlaski and the Office of the State Archives in Siedlce, located in central Poland, and learned that Kupientyn belonged to the Catholic Parish in Sokołów Podlaski, which was destroyed by the Russian Army in 1944 when the town was under German occupation during World War II. The majority of the church archives that contained documents from the 19th century perished in the fire, and those that survived were transferred to the government office, reviving my hope for finding Henryk's death certificate. When I contacted a counter clerk in the State Archives in Siedlce, however, she told me that they did not have any death certificates from the period for which I was searching. The people I contacted were not able to tell me anything about the Catholic cemetery in Kupientyn, but it seemed that the Kupientyn estate did not have its own chapel and the cemetery at the time of Henryk's death. I know from the Internet that there are old cemeteries in the Kupientyn area and I still need to find a way to check if there are any tombs there from 1878.

I am not able to explain why there is no obituary, death card, or condolence letters related to the death of Henryk Freiherr von Richthofen in my family archives, which interestingly enough, contains papers connected to people who were not members of the family. This is one of my family's mysteries that will remain unsolved, I am afraid; but for now it looks as though the memory of Henryk was erased on purpose. Adding to this mystery is a letter written from a lawyer's office in Posen (Poznań) to my great-grandfather Bolesław 12 years after his father's death, which stated that the family should get back money from Mr. N. K., Henryk's debtor since 1867.

In 1879 Maria finished a manuscript recalling her stay on Ischia Island with her parents when she was a child. Perhaps she was just preserving her memories for her children, but it is possible that writing about that carefree time of her youth took her mind off how much her life had changed. Bolesław, her firstborn and beloved son, after graduation from the University in Breslau (Wrocław), came to Kraków to continue his graduate studies.

The university in Kraków, founded in 1364 by Polish King Casimir III the Great, was the oldest in Poland and one of the oldest universities in the world. The golden era of the university took place between 1500 and 1535 during the Polish Renaissance. At the end of the 18th century, during the Partitions of Poland followed by the occupation of Kraków by Austria-Hungary, the university struggled but managed to survive. In 1817 it was renamed Jagiellonian University which today is commonly called "UJ." In the second half of the 19th century, the university was under Austrian influence and German was the mandatory language in lectures. Gradually, the situation changed at the university, reflecting the political fluctuations. Franz Joseph (1830-1916), the Emperor of Austria-Hungary, allowed the use of the Polish language in lectures in the majority of courses in the department of philosophy; therefore, only the history of Austria, the German language, literature, and one of the classical languages were lectured in German. The laboratories of history and philology were divided into two groups, one of which was conducted in German and the other in Polish. The Polish language has been recognized since 1870 as the language of instruction in all courses, except the German language and literature in the Jagiellonian University.

Bolesław studied history and classical languages. Professor Stanisław Smólka, a recognized historian who specialized in the history of the Middle Ages at the Jagiellonian University, was his Ph.D. program advisor. In 1879 Bolesław founded the Society of Philology and Literature with the majority of members coming from the Classical Languages Department of the School of Philosophy at the university. The purpose of the society was to enhance the knowledge of classical and modern literature, build friendships among the students, and help them in their studies. The members met weekly on the weekends. The society founded by Bolesław almost 150 years ago still exists but is known today as the Circle of Classical Philologists of UJ.

In 1881 Bolesław defended his thesis, titled in Latin *De Caesaris Codice Cracoviensi*, which was devoted to the Code of Kraków in the Middle Ages. He received the title of Doctor of Philosophy on July 14, 1881 and then was employed as "Privatdozent" at the Jagiellonian University. The position Privatdozent was introduced in the 19th century in the German universities during the period of school reforms; and a Privatdozent was a lecturer paid by students rather than the university. In 1887, there were 29 Privatdozents at the Jagiellonian University in Kraków.[113]

---

[113] Kronika Uniwersytetu Jagiellońskiego od roku 1864-1887 i obraz jego stanu dzisiejszego wraz z rzeczą o rektorach od czasów najdawniejszych, drukarnia UJ 1887, p. 106.

During his student years at the Jagiellonian University, Bolesław worked as a volunteer in the Jagiellonian Library by assisting in the task of cataloging its huge collection. The director of the library, Karol Estreicher, depended on the help of volunteers because the collection was quickly growing and there was a lack of funds to increase the group of paid employees to manage the cataloging.

> The volunteers, specialists in different fields, cataloged works in their areas and were: Professor Maurycy Straszewski, W. i Fr. Bartynowscy, M. Baraniecki, Adam Asnyk, M. Bobrzyński, Józef Kremer, Józef Szujski, Leon Kulczycki, J. Winkowski, Winc. Zakrzewski, Bronisław Kruczkiewicz, Bolesław Richthofen (who came back as a volunteer in the period 1922-1923). Thanks to help of the volunteers, a total of 83 during 12 years (1869-1881), the majority of the collection of the library, except medicine, biology, ancient classics, periodicals, and incunabula, was cataloged (Lipska, 1936).[114]

When I studied the lives of the von Richthofen brothers, I realized how different their paths of education were due to their individual talents, physical conditions, and circumstances. Stanisław Freiherr von Richthofen, as an officer in the Prussian Army had to be physically and mentally fit and was entirely immersed in his military service. He did not have much time for family and did not marry and start his own family until later in life. His officer rank gave him prestige and privileges, but in exchange he had no privacy and his religious zeal perhaps suffered. As a child Stanisław was raised in the Catholic faith, but I believe he spent more time with Protestants as a youth in school, in the company of his paternal grandfather Wilhelm, and in the army where the majority of the Prussian soldiers were Protestants as well. I believe that Stanisław was not religious when he grew up as he never mentioned his faith and religious beliefs in the letters he wrote to my grandmother. I sometimes ask myself if Stanisław's life was determined by the decisions of his parents, Grandfather Wilhelm, and teachers, to which I could say yes unequivocally. Since he was 12 years old he was raised mainly by the

---

[114] H. Lipska, Żegota Pauli (w 40-lecie) w: Przegląd Biblioteczny, redaktor Edward Kuntze, Rocznik X, 1936 rok, p. 9.

German part of the family and in German schools; and I believe he wanted to fit in and felt more German than Polish at that time.

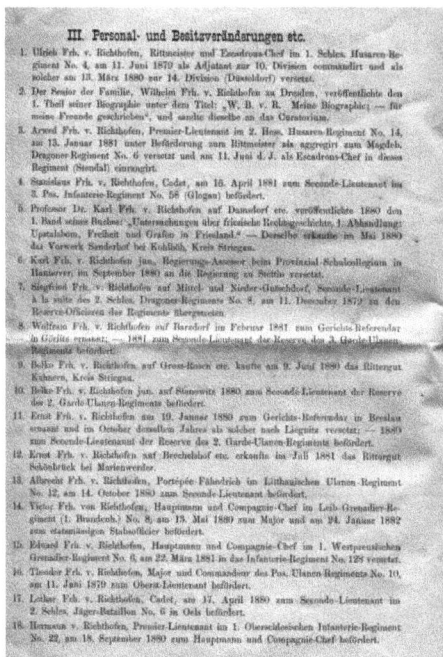

Left: The page from the 1882 von Richthofen family newsletter, in which the second paragraph is a note about Wilhelm Freiherr von Richthofen's autobiography and the fourth paragraph talks about Stanisław Freiherr von Richthofen as a second lieutenant in Glogau (Głogów) in Lower Silesia. *Right*: Stanisław Freiherr von Richthofen's pictures from different periods of his military career.[115]

Maria was the first of the von Richthofen siblings to be married. Her wedding with Józef Miłkowski, the coat of arms of Awdaniec, took place in Kraków on June 30, 1883 in the Capuchin Church, a small building with an interior design that revealed the strict rule of the Order, promoting extreme poverty. I assume that the wedding was small and modest because of the limited finances and decreasing family of the bride.

---

[115] Ivona Tarko's archives.

Maria's father, Heinrich (Henryk) Freiherr von Richthofen, passed away five years earlier; and both sets of grandparents, the Wielogłowskis and the von Richthofens, were deceased as well. Maria's siblings and cousins from the Miłkowski, Objezierski, and Topiński families probably came to Kraków to the wedding, as well as her Aunt Eliza née Freiin von Richthofen Szydłowska, the sister of Maria's father. Maria's husband, Józef Miłkowski, was a close family relative, actually her uncle, but no more than eight years her senior. Maria was 20 years old when she married Józef, son of Fanny née Objezierska Miłkowska, the nephew of Paulina née Objezierska von Richthofen, Maria's grandmother. Józef was the owner of the Serafinówka estate near Chełm, in eastern Poland. I suspect that Maria's marriage was arranged by both families, perhaps with the help of Eliza Szydłowska, who lived in eastern Poland as well.

Their marriage was mutually disappointing for Maria and Józef and ended with a separation after only a few years. Maria was unhappy with Józef, repeatedly suffered stomach and liver pain, and was often frightened because her husband intimidated her with a pistol. The couple did not have children. When Maria's brother, Bolesław, learned about her miserable life with Józef, he went to Serafinówka and took Maria to Kraków where she would spend most of her life. I suspect that she was never officially divorced and remained single the rest of her life.

Was Bolesław's temperament reflective of the average citizen of Kraków from the 19th century as described below by Professor Stanisław Estreicher?

> The average resident of Kraków does not have the energy, mobility, gaiety, and vitality of the citizens of Warsaw. He does not have the same seriousness and severity as the people of Posen. Intellectualism and critical restraint, the lack of emotions, and no tendency to outbursts are the features of the average inhabitant of Kraków. Also, there are more tendencies to criticism and skepticism in Kraków than in any other parts of the Polish lands. The Kraków citizen is usually calm and seldom applauds what he

sees in a theater or at a rally. He has high expectations, and it is not easy to make him happy (Estreicher, 1931).[116]

Bolesław's Ph.D. from Jagiellonian University placed him among the Kraków intellectuals; and as the owner of the Bonarka estate in Podgórze, a small city nearby Kraków, he could also call himself a landlord. His doctoral degree was more important to him than his aristocratic title, however, which he did not put on his business cards. He valued intellectual work, peace, and harmony. He did not like loud people and did not seek large crowds. He loved his mother very much, and she worried about him and wanted him to get married. In one of the letters she composed to Eliza née Freiin von Richthofen Szydłowska, her late husband's sister, Bolesław's mother wrote

> God bless you for your every cordial word, each good and friendly advice, and kindly willingness to come with help for Boleś (diminutive from Bolesław). Buying Bonarka was for us an easy step because the Bonarka estate was not expensive. It does not bring much profit, but it might with some effort if the estate was in a good landlord's hands. Boleś did a lot there and raised the value of the estate by careful cultivation, but the small suburban estate does not bring much cash. It would be much better if a young housewife was here. I do not do much, even if I have the best intentions, especially now when I am so depressed. I did not write to you for a long time because we lived in constant worry and uncertainty. I did not want to write to you when I was in such a low mood. (Richthofen, year unknown).[117]

I believe that Maria felt depressed because of some family misunderstandings, her financial problems, and perhaps the signs of her daughter's unhappiness. Her wish for Bolesław came true when he met Bronisława Sędzimir, who was introduced to him by the wife of his acquaintance Władysław Miłkowski, a publisher from Kraków.

---

[116] S. Estreicher, Znaczenie Krakowa Dla Życia Narodowego Polskiego W Ciągu XIX wieku –Typ Psychiczny Krakowski, 1931.
[117] Ivona Tarko's archives: M. Richthofen to Eliza Szydłowska, Letter.

Anastazja Miłkowska and Bronisława Sędzimir knew each other from their school years in Warsaw. Bronisława was not typical girl from a noble family. Bronisława's father, Julian Sędzimir with the coat of arms Ostoja, gave up his estate Zbrzeznica near Łomża, in central Poland, for the love of theater. He became an actor and married an actress and dancer Julia Klimkowska. My grandmother did not know much about Julia, including the names of her parents. I could not find anything about Julia's background, but her name was among the list of actors performing in the town of Żytomierz in 1858 when Józef Kraszewski, a well-known Polish writer, was the director of the theater. The article devoted to this theatrical group mentioned also Julian Sędzimir, the actor, who played in the theater in the town of Lublin in 1859 and later in Warsaw. He was not very successful in this career so he gave up his life on the stage, moved to Kraków bought a house in the district of Kleparz and rented rooms to the Kraków actors. The love of theater is still present in our family and one of Julian's great-great-granddaughters is an actress in Kraków, Poland.

The beautiful Julia was 18 years younger than her husband and the couple was blessed with four sons: Wacław, Kazimierz, Czesław, and Mieczysław and one daughter Bronisława. In 1870, a tragedy struck the Sędzimir family. Julia had a heart attack when she was swimming in the Vistula River in Warsaw and drowned; she was only 28 years old. Bronisława, Julia's daughter was eight years old when she lost her mother so her father raised her with the help of a governess at home and later sent her to a boarding school managed by a convent. After she finished school, she went to Kraków to live with her father. Brosia, Bronia, and Brona, as she was called by those who knew her, enchanted Bolesław from the very first moment he met her. She was a happy dark-eyed beauty, bursting with laughter, optimism, zest for life, and energy.

A few days before their wedding, Bolesław attached his business card to the bouquet of flowers he sent to Bronia on which he wrote:

My dearest and only, accept these flowers now, please, and I will come around five o'clock. I am waiting impatiently for our meeting. Sincerely yours, Bolesław (Richthofen, 1887).[118]

Bronisława née Sędzimir Freifrau von Richthofen and Bolesław Freiherr von Richthofen, my great-grandparents.[119]

---

[118] Ivona Tarko's archives: B. Richthofen, Business Card.
[119] Ivona Tarko's archives.

They married on October 12, 1887 in the Capuchin Church in Kraków, the same church where a few years earlier Bolesław's sister, Maria, married Józef Miłkowski. Two members of the Miłkowski family, Lieutenant Colonel Emil Miłkowski and Władysław Miłkowski, a publisher, were the witnesses of the ceremony required by the church. I assume that the wedding was not large for three reasons: the Sędzimir family was fairly new in the city and did not have many relatives there, Bolesław did not wish to have a huge celebration, and rather modest weddings were in fashion at the time. I imagine that a small reception followed the church ceremony, but was not very long because the health of Bolesław's mother was declining.

Maria née Wielogłowska Freifrau von Richthofen passed away on the Bonarka estate on October 14, 1887, only a couple days after her beloved son's wedding. This discovery made me think how sad it was that Bolesław and Bronisława started their new life with his dear mother's funeral and mourning that loss. Maria was buried in the Wielogłowski family tomb, beside her parents, in the Rakowice Cemetery in Kraków.

CHAPTER 6 Bolesław Freiherr von Richthofen and His Family

A happy love. Is it normal, is it serious, is it profitable – what use to the world are two people who have no eyes for the world?

~ Wisława Szymborska

The manor house on the Bonarka estate in Podgórze was the first home of my great-grandparents, Bolesław and Bronisława von Richthofen. Podgórze was a small town near Kraków that was a new and rapidly developing center of industry in Galicia at the end of the 19th century. Thanks to the stone quarries and cement plants located there and the small factories that had popped up, Podgórze was becoming one of the 30 most important centers of Galicia as a result of the Industrial Revolution. It likely was not the healthiest place to raise a family with all the industry concerns, but the price of land there was relatively low and affordable for Bolesław. In January 1881, a railway line was built that connected the Bonarka station with the main railroad station in Kraków, which provided easy access to the center of Kraków.

I did not find a photo of Bolesław's manor house in the documents passed to me by my grandmother so I searched old books and the Internet and even asked my family and friends from Kraków for help because the Bonarka estate with its surroundings had been demolished a few years ago. Everything was gone; and the look of the area changed completely when a very modern shopping center, named the Bonarka City Center, one of the largest in Central Europe, was built there in 2009.[120]

In a Kraków local newspaper from 2010, I found an article about the history of the Bonarka estate so, in lieu of a photo in this book, I decided to translate a fragment of that article.

> The building was named a manor house but lost the features of a suburban residence after World War II due to an unfortunate adaptation and remodeling. The only interesting reminders of its old splendor were the statue of St. Florian placed on the façade and a splendid coal stove. Both items disappeared in 2004 (zabytkowo.blox.pl, 2010).[121]

---

[120] http://www.local-life.com/Kraków/articles/Kraków-galerias 05-13-2016.
[121] http://zabytkowo.blox.pl/html/1310721,262146,14,15.html?0,2010 accessed 02-24-2013.

St. Florian has long been revered in Poland as the protector from fire and became the patron saint of firefighters. I believe that the statue of St. Florian was placed on the façade of Bolesław's house at his request. The maternal grandfather of Bolesław, Walery Wielogłowski, was a devotee and promoter of insurance and was one of the founders of the Insurance Company of Fire in Kraków in 1860. In 1874, the company became the Association of Mutual Insurance and began offering property and life insurance policies as well. Bolesław Freiherr von Richthofen worked in the association, which was named by the Kraków citizens "Florianka," before World War I.

Unfortunately, the Bonarka manor house was not preserved, but there are places in Podgórze that remind me of the time of my great-grandparents, such as St. Joseph Church and a few apartment buildings in the church's neighborhood. During one of my recent visits to Kraków I took photos of old Podgórze, which became one of the neighborhoods of Greater Kraków in 1915.

After finally accepting the fact that I would never know how the Bonarka estate looked, in 2015 I found a photo taken there in 1934 posted on a website *"Kraków.fotopolska."* I examined with curiosity the image of the one-story manor house, surrounded by trees, with a veranda that opened to a garden and cathedral ceilings in the center of the house. The Richthofen manor on the Bonarka estate was a modest but nice and cozy home.

My great-grandparents lived on the Bonarka estate and their first child Maria Henryka, a longed-for daughter, came into the world there on July 20, 1888. She was named in honor of Bolesław's parents, Maria and Heinrich (Henryk) von Richthofen, who unfortunately did not live to meet baby Maria. All the grandmotherly duties were assumed with love and enthusiasm by Henryk's sister, Eliza Szydłowska. The parents of Maria, who was called Marylka by the family, were overjoyed upon the arrival of their healthy daughter. Four days after the birth of Marylka, her father wrote a letter to Anastazja Miłkowska that read:

The photo of the Bonarka manor house and the 19th century holy card with the image of St. Florian, whose relics were brought from Italy to Kraków, Poland in the 12th century. [122]

Dear Madame! I am so sorry that I could not be the first to let you know about our blessed event, but I was so absorbed in my newborn daughter and my wife that I did not have time to gather my thoughts to write. Sir Władysław visited us three days after the baby's birth and said that he had already written to you about our happy event. Now I am personally fulfilling my pleasant, although delayed, duty to tell you, dear Madame, who is always generously interested in our matters that our baby - thanks to God, daughter! - is big and healthy, and my wife feels very well. I also would like to thank you for your friendship with Bronia and your kindness to me. I am indebted to you for introducing me to Bronisława which brought us such happiness. May God Almighty reward you! Marynia and Brosia's brothers enjoy their baby niece very much. Brosia is going to write to you, dear Madame, as soon as she is able. She also sends you the most amiable greetings and I ask Madame for your gracious consideration. I have the honor to remain with the deepest

---

[122] http://Kraków.fotopolska.eu/549764,foto.html Photo of the Bonarka manor house, accessed 03- 21- 2015; the image of St. Florian from the archives of Ivona Tarko.

respect, always grateful Bolesław Richthofen, Bonarka, July 24, 1888 (Richthofen, 1888).[123]

I have some comments regarding Bolesław's letter. The young father emphasized his happiness upon having a daughter. It reminded me of hearing from my grandmother that soon after marrying Bronisława, Bolesław told his young wife that he would like to have as many daughters as possible, but he did not desire a son. His conviction was surprising to me because I knew that families at that time preferred a male offspring to pass on their names and continue their family line. A need to carry on a surname, especially in noble families, was often the most important reason to get married and start a family. Why did Bolesław think otherwise?

With delight and assured that the couple was happy, I read Bronisława's letter written on August 16, 1888, to her friend, Anastazja Miłkowska.

> Dear Tazia,
> I remembered your Name Day, which for years we used to spend together and which was always such a nice and joyful time for both of us, but today, being far away, I send you, dear Tazia, these wishes from the bottom of my heart: May God give you health, happiness, and long life to enjoy the wellbeing of your children, and may God reward you for all the good you have done for me. I wish everyone could experience the love you and I share. I cannot find words, dear Tazia, to say how happy I feel upon the arrival of my daughter. Today I am the mother of the dearest being, the baby I love more than my life, and who will love me one day. Today I feel a blissful peace in my soul, an inner satisfaction. When I became a mother, I felt an abundance of joy. My home is my whole world, the place where my husband and my baby are; for them I live and their happiness I breathe. I wait impatiently for your return to show you my daughter and to tell you all the details; I miss you very much, Taziuchna. The childbirth took place without problems, but I suffered a lot; and I

---

[123] Ivona Tarko's archives: B. Richthofen to Anastazja Miłkowska,Letter, 1888.

asked God for a second child no earlier than in a couple years; and Dr. Balicki had the same wish for me. He even said that he would not recommend a new pregnancy soon after this one for the good of my health. Yours Brona (Richthofen,1888).[124]

Sooner than Bronisława planned, she was expecting again; and in less than two years after the birth of Marylka, the second daughter of the von Richthofens came into the world. Bolesław was beyond happy. I again tried to understand why Bolesław wanted only daughters. Was he so disappointed in his father that he did not care to pass on the von Richthofen family name? Was he afraid that a son could carry a personal trait from Henryk like melancholy or some other condition? Was Bolesław afraid that his son would face many more obstacles in life than a daughter? Was he afraid that the sense of belonging, identity, would be difficult for a man with a German surname and a Polish background based on the experiences of his brother and himself? I believe that Bolesław considered himself a Pole while Stanisław a German at that time. Was Bolesław aware of the growing militarism in Germany and was he afraid that his son would be expected to join the army? Bolesław was a philosopher and pacifist so I could not imagine him being happy to have a soldier son. Perhaps when he thought about the comfortable and peaceful life of his Aunt Eliza née Freiin von Richthofen Szydłowska, who married a Pole, he wanted the same for his children. He wanted to guide his daughters to marry Poles and have Polish surnames. If Bolesław had married a German or Austrian woman, this line of the von Richthofen family would not have changed to the Polish one. During his university studies he joined Polish groups of students, had Polish friends, and then took his wife from a Polish family. Bolesław also chose to nurture his children in their Polish heritage.

I also thought about Bolesław's financial situation, which could have impact on his plans as far as the future of his children. Bolesław did not have a prominent estate or large assets to pass to his heirs; he gradually became a member of the intelligentsia, the rising social class in the 19th

---

[124] Ivona Tarko's archives: B. Richthofen to Anastazja Miłkowska, Letter, 1888.

century from the groups of less wealthy nobility and bourgeoisie. In general, the intelligentsia was the group of people who supported themselves with their intellect, such as teachers, physicians, engineers, artists, and clerks. My great-grandfather was a faculty member in Jagiellonian University for a short time and then was a clerk in "Florianka", the insurance company. He most likely was the only clerk with a PhD! Bolesław's income from the Bonarka estate and his job and his wife's share of rental income from an apartment building in Kraków owned by her family, was enough to support the family, take vacations in Europe, and save for a modest dowry for his daughters.

Bolesław's daughters remembered him as a nervous man who hated noise and chaos. For example, Bolesław threatened to shoot a rooster that lived in his neighborhood because he despised hearing its cockcrow early every morning. Bolesław, a bookworm who loved the classic languages, Latin and Greek, longed for tranquility; could he possibly have thought that a house without boys would be quieter? He loved his family sincerely and took good care of them, and in his correspondence always referred to his wife and daughters as "my dearest."

His wife, Bronisława, was a cheerful and social person. Her granddaughter, my mother, remembered her as full of life, even in her senior years, when she chased the kids and played the game of hide-and-seek in a vast Kraków apartment in Matejko Square. The spouses had very different personalities. Bronisława's optimism and vitality helped her in the difficult times of her life, which I believe also served her well in building a good and harmonious relationship with Bolesław.

Elżunia, born on February 17, 1890, named Elżbieta Ferdynanda Bronisława, received her first name in honor of Eliza Szydłowska, her great aunt; the second name in honor of Ferdinand Freiherr von Richthofen, the famous German geologist; and the third name was after her mother, Bronisława. People used to say that Elżunia was as pretty as an angel. She inherited many physical features from her father. The godparents of Elżunia were Antoni and Eliza Szydłowski from the Werbkowice estate. The Richthofen couple with their two daughters lived happily and without any major problems on the Bonarka estate. They did not know then, unfortunately, that those were to be the happiest years of their life together.

Elżunia and Marylka von Richthofen.[125]

I vividly remember the above picture of Marylka and Elżunia from my childhood when I visited Grandma Antonina. A large print of this portrait framed in green velvet hung on a wall in her bedroom. I had probably thought too much about the girls after seeing this picture during my research because one night not long ago, I had a dream in which I saw Elżunia standing by my bed. She turned her head in my direction and informed me without speaking that she was my Guardian Angel.

I wonder if Bolesław stayed in contact with Władysław Wielogłowski, his relative from the Tęgoborze estate in southern Poland who was an avid

---

[125] Ivona Tarko's archives.

Spiritism enthusiast who invited mediums and organized séances in his palace. A mysterious prophecy on September 23, 1893 always will be remembered in Poland because it was about the future of Poland and the world.[126] Nowadays, some people even think that one of the verses about *the anointed one from Kraków* was the Polish pope, John Paul II.

I remember Tęgoborze as a child in the early 1960s when my family spent our summer vacations there. During the Communist era in Poland, my father's employer, the Kraków Company Telpod, owned the palace; and they organized the annual two-week summer vacations in the palace for its employees and their families and subsidized them as well to make them affordable for everyone. There was a large, most likely modern, swimming pool located on the palace grounds, where my father taught me to swim. Meals were served in the huge dining room of the palace. I remember the moment when my mother said for the first time that this palace belonged to the relatives of my great-grandfather and how absolutely stunned I was that one family could have so much space in which to live! You see, at that time my parents and I lived an apartment in Kraków that was no more than 220 square feet; in fact, for a few years, I slept on a cot because there was not enough space for a regular bed for me.

During my trip to Poland in 2013, I visited Oscar Schindler's Enamel Factory located on the street Lipowa 4, which had become the Historical Museum of the City of Kraków. When I stood by the museum gate, I realized that this was also where the Telpod Company had operated during the Communist era, the place where my father worked almost every day for more than 20 years. When I was a child, I knew nothing about Oscar Schindler, the factory, or the people who worked there during World War II. For me it was just a place where my father worked – it was the beginning and the end of the history of this place in my small universe. I had no curiosity about what was there before the Telpod Company. My 2013 visit made me realize that, as we mature and recollect

---

126 https://en.wikipedia.org/wiki/T%C4%99goborze_Prophecy accessed 04-07-2016.

our past and various events and places that took place, it all seems to be connected in a way we could not have imagined when they were happening in our lives. Connecting those dots makes us feel complete and, at the same time, confirms our part of the history we lived.

A tragedy struck Bolesław and Bronisława in 1895 that changes their lives forever. Six-year-old Elżunia became very sick with diphtheria, and the Kraków doctors could not save her life. Her parents and older sister Marylka were devastated and heartbroken. Elżunia's funeral took place on February 28, 1895 at the Rakowicki Cemetery. I found her obituary as well as the copy of a poem composed by Madame Duval, titled *Modlitwa matki po śmierci dziecka* [The Prayer of a Mother after the Loss of Her Child], in the family archives. The poem was copied by Bronisława on a sheet of plain paper and here is what I translated:

> Oh, my Comforter! You will not condemn the tears of a mother. You, who cried upon your friend's death, do not allow to snatch from my heart, pierced with the pain, a word which You do not like. Make it happen that my sorrow will not be despair and do not allow me to give in to anguish with my negligence of duty. In my mourning do not allow me to be indifferent and unjust to what remains in my life (Madame Duval, year unknown).[127]

I also translated Elżunia's orbituary:

> Elżunia
>
> the most beloved daughter of Bolesław and Bronisława Richthofen, passed away in the sixth spring of her life on February 20, 1895. The parents, immersed in deep sorrow, ask family, friends, and acquaintances to attend the funeral, which will be held in the house on Garncarska Street number 8, on Thursday, February 28, at 4 p.m. and thereafter she will be laid in her final resting place in the family tomb.(Richthofen, 1895).[128]

---

[127] Ivona Tarko's archives: M. Duval, Manuscript.
[128] Ivona Tarko's archives: Elżbieta Freiin von Richthofen's orbituary, 1895.

This sad story, which I have known since my childhood, strikes me differently now that I am a mother of two children. It was the lack of mention of Marylka's state of mind or sorrow. Nothing was said about seven-year-old Marylka and how she handled the loss of her younger and only sister, her playmate. I write about this now because I came to the realization during my research that people from previous generations did not pay much attention to children's feelings.

I was told that after Elżunia's death, the house in Bonarka became a very sad place, and the mourning parents did not want to live where everything reminded them of their lost daughter. Bolesław sold the estate to Professor Juliusz Leo, who later would become the Mayor of Kraków, and moved with Bronisława and Marylka to an apartment building in the center of Kraków where the family could sooth their broken hearts without the painful reminders and move on to this new phase of their lives. I wonder if their attempt to detach from any memories of the Bonarka estate affected others in my family as my grandmother and mother never showed any interest in visiting Bonarka, seeing the old manor house on Puszkarska Street, or taking photos of them.

One of the places in Kraków where Bolesław lived with his wife and daughter Marylka was an apartment on the second floor of the building on Łobzowska Street number 8, where a neighboring small house was owned by the Congregation of the Resurrection of Our Lord Jesus Christ (CR). My family was close to the founders of the CR through Bolesław's grandparents on both sides of the family: Walery Wielogłowski and Paulina Freifrau von Richthofen. In Chapters 1 and 2, I discussed my family connections with the CR during the first half of the 19th century.

During my great-grandparents' stay in Kraków, one of the priests of the CR, Fr. Piotr Pietryka, became a close friend of Bolesław and was a frequent guest at the Richthofen family apartment and was even the family's travel companion.

Bronisława's father and her brother Mieczysław, as well as Bolesław's sister, Maria, also lived in Kraków. Maria traveled a lot and visited the senior members of the family, Eliza Szydłowska in Werbkowice and her second brother, Stanisław, in Dresden. My great-grandparents had friends in several Kraków families: the Miłkowskis, Cyrus-Sobolewskis, Mieroszewskis, Sternstein Helcels, Łubieńskis, and Popiels.

Moving from the Bonarka estate to Kraków changed the lifestyle of my great-grandparents; they became city dwellers who lived in the center of various cultural and social attractions and were now closer to their family and friends. Kraków was the center of culture with the Jagiellonian University, the library, and the permanent city theater directed by Tadeusz Pawlikowski. There were frequent celebrations of the anniversaries of important Polish historical events, holidays, and religious occasions. There were also coffee shops and stores. The gardens of Planty became a popular venue for socializing, a great place for Bronisława, who enjoyed both walking and company. When she was tired of walking, she could take the horse-driven tram that operated in the city at the time. In June 1898, the citizens of Kraków celebrated the memory of Polish romantic bard, Adam Mickiewicz, with a ceremony for the unveiling of a monument memorializing the poet in the Main Square, which became an important element of the Kraków landscape.

The month of June 1898 was memorable for my great-grandparents because they welcomed the baby girl. Bronisława had longed and prayed for the baby since her overwhelming sadness had begun to lift and she felt more alive again. On June 13, 1898, their healthy beautiful baby girl came into the world in the Richthofens apartment on Łobzowska Street. I was told that an unexpected emergency accompanied the baby's arrival when a huge glass jar suddenly broke into pieces in the room of the delivery, and the doctor attending my great-grandmother had to leave her and rush to help my great-grandfather who had fainted when he heard his wife groaning and saw blood.

Antonina Julia was the name chosen for the baby by the happy parents because she arrived on the day when Catholics in Poland celebrate the memory of St. Anthony of Padua (in Polish language Antoni) and her middle name was to honor her maternal grandmother Julia Klimkowska.

I imagine the summer day when Antonina was born as sunny, beautiful, and saturated with the aroma of peonies and stock flowers, which in Poland are named gracefully *lewkonia (in Latin Matthiola)*, both of which are always in bloom in early June there. Antonina loved them so my mother and I always visited her on her birthday with a huge bouquet of pink peonies or old-fashioned pale lavender and cream color stock flowers. I also planted peonies in my garden, and I remember how happy I was when I learned that the peony is the state flower of the U.S. state in which I reside, Indiana!

Based on a Polish superstition that the combination of the 13th day of a month and Friday can bring bad luck to a person, some members of my family predicted an uneasy life for Antonina because she was born on Friday, June 13. Who could foresee at that time the personal tragedies that would befall her and the two world wars that brought so much suffering to the people of Antonina's generation? In the year of Antonina's birth, 1898, Jan G. Bloch, who was born in Poland in 1836, finished his six-volume work *The Future of War,* in which he offered his opinions about the development of civilization. Bloch thought that the use of advanced weapons, including machine guns, would bring enormous suffering for humanity and even the end of civilization; therefore, people who are aware of that fact should not strive for war. Bloch believed that nations should seek rational resolutions for disputes, and he saw war as the negation of his thesis. His book is the canon of pacifist literature; and Bloch was nominated for the Nobel Peace prize in 1901 for his writings. He did not receive the prize and passed away before World War I. Sadly, Jan Bloch's son-in-law, Kazimierz Kostanecki, who was the rector of the Jagiellonian University, was arrested by the Nazis in 1939 in Kraków and sent to the Sachsenhausen camp where he died in 1941.

Antonina Julia Freiin von Richthofen was baptized on June 10, 1899 in the Capuchin Church on Loretańska Street in Kraków, where 12 years earlier her parents were married. The senior member of the family, Eliza Szydłowska, became Antonina's godmother and retired General Jan Józef Antoni Hieronim Ziemięcki (1816-1906) was her godfather. The general was the relative of Bolesław Freiherr von Richthofen. Bolesław's great-grandmother, Apolonia née Zaremba Objezierska, and General Ziemięcki's mother, Józefa née Zaremba Ziemięcka were sisters.   My grandmother barely remembered her godfather because he passed away when she was eight years old. I learned through my research that General Ziemięcki graduated from the Cadet School in Dresden and became the aide-de-camp of Prince August of Saxe-Coburg and Gotha, was a general major in the army of Saxony, and later commanded his own cavalry brigade in Prague. After his retirement in 1878, he lived in Kraków where he passed away in 1906.

Traditionally, at the time of Antonina's childhood, senior family members were asked to be a baby's godparents, which meant for the children that they usually did not experience the presence of their godparents very long; both of Antonina's godparents passed away before her First Communion on March 25, 1912, she took at the age of 14, which was customary at that time.

Antonina had a happy and carefree childhood. She was a quiet, kind, and well-mannered child, and was called by family members and friends by her diminutive names: Tola, Tolunia, Toleczka, or Toluchna. Her parents sometimes referred to her as "the child" as her sister, who was ten years her senior, was already a mademoiselle. Antonina loved books and I can imagine her sitting alongside her mother and listening to one of the poems by Stanisław Jachowicz, like the one about a sick kitten that all generations of Polish children were taught, or one of the verses from a book written by Wacław Szymanowski *Dobre dziatki- dobre matki* [Good Children – Good Mothers]. She also knew German poems for naughty children by Heinrich Hoffmann because she was taught German (and French) from her early childhood, but she considered the verses as too frightening, even if they contained useful messages for children such as the warning of the disastrous consequences of playing with matches and fire, like *The Dreadful Story of Pauline and the Matches.*

Left top: General Baron von Nieczuja Ziemięcki, Antonina's godfather. *Left bottom*: Tolunia, Antonina Freiin von Richthofen. **Right top:** The obituary of General Baron von Nieczuja Ziemięcki who passed away in Kraków in 1906. **Right bottom**: The holy picture with the image of St. Anthony de Padua, which Antonina received for her eighth birthday in June 1906.[129]

---

[129] Ivona Tarko's archives.

I believe that at the time the picture of Tolunia was taken, my great-grandmother, Bronisława, was firmly established in Kraków, although some expressions she used in everyday language came from the Warsaw region and stayed in my Kraków family for the next generations. In 1905 journalists still stressed the differences between both cities: Kraków and Warsaw. For example, W. Feldman wrote in a newspaper:

> Those who want to know Polish souls should look for them in Kraków where melancholia is engraved in old pictures, stones, and tombs; those who want to know the future of Poland should go to Warsaw, the city of never ending youth and recklessness with uplifting spirituality and prosperity (Barycz, 1978).[130]

After a few years of living on Łobzowska Street, my great-grandparents moved to another apartment in Kraków, on Batory Street, where they hosted many Kraków families, some of them well-known such as Polish artist Jacek Malczewski and his wife Maria and Polish playwright and poet Lucjan Rydel.

In the apartment building on Batory Street, Antonina met Emilia (Milunia) Bakałowicz with whom she had a cordial friendship her entire life. From their childhood, my grandmother saved a note written by Milunia with a message:

> Dear Tolunia! Please visit me today around 4 p.m. if you can. The grandchildren of Madame Miłkowska are coming. Please come if your mother will allow you. Your Mila (Bakałowicz, circa 1906).[131]

When Antonina lived with her parents in Kraków, her older sister, Marylka, was in Nowy Sącz, a city located in the south of Kraków, where she attended a school operated by nuns from the convent of the Sisters of the Immaculate Conception, founded in Rome in 1857 by Józefa Karska and Marcelina Darowska, with the support of Father Hieronim

---

[130] H. Barycz, Historyk Gniewny i Niepokorny – Rzecz o Wacławie Sobieskim, Kraków, 1978, p. 202-203.
[131] Ivona Tarko's archives: M. Bakałowicz, Business card, year unknown.

Kajsiewicz, CR, whom I mention several times in this book. The school for girls in Nowy Sącz, called "Biały Klasztor" [The White Monastery], which opened in 1897, focused on the humanities and practical skills that could be useful in the households of future wives and mothers and also propagated patriotism and the Catholic faith. Polish aristocratic families held the school in high regard; and one of the students who attended the school, but who was much younger than Marylka, was Maria Jadwiga Sapieżanka, the niece of the Kraków Metropolitan Bishop Count Adam Sapiecha. Marylka liked the school where she learned, along with the academic curriculum, useful skills like cooking and also was able to improve her artistic hobby of drawing. She used to draw flowers on sheets of stationery, which she sent to her parents and other family members. She was fluent in Polish, German, and French.

Marylka encouraged Antonina in various religious practices and devotions during her visits at home in Kraków. The sisters were never playmates because of the large age difference, and they were not soulmates because of their very different temperaments and characters. Antonina loved her older sister unconditionally; but Marylka was certain that her younger sister was spoiled by their parents, which may have been due to Bolesław and Bronisława perhaps being overly concerned about the health and wellbeing of the younger daughter after the tragic death of Elżunia, especially when Antonina turned out to be a delicate child prone to poor health.

Antonina was never sent to a boarding school. When she was a young child, she had French and German governesses at home, from whom she learned both languages well. She started piano lessons early and became a gifted pianist studying under Professor Jerzy Lalewicz, who was the winner of the Third International Piano Competition in Vienna, Austria in 1900. Professor Lalewicz came to Kraków and taught music in the Kraków Conservatory and monopolized the music scene in Kraków society, performing solo or sometimes in duets with Henryk Malcer or Ignacy Friedman.

Antonina's favorite composer was Edvard Grieg, whose music she played with great understanding and passion. I believe that Grandmother Antonina influenced my music preferences because the Solvega Song from Peer Gynt, which she loved, has been one of my favorite musical pieces as well. Professor Lalewicz encouraged Antonina to play in public, but she never did. In 1912, he left Kraków for Vienna where he taught in the Academy of Music. He propagated the music of Frederic Chopin and younger Polish composers such as Ignacy Paderewski and Karol Szymanowski.

Before World War I, Antonina attended a private school for girls owned by Helena Kaplińska in Kraków, where she was a very good student in French, German, history, and literature. Science and mathematics were not her favorite subjects, and she never showed any interest in sewing, knitting, or drawing.

While Bolesław Freiherr von Richthofen worked in the insurance company in Kraków to support his family (he was the only von Richthofen sibling who had children), his brother Stanisław served in the Prussian Army, achieving the rank of major, and spent several years in the Posen (Polish Poznań) area and in Pomerania in Swinemunde (Polish Świnoujście) by the Baltic Sea. Stanisław loved his siblings and Bolesław's entire family. On one of the postcards he sent to his sister-in-law, Bronisława, he wrote in Polish:

> On my way to Swinemunde,
>
> Dear Brońcia, I often think about all of you during my very pleasant trip. When I visit the places where I was on military duty in the past, many memories, usually nice, come back to me. Today I am on a ship, but tomorrow after 5 p.m. I should be in Swinemunde where I will stay for a few days. We had a stop in Sopot on our way, and then I saw from the distance the peninsula Hel; the Gdynia Bay was in fog. (Richthofen, circa 1910).[132]

---

[132] Ivona Tarko's archives: S. Richthofen to B. Richthofen, Postcard, [1910].

The chain of events that occurred in the town of Września in Wielkopolska in the western part of Poland in 1901[133] had an impact on Stanisław's career and life. First, I would like to describe briefly what I learned about Stanisław from my grandmother, but I feel obligated to provide chronological evidence about the movements from the region of Wielkopolska that steered Stanisław's action.

In 1873 German became the language of instruction in schools in Wielkopolska (the region annexed by Prussia during the partitions of Poland at the end of the 18th century) with two exceptions: religion and music were taught in Polish. In March 1901, the German administration ordered the religion classes to switch to the German language, but the students refused to say a prayer in German and to accept new German textbooks. The teacher used detention and corporal punishment to force children to accept the new policy. The students' parents protested against the punishment of their children by gathering in front of the school so the police were called by the school authority to force the protesters to leave the premises, and the adults involved in the protests were put on trial for public disturbance and trespassing. Twenty six people were officially charged, and on November 19, 1901, twenty persons were sentenced to imprisonment from several weeks to over two years. The Polish activists formed two committees to support the families whose members were imprisoned. The German administration soon disbanded the committees and in turn charged the activists.

The prosecution of the Polish children and their parents from Września in 1901 greatly angered not only the inhabitants of the town and the region but the majority of Poles from all the Polish lands as well. Two letters written by the Polish writer Henryk Sienkiewicz in which he criticized the Prussian policy against Polish students were printed in 1901 and 1906 in the Kraków newspaper *Czas* [Time]. Another Polish writer, Maria Konopnicka, openly supported the Września strike, as well as Ignacy Paderewski, the Polish composer and pianist. In 1901 in Kraków there was a rally organized by some women to support the Września parents.

---

[133] https://en.wikipedia.org/wiki/Wrze%C5%9Bnia_children_strike accessed 04-08-2016.

Stanisław Freiherr von Richthofen sympathized with the families from Września and Wielkopolska, the land of his childhood. The teacher from the Catholic School of Września who participated in the strike, Bruno Edward Gardo, four years younger than Stanisław, was born in Ostrowieczko, the village owned by Stanisław's father. The situation in Września left Stanisław morally torn. How could Stanisław, the son of a Polish and Catholic mother, accept the whipping of Polish children by German teachers for refusing to use the German language in their prayer? Would he be able to accept a hypothetical situation in which his brother, Bolesław, might be punished or sent to prison if he had been one of the parents from Września? Love for his family and attachment to his nieces made Stanisław even more sensitive to the problem. His older niece, Marylka Freiin von Richthofen, was 13 years old in 1901 and attended the White Monastery Catholic School; could Stanisław tolerate the punishment of Marylka if she had been one of the students from Września? Certainly not. Stanisław's brother and his family spoke Polish at home and even Eliza née Freiin von Richthofen Szydłowska, Marylka's great aunt, sent her a postcard with a patriotic poem composed by Władysław Bełza *Modlitwa Polskiego Dziewczęcia* [The Prayer of the Polish Girl][134], which I found in my archives. The first verse of the poem reads:

> I know I am a Pole, the child of this earth,
> Because my mom told me.
> I know how Poland is precious to me,
> Because I learned a prayer in Polish language.
> The Polish floodplain fed me with grain for bread
> And birds taught me Polish songs.
> Because there, in the sky, guards me the Lady from Częstochowa,
> The Queen of Poland.

The poem ends with the words: Lord, we ask that you give us a homeland and freedom.

---

[134] The poem became a song which is available in Polish language on YouTube: https://www.youtube.com/watch?v=S4q6lYojGL4 accessed 06-13-2016.

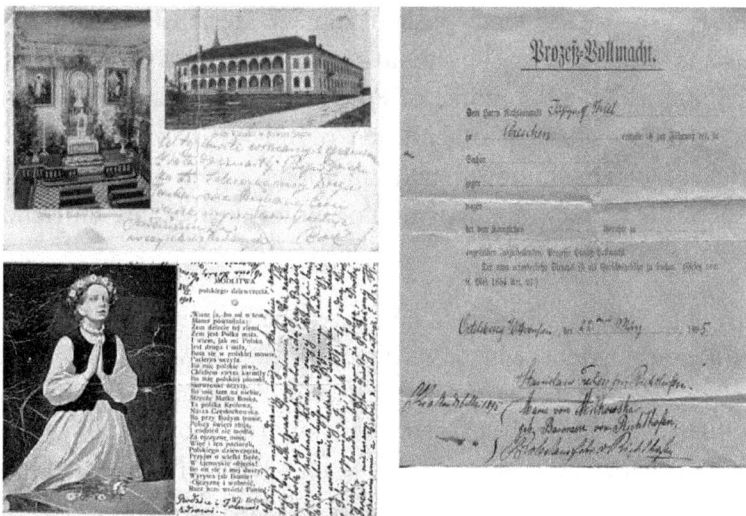

Left top: *An old postcard with the image of The Convent of the Sisters of the Immaculate Conception and The White Monastery School, which Marylka Freiin von Richthofen attended in the early 1900s.* **Left bottom:** *The postcard with the poem Modlitwa Polskiego Dziewczęcia [The Prayer of the Polish Girl] from Grandmother Antonina's collection.* **Right:** *The authorization form signed on March 22, 1895 by the von Richthofen siblings: Stanisław, Maria, and Bolesław for a lawyer from Wreschen (Września), Wielkopolska.*[135]

The postcard with the image of the White Monastery School showed above was sent by Bolesław to Eliza Szydłowska and included his handwritten note to Aunt Eliza about Marylka's exam:

> At this moment, we are coming back from an exam. Sha passed it and was accepted to the fourth grade. Thank God for this. Recommending my dear [daughter] to the kindness of her dear aunt, I cordially kiss your hands. I send my cordial wishes to all of you, my dearest. Bolesław (Richthofen, circa 1900).[136]

According to my grandmother, Stanisław Freiherr von Richthofen decided to leave the Prussian Army following the Września strike. I could imagine Stanisław's state of mind: a decent man who thought about the honor and the good of the country and its citizens. I believe that his

---

[135] Ivona Tarko's archives: B. Richthofen to Eliza Szydłowska, Postcard, [1900].
[136] Ibid.

German-Polish background pushed him to seriously ponder which citizens and which country he should support. This question of the extent to which Stanisław felt German or Pole made me think about identity in general and the situation of children of mixed marriages. Different countries of origin, cultures, and traditions enrich families until the interests of the two are in opposition or, unfortunately, are unfriendly or even hostile to each other.

I believe that Stanisław's decision to leave the Prussian Army came after a careful examination of his conscience and his heart. It most certainly was not an easy choice for him, especially from a practical point of view. The military was the only career Stanisław had known and he was not prepared to change after being detached for years from a civilian life. He did not have a wife and children, and at the age of 41 he was single and lonely. Stanisław and his life was a tragedy from my point of view. His German-Polish background was the source of the challenge he faced when he decided to leave the military; but at that time, he did not know that his future would be even more challenging. He hoped for an early quiet retirement and could end the monotony of his life by traveling and visiting family, but fate placed him in a world full of uncertainty and difficult choices until the end of his life. As a civilian he lived in Dresden, the town he always liked, until World War I.

Maria, Stanisław's sister, persuaded him to move to Kraków where she and Bolesław lived because she worried about him. He refused and she kept visiting him, writing to Bolesław about her observations.

> Stanisław and I organize frequent trips but his bad appearance and loneliness worry me very much… [Miłkowska, 1912].

In another letter Maria wrote again:

> I worry very much to see my dear Stanisław looking so bad but I could not show him my convictions. His loneliness concerns me and the fact that he completely dropped the idea of moving to Kraków; he says that the dirty city of Kraków and the prevailing relations, the lack of punctuality, and high prices make him pull back. I must say that even if we do not like Germans, we have to

admire their culture, exemplary order, cleanliness, and meticulousness [Miłkowska, year unknown].[137]

Before the war, Stanisław appeared to be the main liaison between my family and the other branches of the von Richthofen family. A leaflet written by Emmo Groto and published in 1907 in Silesia about Karl Freiherr von Richthofen and his wife Teresa Groto, which I found in my grandmother's archives, is a token of the interest of my great-grandfather for the von Richthofen family, but I do not have any evidence that Bolesław was in touch with his father's family.

A few years before World War I, two sad events, both related to the senior members of the family, touched my family in Kraków. In summer of 1909, Julian Sędzimir, maternal grandfather of Antonina Freiin von Richthofen passed away and two years after Julian, in 1911, on Christmas Day, Eliza née Freiin von Richthofen Szydłowska died. Both funeral Masses were celebrated in the familiar church of the Congregation of the Resurrection of Our Lord Jesus Christ on Łobzowska Street in Kraków. One of Bolesław's friends, Jan Mieroszewski, called Eliza "the best aunt anyone could imagine" in his condolence letter to my great-grandparents.

Eliza Szydłowska's death brought not only sadness and personal loss to the family but also ended the family link to the Werbkowice estate, which Eliza née Miłkowska Ślaska inherited. For my grandmother, it meant the end of her summer vacation in Werbkowice. Years later, when Antonina was an adult, one of my grandmother's cousins, Zofia Lamparska from Poznań, wrote to her:

> For me you remain forever the little Tolunia from Werbkowice, who we, the older cousins, loved very much (Zofia Lamparska, year unknown).[138]

Lizia [Eliza] Ślaska who was rewarded very generously for accompanying and taking care of her cousin Eliza Szydłowska,

---

[137] Ivona Tarko's archives: M. Miłkowska to B. Richthofen, Letters, [1912].
[138] Ivona Tarko's archives: Z. Lamparska to A. Richthofen, Letter, year unknown.

unfortunately did not enjoy her inheritance very long as she lost it by gambling in Monte Carlo according to my grandmother. One of the postcards written by Lizia to my great-grandmother includes the image of Un Coin de Casino.

My grandmother recalled numerous trips from Kraków to Zakopane, the charming town in the Polish Tatra Mountains, where she stayed with her sister to gather strength and improve her immune systems. Bronisława, their mother, loved the mountains and believed in the healing power of fresh air and outdoor activities and the "Kneipp Cure," a naturopathic medicine propagated by Sebastian Kneipp, the Bavarian priest. Bolesław, who had a full-time job, used his limited vacation time to travel to Western Europe, usually with his family. Antonina had a huge collection of postcards, which were the most popular way to communicate at that time, from relatives and friends from different parts of the world with holiday or birthday wishes or greetings from vacations.

The year 1914 started joyously for the von Richthofen family in Kraków as they prepared for the wedding of Maria Henryka Freiin von Richthofen, called Marylka, and Juliusz Gawroński, son of Sobiesław, the family coat of arms Rawicz, and Maria Toczyska. Juliusz was a lawyer and a very talented pianist and student of the Polish composer and pianist Władysław Żeleński. Juliusz was frequently praised for his spectacular performances and was asked to visit the USA for a recital in the 1890s. However, he decided not to pursue a career as a pianist, and chose to be a lawyer and a banker instead. He never stopped playing for himself and his family, and in the independent Poland he became the president of the Music Association in Kraków. The wedding ceremony of Maria Henryka Freiin von Richthofen, the older daughter of Bolesław, and Juliusz Gawroński took place by the high altar with the effigy of St. Florian painted in the late 17th century in St. Florian Church on Warszawska Street in Kraków, which was followed by a reception in the Grand Hotel.

Soon after the wedding, Maria and Juliusz left for Vienna, Austria, where Juliusz was the director of the Central Credit Bank. My great-grandparents decided to spend a summer vacation in Belgium with their younger daughter, Antonina. It was June of 1914 when Stanisław Freiherr von Richthofen accompanied them to Knocke-sur-Mer at the seaside in Flandria and then traveled to Brussels. In Knocke-sur-Mer they all stayed in the Zomer guesthouse at Avenue del a Reine. They tried to enjoy their vacation, but it was spoiled somewhat by bad weather. At the end of July, Bolesław celebrated his Name Day, which I was reminded of by a card preserved in my family archives that included cordial wishes for Bolesław from his friend, Fr. Piotr, from the town of Zakopane.

*Left: Maria Henryka Freiin von Richthofen, Bolesław's daughter, on her wedding day, February 14, 1914. **Right**: Group picture of the newlyweds with their wedding guests in the Grand Hotel in Kraków: in the center Maria and Juliusz Gawroński; on the side of the bride is her mother Bronisława Freifrau von Richthofen and by Bronisława's side is the groom's mother, Maria née Toczyska Gawrońska ; the father of the bride, Bolesław Freiherr von Richthofen, is sitting first on the right; Maria née Freiin von Richthofen Miłkowska is sitting third from the right; Stanisław Freiherr von Richthofen is standing in the last row third from the right; and Antonina Freiin von Richthofen, the bride's sister, is standing second from the left.[139]*

I believe that none of my family members foresaw the possibility of war on the horizon. According to the corespondence I have, the only problems of the vacationers were the weather and overpriced hotel rooms. On July

---

[139] Ivona Tarko's archives.

167

29, 1914, Stanisław Freiherr von Richthofen wrote to his brother Bolesław.

> My dear brother, first I would like to thank you once more for your great hospitality and kindness to me during my stay in Knocke. I am sending greetings to the owners of the guesthouse. I wish you a pleasant stay with better weather (Richthofen, 1914).[140]

One day before Stanisław wrote to Bolesław, Austria-Hungary declared war on Serbia. On July 31, 1914, posters were distributed in Kraków announcing mobilization in the countries which belonged to the Austria-Hungary monarchy. Serious political events followed quickly, almost day by day; then Germany declared war on Russia and a few days later on France.

Rainer Maria Rilke, the Bohemian-Austrian poet composed in July 1914 a poem *Lament,* which the first verse I cite below.

> To whom, heart, would you lament? Ever more avoided
> your path struggles through incomprehensible
> humankind. The more in vein perhaps
> since it holds to the course,
> holds the course toward the future,
> toward the lost.[141]

Under the cover of night, on August 3, 1914, the German army invaded neutral Belgium. My great-grandparents decided to leave Belgium and tried to reach Kraków by train. The journey was long and dangerous as they were passing through a region where there were landmines. They were in grave danger once but reached Kraków safely, only to see that its residents faced hunger and were afraid of the possibility of a Russian siege of the city. In the fall of 1914, the peasants who lived I, nearby

---

[140] Ivona Tarko's archives: S. Richthofen to B. Richthofen, Postcard, 1914.
[141] R.M. Rilke, Uncollected Poems, Selected and Traslated by Edward Snow, Bilingual Edition, New York, 1996, p. 95.

villages were forced to leave by the Austrian authority, and the villages were burned to create an unappealing enviroment for the coming enemy. Forts and ramparts were erected. In Kraków, the residents who did not have enough food supplies to last three months were forced to leave the city. Grocery stores were closed and restaurants and coffee shops were open only for few hours a day. Bolesław decided to take his wife and daughter Antonina to Vienna, where his older daughter Maria and son-in-law lived.

Bolesław, Bronisława, and Antonina stayed in Vienna in the apartament of Maria and Juliusz Gawroński on Schmerligplatz 3, where today Expat Center Vienna is located. Maria was delighted to have her family living with them because she was lonely and homesick. Juliusz was ocupied by his demanding job and she did not have many friends there. At the beginning of the war, more Polish families from Kraków came to Vienna. My grandmother recalled that living in Vienna at that time felt almost like living in Kraków as there were many Poles and many Catholic churches.

One of my relatives saved a leaflet with *Modlitwa Polaka w czasie wojny* (The Pole's Prayer at the Time of War), which I found in my grandmother's archives. This prayer, which was published during World War I, was composed by Bishop Wł.B. (I believe the initials belonged to Bishop Władysław Bandurski). Poles were hoping that the end of the war would bring changes in Europe and that they would live in an independent Poland again. The prayer's words were very powerful to them.

> I beg You, God, for mercy on an unfortunate nation
> For the end of our misery and wandering.
> Raise us from the abyss of slavery and the darkness of the grave.
> Give us, Lord, a free and happy homeland; connect all Polish lands again.
> God of the Piasts, Jagiellonian, and Sobieski, have mercy on us.
> God of Kordecki and Kościuszko do not leave us (Bishop Wł.B.).[142]

---

[142] Ivona Tarko's archives: WŁ.B, Modlitwa Polaka w czasie wojny.

My grandmother spent her 17th birthday on June 13, 1915 in the Felicitas guesthouse on Josephsgasse 7 in Vienna. Her cousin, Aniela Sędzimir, sent a birthday card and wished her to live soon in free Poland and be one of the strong links to connect, unite, and inspire Polish society.

Antonina (Tolunia) returned to Kraków with her parents in the fall of 1915 and resided in an apartment building owned by the Sędzimir family in Matejko Square. The city seemed to be peaceful, and people did not pay much attention to airplanes overhead or distant cannon shots. Hunger remained the biggest problem in the city because the rationed food was inadequate and the black-market prices were skyrocketing.

Clippings from Der Tag, the Berlin newspaper, from April 23, 1918 with an article devoted to the life and death of Manfred Freiherr von Richthofen with a handwritten note by a member of the family perhaps, found in Grandmother Antonina's archives; and from Ilustrowany Kurier Codzienny, the Kraków daily newspaper, from April 24, 1918. [143]

Stanisław Freiherr von Richthofen spent the years of World War I in Dresden and I often wonder what his life was like there and whether he stayed in touch with other members of the von Richthofen family from Germany. My great-grandfather and Stanisław followed the news about

---

[143] Ivona Tarko's archives.

the ace German pilot Manfred Freiherr von Richthofen. One of them preserved Manfred's picture and clippings from newspapers about his death, which I found in my family archives.

The clipping from *Ilustrowany Kurier Codzienny* [Illustrated Daily Courier] read:

> After the death of Baron Richthofen; Vienne, April 26; accommodation of war news report: On the occasion of the death of Captain baron Richthofen, the Emperor [of Austria-Hungary] sent a telegram to the German Emperor, to which the Emperor responded by thanking him for the words of sympathy. (B. Correspondent, 1918).

Manfred Freiherr von Richthofen, aka The Red Baron (1892-1918).[144]

---

[144] Ivona Tarko's archives.

I sent the copy of the clipping from *Der Tag* newspaper to Dr. Karl-Friedrich Freiherr von Richthofen asking him to decipher the handwritten note, but the handwriting was barely understandable so he asked for help from Dr. Joahim Castan, the author of the Red Baron's biography. Dr. Castan said that the note included a combination of abbreviations in German and Latin languages and the message was unclear to him. Perhaps my great-grandfather used his knowledge of the classical language to make comments on an article he read. I would never know. The article, written just two days after the Red Baron's death, reminded people of Manfred von Richthofen's bright career and high esteem as a pilot and colleague. It was the first step in building the legend of the Red Baron.

Manfred Freiherr von Richthofen, who was born on May 2, 1892 in Borek close to Breslau (Wrocław), was six years older than my grandmother and was her couisin in the fourth line. Manfred's great-great-grandfather was Andreas Ludwig von Richthofen, brother of Wilhelm Ludwig, my grandmother's great-great-grandfather. I wrote about them in Chapter 1. Manfred wrote in his memoir that the majority of the von Richthofens were landlords with estates in the Breslau [Wrocław] and Striegau [Strzegom] area and had seldom participated in wars in the past, but his father was an officer and Manfred, a great athlete, liked the idea of pursuing a military career.

When World War I began, my grandmother was 16 years old, and Manfred Freiherr von Richthofen was 22. He started his career in the German Air Force in May 1915 after serving as a cavalryman and in the trenches for a short period of time. He took his first solo flight on October 10, 1915 after only 24 hours of flight training. He was appointed commander of the Flying Circus in June 1917, a new unit that was highly mobile and could be quickly sent to any part of the Western Front where they were most needed. Manfred Freiherr von Richthofen was a very skillful and brave pilot and was known as the Red Baron. He scored 80 confirmed kills during the air war; but his short life ended on April 21, 1918 when he was shot down over the valley of the Somme. My grandmother never talked about any social contacts she may have had with him or his immediate family in Breslau (Wrocław) before or during the war.

The German army was successful on the Western Front until July 1918. The turning point came at the Battle of Amiens on July 18, 1918 when the coalition forces, the Allies (based on the Triple Entente of the United Kingdom/British Empire, France, and the Russian Empire) launched a counteroffensive. The war continued until the end of October 1918.

On November 3, 1918, a ceasefire was signed on behalf of the Austria-Hungary monarchy and Kraków became a Polish city again. Everywhere in the city the signs of Austrian control began disappearing and the Polish government began taking control. Antonina Freiin von Richthofen and her parents lived to see the revival of an independent Poland. I wonder how the inhabitants of Kraków reacted to German surnames and if my family faced any disrespect. In December 1918, an article was published in the local Kraków newspaper *Ilustrowany Kurier Codzienny* [Illustrated Daily Courier] in which the publisher recommended a boycott of New Year's Eve balls because they were seen as a German custom.

Below is one of my favorites postcards, a German card from Antonina's collection, with the image of a girl raising a glass of steaming grog on New Year's Eve. This card reminds me of a childhood conversation with Grandmother Antonina when I asked her what grog was, a word I had just heard for the very first time. She told me that grog was a drink of juice mixed with rum or wine, which a person drank to warm up. I could not hide my bewilderment to learn that somebody gave an alcoholic drink to the little girl on the postcard as I realized at that moment that the world had changed very much since my grandmother's childhood because I was never allowed to drink anything that contained alcohol!

In Kraków, Antonina studied literature at the Baraniecki's Seminary for Women, founded in 1868 by Adrian Baraniecki, a phisician and philantropist. The seminary was the only place of higher education for women in Kraków from 1868 to 1894, until the Jagiellonian University allowed women to study. The Baraniecki Seminary for Women operated until 1924 and offered classes in literature and history.

Top left: *My favorite German postcard from Grandmother Antonina's collection.* *Top right*: *My great-grandfather Bolesław Freiherr von Richthofen with his wife, daughter Antonina, and Fr. Piotr Pietryka in a photo taken shortly before the outbreak of World War I.* *Bottom*: *Breslau (Polish Wrocław) before World War I, postcard from Grandmother Antonina's collection.* [145]

[145] Ivona Tarko's archives.

When Poland became an independent country, Maria née Freiin von Richthofen Gawrońska and her husband, Juliusz, moved from Vienna to an apartment in the building in Matejko Square in Kraków. Both of Bolesław's daughters now were living in Kraków. Juliusz began working as the director of the Małopolska Bank. A few years after moving to Kraków, on April 30, 1923, the first daughter of Maria and Juliusz came into the world. She was named after her mother, Maria, but the family called her "Maninia." Four years later, their second daughter, Teresa, was born, called "Niutka" by the family.

After the end of War World I, Bolesław's sibilings, Stanisław Freiherr von Richthofen and Maria née Freiin von Richthofen Miłkowska also went to live to Kraków; and they had their own apartments in different parts of the city. The family was reunited and was ready to start a new chapter of their lives in independent Poland.

In Kraków after the war, the shortage of food and money was a grave problem. Coins, in particular, were scarce because they were made of silver and had more value than paper money so people preferred to keep, rather than spend, them. Securities had becme "unsecurties." When winter came, fuel shortages became a problem as well.

In 1921, three years after the end of the war, 183,706[146] persons lived in Kraków. Among them, blue collar workers were the largest group and white collar workers were the second largest, but they all were rapidly becoming poor. My great-grandfather, 67 years old at that time, worried about the precarious financial situation of his family and his failing health was getting worse. He tried to find out what happened to land that one of his maternal ancestors had purchased in New York, hoping that he would inherit something and make his situation at home better. Nothing came from his research due to the lack of documented information and the distance. The idea that an ancestor once had a piece of of the city of New York remains a myth in the family. Hiperinflation in Poland only increased my great-grandfather's anxiety. Antonina apparently was more

---

[146] M. B. Michalik, Kronika Krakowa: W Polsce Znów Niepodległej, 1996, p. 297.

practical than her father in looking for an additional income, and she decided to work as a clerk in the Bank Małopolska, where her brother-in-law was a director.

Bolesław thought that Tolunia was not qualified for the job, and he was fearful that his spoiled daughter did not have the constitution for it. Luckily, she proved him wrong. Antonina worked in the bank for a few years and brought home a small but steady income.

Bolesław worked as a volunteer in the Jagiellonian Library from 1922 to 1924. He became seriously ill in June 1924 and passed away at the end of that month on June 29, 1924. His final resting place was the Wielogłowski family tomb at the Rakowice Cemetary in Kraków, where he was laid to rest beside his beloved mother Maria née Wielogłowska Freifrau von Richthofen, his daughter Elżunia, and his maternal grandparents, Konstancja and Walery Wielogłowski.

I read with sadness my great-grandfather's death certificate, on which a clerk made a note that the deceased did not leave any assets. I believe the note was important for the widow for financial purposes, perhaps according to the succession law in Poland.

Grandmother Antonina told me about the currency reform in Poland in April 1924 when the Polish mark was replaced by the Polish zloty, which meant the money the family had left was worth even less. There whole "fortune" amounted to just about enough to buy a pair of shoes. Antonina was very attached to her father so his illness and death was a traumatic experience for her. She looked for inner strength in prayer and even considered entering a convent.

CHAPTER 7 Between the Wars: Bolesław's Daughters

To the soul, there is hardly anything more healing than friendship

~ Thomas Moore

Soon after the death of her father, Antonina experienced another traumatic separation. This time it was her best friend and confidante, Milunia (Emilia) Bakałowicz. They grew up in the same building on Batory Street in devout Catholic families and spent most of their childhood years together. In her 20s Milunia felt called to the contemplative life as Sister Maria Immaculata of the Order of the Dominican Sisters in Kraków. Milunia described the day she took her eternal vows as the happiest day of her life. My grandmother obviously did not feel called to cloistered life and chose to marry and raise a family. Fortunately, their strong bond was not to be broken; and for the next 50 years they stayed in touch by correspondence and visits at the monastery.

Antonina was to meet her future husband, Adam Strzelecki, doing something she enjoyed: taking one of her daily walks with her mother, Bronisława Freifrau von Richthofen, in the Planty Park in Kraków, which was close to where they lived in Matejko Square. As you may recall, Bronisława was faithful to the methods of Dr. Kneipp and believed that fresh air was one of the most important necessities of life and that walking not only strengthens muscles but improves the condition of the whole body by increasing blood circulation.

Adam walked the Planty Park every day on his way home from work and noticed Antonina's modest, even old-fashioned, long dress, braided hair, and no makeup, which were refreshing to him in 1920s Kraków when most of the young women were wearing short skirts, bobbed hair, and lots of makeup.

A graduate of the Jesuits High School in Chyrów near Przemyśl and the Jagiellonian University, where he received a Ph.D. before World War I, Adam was a history major. The promoter of Adam's dissertation, *Sejm 1605* [the Diet 1605] was the noted historian Professor Wacław Sobieski, who was "unusual, controversial, and unconventional" [Barcz, 1978].[147]

---

[147] H. Barycz, Historyk Gniewny i Niepokorny – Rzecz o Wacławie Sobieskim, Kraków, 1978, p. 357.

The outbreak of World War I postponed Adam's academic and professional career because he was called to military service in the Austrian Army and was sent to the war front on October 1, 1914. He served until the end of the war, and the months he spent in the trenches damaged his health because he became ill with arthritis. On November 2, 1918, he returned to Kraków, his hometown, and volunteered to organize the first Polish artillery formations for the Polish Army. He became the adjutant of General Paweł Cyrus Sobolewski.

In May 1919 Adam was assigned to the Corps of Cadets as a history professor, but his career was interrupted by the Bolshevik invasion and the outbreak of the Polish-Soviet War of 1919-1921. Adam volunteered for the front at the beginning of the war and fought for the Polish Army until September 24, 1920 when he was moved back to his teaching position in the Corps of Cadets. On October 25, 1921, he began serving in the reserves at the rank of captain. The Austrians awarded him the Signum Laudis (the Military Merit Medal) of the Empire of Austria-Hungary and the Karl Troop Cross. He also received from the Poles the Badge of Honor for organizing the Polish artillery and the Orlęta Badge [the Eaglets Badge].[148]

When Adam left the army, he taught history at the private Catholic University of Lublin, Poland for a short time. In 1923, he decided to return to Kraków, where his parents lived, which was still the thriving center of academic and artistic life in Poland. He took a history teaching position at the Baraniecki's Seminary for Women[149] and the State Teacher's Seminary.[150]

Adam's only sibling, his brother Tadeusz Strzelecki, studied law at Jagiellonian University and left Kraków to fight the Russians for independent, post-war Poland with the First Brigade of Legions formed by Józef Piłsudski in 1914. Sadly, he died in 1918 as an enemy captive without his family ever locating his gravesite. After World War I, his

---

[148] Ivona Tarko's archives: A. Strzelecki, Curriculum Vitae, Kraków, May 14, 1933.
[149] Wyższe Kursy dla Kobiet im. Dr. A. Baranieckiego w Krakowie.
[150] Państwowy Wyższy Kurs Nauczycielski w Krakowie.

parents donated money to restore the Royal Castle on Wawel Hill in Kraków and honored Tadeusz's memory by engraving his name on one of the Wawel bricks placed on a wall located along the northern entrance to the castle.

Jan Strzelecki was the father of Adam and Tadeusz and owned the Sidzina estate near Kraków. An ichthyologist,[151] Jan tried his luck with a carp fish farm on the estate; but according to my mother, it was an unfortunate fiasco and was likely why the Strzelecki family moved to Kraków. Adam's mother, Julia née Brzezińska Strzelecka, was the daughter of Paweł Brzeziński from Kraków, who was a mathematician and the founder of the Technical Institute in Kraków, which over the years developed into Kraków Polytechnic. Julia's mother was Bronisława née Krzyżanowska Brzezińska.

Once Adam became aware of Antonina, he looked for her in the Kraków social circles so that he could be formally introduced, but Antonina, mourning her father and occupied by her work in the bank, was not participating much in Kraków social life. As Adam continued to look for ways to meet Antonina, he asked for help among his fellow historians who remembered Antonina's father, Bolesław Freiherr von Richthofen. I believe he was finally introduced by a friend of Bronisława von Richthofen, Maria née Cyrus Sobolewska Skowrońska, sister of General Paweł Cyrus-Sobolewski.

They married exactly two years after the death of Antonina's father on June 29, 1926, in Antonina's parish church, St. Florian. She was twenty eight years old, and Adam was eight years her senior. The couple's photo and several telegrams, a trendy way at the time to send best wishes, tell the story of the ceremony. Surprisingly, my grandmother never told me about the wedding reception. The closest members of the families present at her wedding were Antonina's mother and her sister and brother-in-law; Adam's parents, Stanisław Freiherr von Richthofen and Maria née von

---

[151] J. Strzelecki, O rentowności gospodarki rybnej, Okólnik Rybacki, organ Krajowego Towarzystwa Rybackiego w Krakowie numer 119 wrzesień i październik 1911.

Richthofen Miłkowska; and some if not all, of her uncles with their wives and children from the Sędzimir family, with whom Antonina was very close.

My grandparents, Antonina (born Freiin von Richthofen) und Adam Strzelecki on their wedding day.[152]

1926 was a memorable year in Poland because of the May Coup d' État in Warsaw undertaken by Marshal Józef Piłsudski, who wanted to end political chaos and instability in the Polish government and parliament. The new independent Polish state faced vast challenges in building the

---

[152] Ivona Tarko's archives.

Second Republic, which was split among many political factions. After more than 100 years of living under occupation by three powerful monarchies (Prussia, Austria-Hungary, and Russia), the Poles hungered for independence and set out to organize a new, united, and modern society after World War I. In May 1926, in the process of replacing the President and Prime Minister, Marshal Piłsudski rejected the offer to become the president of Poland but remained the most influential politician in the country until his death in 1935. Jan Strzelecki, Antonina's father-in-law, absolutely admired Marshal Józef Piłsudski, but Antonina criticized some of the Marshal's actions.

Professor Wacław Sobieski, in a letter addressed to Adam written four days before my grandparents' wedding, apologized that he would be not able to attend the ceremony but wished the groom and his bride much happiness on their new life together and said:

> Let heaven send rays of sunshine to cheer your new nest. Your new home is the new torch of the national spirit: a serious and great thing in our country incited by Bolshevism and anarchy (Sobieski, 1926).[153]

The newlyweds first lived in an apartment in the building owned by the Sędzimir family in Matejko Square, where Antonina's mother and Sister Maria and her family lived. After a few years, they moved to a new, modern, and up-to-date district in Kraków, where they rented a contemporary apartment at Słowacki's Alley 56. Adam always dreamed about building a house; and in the early 1930s, he had a villa constructed according to his plans in the Prądnik Valley by Ojców in the Kraków–Częstochowa Upland. My grandmother remembered it as a scenic spot surrounded by forest and rocks in the Prądnik Valley, which now is part of the Ojców National Park. My grandparents spent their summer vacations in Ojców.

---

[153] Ivona Tarko's archives: W. Sobieski, Letter to Adam Strzelecki written on 06-25-1926 (I believe Professor Sobieski wrote 1925 by mistake).

The other place that my grandmother recollected was Przyszowa near Limanowa, the estate owned by her Uncle Aleksander Żuk Skarszewski, a physician, who opened the center of hydrotherapy and had two guesthouses, which was a new trend in the circles of Polish landlords in the 1920s. The Przyszowa guesthouses had a good reputation and were successful until World War II.

Antonina and Adam had a harmonious marriage despite their different personalities. He enjoyed life and was easy-going, energetic, passionate, and sometimes even slightly coarse, while she was quiet, melancholic, and a little bit nervous; but both were honest and responsive to each other's sufferings and injustices and valued the same ideals. However, as I previously stated, Antonina did not admire Marshall Józef Pilsudski, the Chief of State (1918-1922) and the leader of the Second Polish Republic as much as Adam and his family and criticized some of his political decisions and his private life.

The correspondence I found between Adam and Antonina contained words and expressions that indicated their mutual love, affection, and fondness. Their early married life was centered on Adam's duties as a history teacher and then as the director of the Higher Teacher Education Courses from 1930 until his death.[154] He worked in one of the buildings on Wawel Hill in Kraków, which were occupied by the Austrian Army before the end of World War I and then abandoned in 1918.

My grandmother told me how much she enjoyed the anecdotes and stories from the past shared at the dinner table by my grandfather, the historian. He also was a good educator and was popular among his students, who sent him postcards, letters, and best wishes on the occasion of his Name Day or holidays, even years after their graduation. On December 24, 1927, one of his former students wrote:

> Beloved and Dear Professor,
>
> Please forgive my boldness, but I could not find other words and expressions that would be more appropriate for you as the

---

[154] Państwowy Wyższy Kurs Nauczycielski w Krakowie.

memories of working with you remain with me. With deep affection and sincerity and unwavering kindness and love, I send you cordial wishes on your Name Day. May God bless you with good health, satisfaction, and joy. Continue to be an example, Dear Professor, of a person who loves science and everything that is beautiful but always is joyful. Let your goodness of heart be the ray of sunshine throughout our lives. Have a long life ahead, Dear Professor.

Your grateful student, Karol Kowicki.[155]

A Name Day party for my grandfather was organized by his parents every year on December 24 at lunch time, in their apartment located on Strzelecka Street 9 in Kraków, close to the Main Railway Station. Julia, Adam's mother served meatless dishes to the guests because it was Christmas Eve day in keeping with Catholic tradition in Poland. Julia Strzelecka usually served seafood and fish at the party, and my grandmother's favorite dish was crayfish in dill sauce. Some members of the family not only did not eat meat but fasted before their Christmas Eve supper, which was, and still is, our most important family gathering at Christmastime.

The Christmas Eve supper was organized by my grandparents in their apartment and they invited Adam's parents, Antonina's mother and family, including Stanisław Freiherr von Richthofen, who became the head of the family and surrogate father for Antonina after the death of Bolesław Freiherr von Richthofen. The dining room table was filled with an abundance of fish, of which carp was the most important among them according to Polish Christmas Eve tradition. Grandmother Antonina recollected one of these family suppers when her beloved Adam was choking on a carp bone but was luckily saved. After that near disaster, she was anxious when carp was served, and at every Christmas Eve dinner she instructed me to be alert when I had a piece of carp in my mouth. I

---

[155] Ivona Tarko's archives: K. Kowicki to A. Strzelecki, Letter, year unknown.

never liked carp and gradually could not bear to eat it; I broke this family tradition when I began organizing Christmas Eve suppers for my family.

The presence of carp on the holiday table was so expected for Poles that Professor Wacław Sobieski wrote about it on a Christmas card sent from Paris to my grandparents:

> Instead of Polish carp this year, I only ate oysters (Sobieski, 1929).[156]

In Poland, the Christmas holiday includes three days of celebration, December 24, 25, and 26; customarily, Christmas Day Eve and Christmas Day were celebrated in the circle of family, and December 26 was spent visiting and hosting friends. My grandmother Antonina and her brother-in-law, Juliusz Gawroński, sometimes played piano duets at the family gatherings, and at Christmastime they played Polish carols which the family sang together.

In their first year of marriage, Antonina and Adam took part in the funeral of the Polish bard, Juliusz Słowacki, whose ashes were brought by train to Kraków from Paris, where he died in 1849. I wrote about the poet's connection to my von Richthofen family in Chapter 2. On June 27, 1927, the funeral of Juliusz Słowacki processed from the Main Rail Station to the Barbican, a round bastion constructed in Kraków in the 15th century, where the coffin was placed for one day to allow the residents of the city and delegations from other towns to pay homage to their beloved Polish bard. The next day the funeral ceremony took place in the court of the Wawel Castle during which Marshal Józef Piłsudski delivered a speech that was considered one of the best of his political career. The coffin containing Juliusz Słowacki's ashes was placed beside another eminent Polish poet, Adam Mickiewicz, in the chapel below the Cathedral on Wawel Hill. Today this is one of the famous tourist destinations in Kraków. The Cathedral, which initially was the last resting place of Polish kings, became the place of entombment for outstanding Poles who

---

[156] Ivona Tarko's archives: W. Sobieski to A. Strzelecki, Postcard, 1929.

devoted their lives to the country. Marshal Józef Piłsudski also was buried in the crypt under the Wawel Cathedral in 1935.

I learned about my family's life in the Second Polish Republic from my grandmother's stories and family correspondence. Antonina and Maria devoted their lives to their families and children and did not work outside the home, which was very common in their social circles. Their husbands' work provided financial security and comfort to their families in challenging times when many other citizens were less fortunate. Kraków was still the vivid cultural capital of Poland with its influential university, a symphony orchestra, movie theaters, and an opera, which did not have its own building but rather held their performances in the Juliusz Słowacki Theater. My grandparents enjoyed attending operas, classical music concerts, and performance theaters.

In addition to his duties as a professor and director of the Higher Teacher Education Courses for teachers, Adam Strzelecki worked on his post-doctoral thesis and planned to teach in the university. Antonina worried about Adam's health because he had suffered arthritis for years; and after their marriage he was diagnosed with a heart condition called angina pectoris. He did not stop smoking, a habit he started during wartime, and did not sleep much because he spent many late evening hours studying or evaluating his students' papers. He responded with jokes and wit to all of Antonina's commentaries about his unhealthy lifestyle. To repair his health Adam began spending vacation time in sanatoriums and spas.

After three years of marriage, Adam and Antonina were childless, which concerned them, but they were the godparents of Teresa, younger daughter of Antonina's sister Maria, whom they loved dearly.

In May 1929 in the Polish city of Poznań the "PeWuKa," the Polish National Exhibition was organized to celebrate the 10th anniversary of the independence of Poland. The purpose of the exhibition was to present the Polish economic and cultural achievements during the past ten years. Stanisław Freiherr von Richthofen, Antonina's uncle, visited the exhibition and shared these insights with the family.

186

The exhibition is imposing in every way, but visiting everything requires good health and stamina. Although I spent five hours every day sightseeing during my eight-day stay, I completed only a cursory examination. I think it would take a few years to see every detail of the exhibition (Richthofen, 1929).[157]

The exhibition was organized in 111 buildings that were located on 65 ha (160.61849765 acres).[158] The von Richthofen sisters, Antonina and Marylka, and their husbands went to Poznań in August 1929 to visit the exhibition. The trip and the hours of sightseeing were exhausting for Antonina, who was expecting her first child.

The weather in 1929 Kraków was very unusual. People were exposed to extremely cold record low temperatures in January and February (-31 F); the previous record low was in 1870. Then, an average summer was followed by an unusually warm fall and winter where the daisies and pansies in the Planty Park bloomed again in November and in the first half of December and fresh wild mushrooms and raspberries were picked in the Kraków area and sold in the city markets.[159]

On December 4, 1929, the first child of Antonina and Adam came into the world, daughter Krystyna. My grandmother, despite her deep devotion to the Catholic saints, followed a new trend and wanted to give her daughter a modern first name, which was taken from literature rather than the Bible. Krystyna, called by family and friends "Krysia," received two more names (Maria and Barbara) because she was born on the feast of Saint Barbara, the patron of miners in Poland, and Maria was a traditional name in Antonina's family.

After Krystyna was born, Antonina spent some time outside Kraków during the summer with her sister Maria and her daughters, Maria and

---

[157] Ivona Tarko's archives: S. Richthofen to B. Richthofen, Postcard, 1929.

[158] https://pl.wikipedia.org/wiki/Powszechna_Wystawa_Krajowa accessed 06-25-2015.

[159] M. B. Michalik, Op. Cit., p. 1929.

Teresa. Krystyna was only two years younger than Teresa so they became good playmates and then good friends.

Sadly, my grandparents are not among us so I could not ask them about Adam's visit to the Royal Castle in 1930, where he was invited to tea with the President of the Second Polish Republic, Ignacy Mościcki, or glamorous receptions organized in the Royal Castle on Wawel Hill. The invitations in my grandfather's name that I found in my family archives reminded me of the high regard in which he was held.

Adam was preoccupied with his post-doctoral thesis about reformation and heresy in the 17th century Poland about the time of these invitations. His advisor, Professor Wacław Sobieski, was not only a mentor but also a friend. I have in my archives the first volume of *Dzieje Polski* [The History of Poland] by Wacław Sobieski with a handwritten dedication to my grandfather and a few pieces of his correspondence. My grandfather was one of his first and oldest students so when Professor Sobieski celebrated the jubilee of his academic work, my grandfather had the honor of speaking at the ceremony.

My grandfather's manuscript started this way:

> Dear and Venerable Professor!
>
> Today, this solemn day of your jubilee of scientific and pedagogical work, I stand before you, as one of your oldest students, to express our tribute and gratitude and to wish you the best of everything for the future. I have two feelings: joy and some concern. I am joyful as I was given the honor and the very pleasant duty of expressing the high regard we have for you, Venerable Master; and concern, because I do not know if my words are adequate to express our reverence for your merits and our feelings for you. Venerable Celebrator of the Jubilee, it is not easy in this short speech to talk about all your manifold merits as the eminent historian researcher, the great professor, the enlightened and understanding manager of our first steps in the history field, and the sacrificial mentor in our later research, with

whom we were united by even closer ties than the usual bond between a professor and his students within the walls of Almae Matris (Strzelecki, 1932).[160]

The ceremony to celebrate Professor Wacław Sobieski's 35 years of academic work was held on December 11, 1932 in one of the lecture halls in the Jagiellonian University.

My grandfather's career was going well as was his family life. On July 24, 1933, my grandparents welcomed their second daughter, Alicja Maria Anna, called "Alinka," who 25 years later became my mother. Antonina was 35 years old and Adam 43 at the time of Alinka's birth.

In 1934, my grandfather's new assignment as a member of the examination committee in the State Teacher's Seminar Extension Program required him to make mandatory trips for a few days away from Kraków during the school semesters. He was bound by the contract until 1937, and the overwhelming duties and stress worsened his health.

Recently, after I read the biography of Professor Wacław Sobieski, I started to wonder how much Professor Sobieski's situation had an impact on my grandfather's career and life. A couple years after the festive jubilee, Professor Sobieski found himself in the disgrace of the Regime of Sanation[161] in Poland and the Cathedral of Universal History in Jagiellonian University, where he was the head, was closed and he was forced into retirement.

I believe that my grandfather hoped to get a job at the Cathedral of Universal History after finishing his post-doctoral thesis so termination of the cathedral was a blow to his career. He then was stunned to lose his mentor and friend forever as Professor Sobieski passed away on April 3, 1935, soon after he left the university. Unpredictably, Marshal Józef Piłsudski died three weeks later on May 12, 1835.

---

[160] Ivona Tarko's archives: A. Strzelecki, Manuscript, 1932.
[161] https://en.wikipedia.org/wiki/Sanation accessed 06-01-2016.

On December 4, 1935, my grandfather passed away in the town of Sosnowiec, where he was participating in an examination committee organized by the State Teacher's Seminar Extension Program.[162] He was only 45 years old and he left behind in mourning his wife, mother, and two very young daughters. Very sadly for Krystyna, he died on her birthday.

My grandfather died of a cardiac arrest and was found in a hotel room beside a table full of students' papers that he was evaluating. The below obituary in the magazine *Reformacja w Polsce* [Reformation in Poland] recalled my grandfather's career.

> Dr. Adam Strzelecki, a former professor at the Catholic University of Lublin and the Director of the Higher Teacher Education Courses in Kraków, passed away during the preparation of his yet to be published post-doctoral thesis and did not finish his corrections. With his sudden death, Polish historiography lost a talented and accomplished researcher. His mentor, the late Wacław Sobieski, steered him to study the Zebrzydowski rebellion and he devoted many years to the huge collection of manuscripts. It was a great loss that he passed away before finishing his main work, but he left the evidence of his thoroughness and methods source. Honor his memory! ((Redakcja Ref.w.P.).[163]

My grandfather's funeral took place in Kraków before Christmas at the Rakowicki Cemetery where he was laid to rest in the Brzeziński family tomb, which dates back to the 19th century and his maternal grandparents. The family and a crowd of colleagues and students attended the ceremony on a cold and snowy winter day. Both daughters were kept at home because they were sick with chicken pox. My mother was too young to remember her father, but Krystyna had some vague memories of him. As an adult, she recollected Christmas 1935 as the saddest holiday in her life; without her father in the company of her stunned heartbroken mother. The

---

[162] Ivona Tarko's archives: Protocol written by Dr. Witold Wasilewski; Protocol from Państwowe Sem. Naucz. Męskie im. A. Mickiewicza, Sosnowiec, 1935.
[163] Ivona Tarko's archives: Reformacja w Polsce, Rocznik VII-VIII 1935-1936, p. 184.

only person who tried to cheer the children up was their grandmother, Bronisława Freifrau von Richthofen.

Antonina wanted her children to have a happy childhood, but her financial situation changed after Adam's death. She received a widow's pension from the Polish government and her daughters an orphan's pension until they were 18 years old. After talking with her mother and seeking financial advice from her brother-in-law, Juliusz, whom she trusted, she decided to leave the apartment at Słowacki Alley and move to her mother's apartment in Matejko Square and with her help to raise the children. She kept her house in Ojców where she spent the summer months with her children and mother.

Antonina found support in her circle of devoted friends: Maria called Uta Łubieńska, the owner of the Catholic Bookstore in Kraków on Mikołajska Street; Helena Grocholska; Zofia Brzezińska; and Helena Skowrońska, the niece of General Sobolewski. Sadly, in 1937, Anastazja Miłkowska, the loving and helpful best friend of my great-grandmother and our family, passed away.

My grandmother's friends were supportive and not critical of her, which was in contrast to some members of her family who thought she was too naïve and impractical because she was eager to share with a person in need even her last slice of bread. Some people used her, but fortunately many of those she helped appreciated and remembered her kindness.

My grandmother loved her daughters very much and wanted to create a happy childhood for them. Her decision to return to the apartment in Matejko Square was good for the children, who spent a lot of time with their cousins, Maria's daughters. All of them lived in the same apartment building. Krystyna recollected games played together, Tuesday social gatherings organized by the girls' grandmother, Bronisława Freifrau von Richthofen, where fantastic desserts were served (all of them had a sweet tooth), and daily walks in the Planty Park.

In the fall of 1936, Antonina enrolled older daughter Krystyna in a private seven-grades school named "Instytut Marii" (Maria's Institute), which was operated by the monastery sisters of the Congregation of the Daughters of Divine Love on Pędzichów Street in Kraków; Maria's daughters attended another Catholic private school named "Szkoła Prezentek" (The School of the Congregation of the Virgins of the Presentation of the Blessed Virgin Mary). Krystyna recalled that the last happy family gathering before the outbreak of World War II was the day of her First Communion on April 16, 1939.

CHAPTER 8 The Last Polish von Richthofens

Forget the suffering you caused others. Forget the suffering others caused you. The waters run and run, springs sparkle and are done, you walk the earth you are forgetting

~ *Czesław Miłosz*

Grandmother Antonina spent the summer of 1939 with her daughters in their Ojców home, which was a tradition for the family. They planned to return to Kraków just before September 1 when all the Polish schools traditionally started a new school year. Krystyna, as a grown-up, described how that summer ended as World War II began. She was in Ojców with her mother, grandmother, and a maid and was preparing to leave for Kraków before the beginning of the school year when they learned about the outbreak of war. They had to stay in Ojców, where they felt fairly safe until the day they saw airplanes fighting in the sky. Villages around were burning, and that night they went to hide in caves because people said that the Germans were approaching. Although it was only a German horse patrol terrorizing the valley that had since left, they were certain they were under German occupation. They learned that Kraków was already occupied by the Germans, but they still hoped to go home. Unfortunately, they all got sick with influenza and stayed in Ojców until the beginning of October. When they finally began their journey to Kraków, it was on a peasant wagon because buses were not operating.

The day the German troops entered Poland was a painful blow to my great-grandmother and grandmother as both were Polish patriots who prayed for the independence of Poland and an end to war. When they returned to Kraków, they saw German flags with swastikas everywhere and there were many Germans on the streets of Kraków, which certainly was a disheartening sight for them.

During the severe winter of 1940, Krystyna recalled that my grandmother was always helping the poor. One of them was an old Jewish man to whom she gave food and her late husband's clothes. After some time, he stopped showing up at their home, and they guessed that perhaps the Germans had taken him to a ghetto. A seamstress who lost her apartment on Pawia Street when Germans bombed her building at the end of summer came to live with them as well… (Strzelecka, 1986).[164]

---

[164] Ivona Tarko's archives: K.Strzelecka-Dymek, Żywot mojej pobożnej matki śp. Antoniny z Richthofenów Strzeleckiej: napisany przez jej córkę Krystynę Strzelecką-Dymek dla zbudowania dusz pobożnych, Kraków, 1986.

The homeless seamstress my grandmother invited to live in her home was Ms. Elżbieta Pantak, whose name I learned from my mother. My mother also told me that she heard from others that, for a short time, a Jewish family was hiding in my grandmother's villa in Ojców.

On November 6, 1939, the Nazis operation called "Sonderaktion Krakau" occurred, which was a terrible blow to higher education in Kraków as 184 academics were arrested. The majority of the professors and lecturers were from Jagiellonian University, but professors and doctors from the Kraków AGH, AE, and a few from Lublin and Wilno universities also were taken away. These academics, along with an additional 13–15 university employees and students from Jagiellonian University, were sent to the Sachsenhausen-Oranienburg concentration camp near Berlin. Among the professors who died in the camp were Ignacy Chrzanowski, Stanisław Estreicher (whose words I cited in Chapter 5), and Kazimierz Kostanecki.

When Antonina heard the sad news about the fate of Kraków's professors, she thought about her late husband who would have been among them; and for the first time in her life, she accepted his death.

Henryk Rowid (born Naftali Herz Kanarek), my grandfather's colleague and the founder of the National Pedagogium before World War II, was not arrested during the Sonderaktion Krakau operation and became active in the Secret Teaching Organization, which was a large group of professors and teachers who organized underground high schools and universities because all the Polish institutions of higher education were closed. Older children in occupied Poland were given the option to go to vocational schools or take courses which would prepare them for factory work. Only the elementary schools were allowed to stay open under Nazi occupation. This underground teaching system organized by Poles took the name of the "Flying University" because it was constantly changing its location in various private apartments for small groups of students. Teachers and students, who participated, risked imprisonment and even death. Sadly, Henryk Rowid was one of those captured and arrested by the Nazis in August 1943. He later died in the Auschwitz concentration camp.

During the first few months of the war, my great-grandmother, Bronisława Freifrau von Richthofen and daughters Antonina and Maria and their families lived in an apartment building in Matejko Square in Kraków. It was the same building where Bolesław Freiherr von Richthofen lived with his family before World War II. From her apartment window Antonina could see the church of St. Florian, where Antonina and Adam made their wedding vows, and the Grunwald monument where her daughters sometimes played. The Grunwald monument, which was the work of Antoni Wiwulski, had special meaning to Kraków's citizens and was a symbol of Polish national pride as it was erected in 1910 on the 500th anniversary of the victory of Polish King Jagiełło over the Knights of the Teutonic Order in the Battle of Grunwald. In fall 1939, the Nazis hid the monument from view to the public by constructing a wooden fence around it while they demolished it piece by piece. The bronze figures from the monument were carried away by the Germans to foundries to recast it for war equipment and the magnificient granite blocks were removed from the site; it was as if it never existed.

Years after the war, Krystyna composed a poem, *Pomnik Grunwaldzki* [The Grunwald Monument] which my son, Adam, translated into English.

> A stone skirmish of figures
> Intertwined with each other in the drudgery of battle,
> And at the peak of the monument the King Jagiełło
> Sits victoriously on horseback.
>
> Over the recollection of my childhood
> A fiery glow burns bloody.
> I saw in the first year of the war
> This monument mined by the German soldiers.
>
> My childhood was torn down along with the shrine
> My happy home, my peaceful harbor.
> Although I had only just finished ten years

I knew then - what war means…

My childhood years – carefree and innocent,
Recalled with a hint of sadness,
Awaken the memory of this monument
Which once was exalted by Paderewski.

Then came years dark and gloomy
Matejko Square - rendered empty
The winds of war drove us from our home
Which became hollow (Strzelecka, year unknown).[165]

As a result of the invasion of Poland by Nazi Germany and the Soviet Union during World War II, the Second Polish Republic was split into three zones: 1) Nazi Germany annexed the Polish areas in the west, 2) the Soviet Union annexed the Polish areas in the east, and 3) the General Government was established at the center of Poland with its capitol in Kraków. Krystyna continued to attend the same elementary school she had since 1936 during the war and occupation (1939 until 1945). Since the school was controlled by the Nazi regime then, however, her student ID below was issued in both Polish and German and was stamped with the German eagle/swastika insignia.

On April 14, 1940, my great-grandmother, Bronisława née Sędzimir Freifrau von Richthofen passed away at 78 years of age. Her last resting place was the Wielogłowski family tomb in Rakowice Cemetery where her husband and daughter Elżbieta already were buried. There were only a few attendees at her funeral because there were significantly less family members by that time; and every living Pole was preoccupied with struggling to live from day to day and was avoiding public gatherings out of fear.

---

[165] Ivona Tarko's archives: K. Strzelecka, Pomnik Grunwaldzki, year unknown.

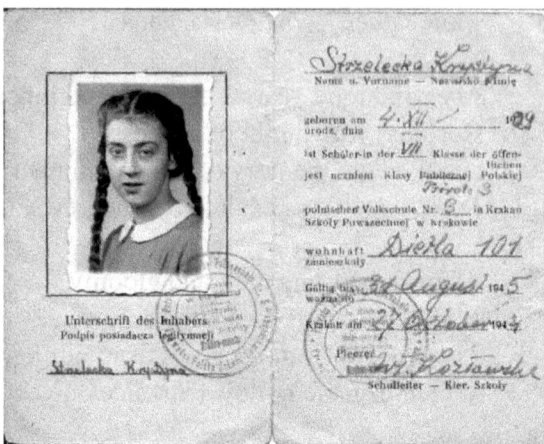

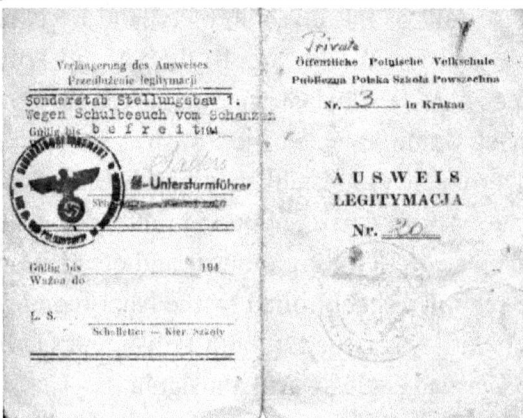

Left top: Antonina's photo from her Kennkarte, the ID issued by the Nazis for non-German citizens. *Left Bottom:* The Grunwald Memorial in Kraków. *Right:* Two pages of Krystyna Strzelecka's school ID from Maria's Institute in Kraków issued October 27, 1944.[166]

In the eyes of Karolina Lanckorońska, however, life in Kraków in the spring of 1940 appeared much closer to normal than in Lvov during the war. Kraków was not damaged and was sunny and loud, but she saw many Germans on the streets and noticed a sign *Nur fur Deutsche (Only for Germans)* on better restaurants and stores. In spite of this German presence, life in Kraków on the surface looked essentially unchanged.

---

[166] Ivona Tarko's archives.

The majority of her acquaintances still lived in their own apartments and invited her for breakfast, often modest, but always served it on china with silver spoons and forks. She was surprised when she returned to her home on the first day of her stay in Kraków and found a business card left by Professor Stanisław Kutrzeba and thought it was funny that the people in Kraków still needed such meaningless things during war (Lanckorońska, 2003).[167]

In spring 1940, many Poles hoped that the war would end soon; but after the capitulation of France, hope faded and some Kraków residents chose suicide to escape. The fear of random capture by the Nazis on the streets of Kraków became a part of everyday life, even for people not engaged in politics like my grandmother. After she lost her mother, my grandmother had to move on; and while her faith and love for her daughters kept her spirits up, the shortage of resources was growing, which became a daily struggle in occupied Kraków. Her extended family, mainly her cousin, Dr. Aleksander Sędzimir, occasionally helped her with financial difficulties, but she had to sell her valuables on the black market to buy food; first her jewelry, including her wedding bands, and later some antiques. The portions of bread rationed by the Nazis were perhaps enough for her, but not for her two young daughters.

When the General Government was created by the Nazis, the Polish railroads including the train stations were under German control; and buildings in the surrounding area of the main railway station in Kraków were seized by the German authorities. My family's home in Matejko Square was one of those properties. The owners and residents were given 24 hours to leave their apartments to make them available to the Germans. Grandmother Antonina had one day to take all her furniture and belongings from her four-bedroom apartment and quickly find storage and a place to stay. Krystyna recollected that Fr. Kozłowski, the rector of St. Florian Church, a decent and good man who knew my family for years, helped my grandmother by offering a place in the parish building to store all of her furniture and then kept it until she was able find a new

---

[167] K. Lanckorońska, Wspomnienia Wojenne, Kraków, 2003, p. 61-62.

apartment. Krystyna sensed that the heavy burden of everything was solely on her mother's shoulders when they left their Matejko Square apartment. She recalled how she had to negotiate with the movers of the furniture and belongings because they wanted too much money; and one of the movers threw a chest on the pavement that contained the Richthofen precious old German china because he was angry about the low payment. The china broke into many pieces and they were only able to salvage shards of porcelain. On that day her mother sold her treasured grand piano because there was no space to store it. That piano was the only one she ever owned. Once all the pieces of furniture were transported to the rectory, the last question remained – where would they stay?

My grandmother's sister, Maria, and her family also had to leave their apartment at the same time. Maria was with her daughters outside Kraków so her husband Juliusz supervised the move, but deciding to delay his wife's grief, he did not inform her about the situation before she returned to Kraków. She learned that she no longer lived in Matejko Square from her husband when he picked her up at the railway station.

Grandmother Antonina and her daughters were invited by her Aunt Maria née Freiin von Richthofen Miłkowska to stay with her. They were grateful and stayed there for a while, but Antonina did not want to impose on her aunt's generosity, who gave her own bedroom to my grandmother and her daughters. Aunt Maria was 78 years old and had health problems and lived in a small apartment on Ansyk Street in Kraków with her housekeeper at the time. Another close relative of Antonina, her Uncle Stanisław Freiherr von Richthofen was 80 years old in 1940 and lived on Słowacki Alley in Kraków. I believe that his housekeeper, Kasia, lived in the same apartment.

In the fall of 1940 Grandmother Antonina rented a room in the convent of the St. Felix order on Kołłątaj Street in Kraków, where the nuns ran a nursing home for the elderly. Fortunately, they had rooms available when Antonina and her daughters were looking for a place to live. They stayed at the convent until spring 1941. Krystyna and Alicja attended a school managed by the St. Ursula order in Kraków on Starowiślna Street. Shortly thereafter, Antonina found an apartment available in a neighborhood close to her children's school.

It was not easy to get an apartment in overcrowded Kraków; many Germans came to Kraków to work and live because Kraków was the capital of the General Government. General Hans Frank, the Nazi Governor, made Wawel Castle his residence. During this influx of new residents, the Nazis forced the majority of the Jewish population to leave the city for a ghetto organized in spring 1941 in the Podgórze district of Kraków. This German decision led to a new resettlement of Poles; my grandmother was offered an apartment to rent on Dietla Street, which before the war belonged to a Jewish family. Maria, Antonina's sister, rented an apartment with her family on the same street, within five minutes walking distance from them.

Grandmother Antonina's apartment consisted of three rooms in enfilade (a suite of rooms with doorways in line with each other), a kitchen, an entry hall, a bathroom, and a toilet. The apartment was located in an annex on the fourth floor without an elevator. The source of heating was coal stoves. Coal could be kept in a cellar, which every family had, but during the war it was extremely difficult to buy coal so they often used anything flammable to heat the room in the winter, usually old papers, sometimes books, and pieces of wood. They had a gas oven in the kitchen, and gas was usually available; but they did not have much food to cook (my grandmother never learned to cook anyway) so they mostly used the kitchen oven to heat a kettle with water for tea or coffee. Some of Antonina's friends and her sister were more gifted and creative in the kitchen and sometimes brought meals to share. My mother especially remembered cakes made of carrots or beets; and as she got older, she started to prepare simple meals from everything she could get to eat. They felt blessed that they had a home and their furniture, which was brought back from the storage. Of course, my grandmother, no matter how much she had, continued to share with friends and family members or took in strangers who needed shelter. My grandmother's Uncle Mieczysław brother of Bronisława, shared the apartment with my grandmother and her daughters for at least a few years during the war.

In 1941, my grandmother was summoned to the offices of the German administration in Kraków, according to her daughter Krystyna, and was asked if she wanted to have German citizenship because she had the German maiden name Richthofen, which was well known in Germany. My grandmother considered herself a Pole and rejected the offer with indignation, preferring to face misery and scarcity with her children during wartime than change her citizenship. After she rejected the offer, she was not forced to change her mind and was left alone. My grandmother's sister, according to my own sources, received the same offer to change her citizenship to German as well and also refused.

In the same year, disturbing news reached my family in Kraków about Antonina's cousin's family from Lvov, Teresa née Sędzimir Nechaj (niece of Bronisława von Richthofen), her husband, children, and mother. They had been arrested by the Soviets. Teresa's husband, a Polish officer, was sent to prison in the city of Kijev most likely, and Teresa and her two small children and elderly mother were deported to the steppes of Kazakhstan. Teresa and her children survived and came back to Poland after the end of the war and her son later wrote a memoir about their life in exile.

During the war my grandmother sold her home in Ojców because she desperately needed money and did not have a job or a regular income, but she did not complain. How could she? She and her daughters were alive, and nothing else was important. Krystyna remembered her mother often reciting the verse of a poem that went like this.

> Do not be saddened by anything.
> Do not tremble before the scourge of bad fate.
> Everything is just dust.
> God is absolute.
> Your aim is radiant.

To add to their difficulties in occupied Kraków, my grandmother had a health issue that required immediate surgery. Thankfully, her cousin, a physician, took care of her in the hospital; and her friend, Helena Skowrońska, whom the girls liked very much, came to live with Antonina's daughters in their home during her absence.

Many years after the war, I still remember Helena from my own childhood as a tall, sturdy woman with a heart of gold. She was the personification of gentleness to me. I can still see this elderly woman wearing old fashioned hats with a beautiful pin that she would talk about with me, a little girl at the time. She always brought a sparkle of excitement to my drab Communist reality, and she still has a very special place in my heart.

Antonina's daughters remembered the summer vacation of 1944 when they were invited by the sister of Elżbieta Pantak (the seamstress who used to live with my grandmother in 1939 because her apartment was bombarded by the German army) to a village in the Tatra Mountains, close to Zakopane. They thoroughly enjoyed the mountain and forest surroundings, the abundance of fresh blueberries and Riga mushrooms, fresh milk, and cheese made from sheep milk, called Oscypek.

Krystyna recalled the moment in August 1944 when they learned about the Polish Uprising in Warsaw and how this news affected her family. Everyone was shaken by the news coming from Warsaw; and in a church in Jaszczurówka, people sang the Polish patriot song *Z Dymem Pożarów* [With Smoke of the Fires].[168] When September came, Krystyna remembered that her mother did not know whether she should go back home or stay in the mountains because the war front had moved close to Kraków. They decided to stay until the end of September and went by train to Kraków. There were many people on the train who had escaped burning Warsaw. The train stopped in the area of Chabówka station but could not go further because a bridge had been blown up by the soldiers of the Polish Underground Army so they had to spend the night there. The

---

[168] Text by Kornel Ujejski, music by Józef Nikorowicz: http://a-pesni.org/polsk/choral.php accessed 09-01-2016.

next day the railroad tracks were repaired and the train continued to Kraków, where they met more people who fled from Warsaw; one of them was Miss Feliksa Suchecka who came to live with them for some time. She baked cookies with my grandmother, which they were selling in a pastry shop in Kraków. Two nieces of the Veraneman couple, my grandmother's tenants, came from Warsaw and stayed in the apartment as well.

In 1944, because of the shortage of apartments in Kraków, the German administration started forcing people with apartments to take in at least one tenant or an entire family. Complete strangers had to live together and share a kitchen and a bathroom. Therefore, in May 1944 my grandmother, as the main resident, had to agree to take in a couple who would share some expenses. My family lost one room, and because Antonina had already let the other room to her uncle, she and her children ended up in the middle room of the enfilade.

Grandmother Antonina lived with her daughters in that apartment to see the end of war. They experienced the most severe cold and hunger in the middle of January 1945 when the Soviet war front was approaching Kraków. They could not buy anything to eat and the only food they had at home was old, dry bread crusts, collected in paper bags by Antonina's uncle. He could not eat the bread crust, but he was too frugal to toss it away and stored everything "just in case." The bags of bread crust saved my grandmother and her daughters from starvation because they had nothing to eat but the bread crust for a week. They suffered extreme cold in their apartment because all the glass windows were shattered when the bridges over the Vistula River were bombed by the German army.

They remembered very well the first meal they ate after that week; it was cooked beans. They got the handful of hard-shell beans from their former maid, Marysia, who found them when was passing through downtown Kraków and happened upon people who had entered a grocery store abandoned by the Germans and were taking whatever was left. She found the beans and because there were not any bags in the store, she just put some beans in her pockets and brought them to my family.

My mother remembered that shortly after the Soviets drove out the Germans from Kraków and people went out on the streets, she went to an empty kitchen of one of the German offices on Wielopole Street. On a table, she saw fresh peeled potatoes, but she was afraid to take the food. She only took some coal she found in the kitchen to warm up their icy cold apartment.

They were overwhelmed with joy that the end of war had come. Grandmother's niece, Teresa, came back to Kraków from the Sandomierz area, where she was trapped for a few months by the approaching war front. They were extremely happy to have survived the six years of the Nazi occupation, but they were anxious about the future because they did not know what to expect. Unfortunately, the coming months brought new worries and disappointments and the growing conviction that there would be no return to pre-war Poland. The surviving Polish soldiers of the Underground Army who bravely fought the Germans were accused by the Communist government imposed by the Soviets for collaboration with the Nazis and for actions against the Soviet Union. Many Polish patriots were arrested, sent to prison, and killed by the new Communist regime. Grandmother Antonina and her sister Maria were not involved in politics, but their maiden name of von Richthofen became troublesome.

In July 1945 Maria née Freiin von Richthofen Miłkowska, sister of Bolesław, and aunt of Antonina and Maria, passed away in Kraków. One month before her death, she sent birthday wishes to my grandmother and a note describing her sadness. She said her day consisted of going to the church of the Divine Mercy on Smoleńsk Street in the morning and then went home to lie down. She felt that her life would end soon, but it did not terrify or worry her. Thirty days later, she passed away. Maria Miłkowska obviously had found inner strength and peace nearing the end of her life. She was laid to rest in the Wielogłowski family tomb beside her brother, Bolesław, at the Rakowice cemetery.

The loss of Aunt Maria was followed by another painful experience in the family. The Polish authority decided that 85-year-old Stanisław Freiherr von Richthofen was a German citizen, and he was forced to leave Poland.

His apartment and all his belongings were taken by an operative of the regional Office of Public Safety.[169] Stanisław was allowed to take only a few personal things; and his possessions were placed in garbage cans in the yard. Our family pictures and mementoes were found in Stanisław's apartment. Stanisław's neighbor contacted my grandmother's sister and told her what he saw. Maria and Antonina went to pick up some of the mementos.

The spring of 1946 was already ending when my grandmother received a letter from Germany, written in Polish by Stanisław, describing what had happened to him since he left Kraków in October 1945.

> Stanislaus V. Richthofen, Germany
> Postcode Koło
> Ratcherz, Kuis Pirna May 22nd, 1946.
> Diakonissenheim Felsengrund
>
> Dear Tolunia,
>
> I learned at the post office that sending correspondence written in the Polish language is again allowed. I assume that this information is correct; otherwise, this letter would not reach you.
>
> More than seven months already have passed since October 16th, 1945 when I became a wanderer, and the lack of information from all of you is very painful for me. From the day I was expelled from Poland, I wrote twice to all of you, sending my letters to Julek. The first one, which I put in a mailbox myself at the Polish mail office in Koźle (Cosel) on October 25th, 1945, you should have received by now. I have doubts about the second one, which I wrote on November 6th, 1945 and handed over to my escort, the member of the People's Guard, asking him to mail it from the railway station. Later he behaved like a bandit because he did not steal but rob me of my pocket watch. The police in Gorlitz

---

169 http://ipn.gov.pl/strony-zewnetrzne/wystawy/twarze_Krakowskiej_bezpieki/content/wprowadzenie.html accessed 06-26-2015.

(Gorlice) advised me against further action in the case; they argued that it would bring no result.

After crossing the border on November 15th, 1945, I learned to my greatest horror at the post office in [Gorlice?] that the postal connection with Poland, and it seemed so with all abroad, had stopped.

All of my attempts to contact you, my Dear, failed: twice in December, from Berlin through the Soviet scoundrels and somebody else, and then through the unfriendly director of the Saxon National Bank.

I was happy to learn at the end of April that international postal connection was back with the exception of Japan and Spain, with which I do not correspond.

I sent a 12-page letter on April 20th to the hands of dear Julek, but written to all of you with a letter attached for my good Kasia. On April 23, I sent a letter to my beloved Marysieńka, with wishes for her Name Day which she celebrates on May 3rd. All these letters were written in German and did not include any harmful information.[170] You should receive them, but maybe I am too optimistic and the delivery time is longer.

After this long introduction, let me tell you the main reason for this letter: your coming Name Day on June 13th, dear Tolunia.

I hope that the period of these almost eight months when I did not have contact with you was not a time of great apprehension and indisposition, and I hope that you could look into your and your daughters' futures with some glimmer of hope. Good health, endurance, and knowledge are needed to see a brighter future. We need to admit that we live in such a transformative time that

---

[170] I believe that Stanisław wanted to say that there was nothing politically incorrect in his letter.

humanity has never experienced before. I hope that you will have good health, but endurance is more likely the result of a strong personality and stamina than of physical development. If I did not have them, I would break down during my unwanted monthly journey.

This historic change has a particularly great significance for women. The terrible killing of World War I, and especially World War II, caused a shortage of men to fill all posts that were previously reserved exclusively to them. Although the shortage of men has forced many women to give up marriage, they have much more opportunities to work. We need to welcome this with gratitude, especially now when we witness global impoverishment. To get a better job, adequate education is required. It seems that all humanity is subject to the obligation of work, except the very young and very old. This applies in our family to the youngest generation because even dear Krysia is in the group which must work. I would appreciate information how our dear Mademoiselles are affected by their new condition.

Now, about me. I miss you all: family, relatives, acquaintances, friends, and my good Kasia. I ask you all for even a short note to let me know if any of my letters have reached you. I do not want to be a financial burden, even through small expenses, to anyone; please pay for your mail to me with money from my bank account; something still should be there, as I informed you in my letters.

Please, let me know what happened to my apartment. Was everything taken? Did anybody oppose? Do I still have anything or in the process of this soulless bureaucracy, have I become a beggar at my old age? What happened to my good Kasia, who for 27 years of life shared with me good and bad moments?

If I die in poverty, it will also have an impact on your situation. In spite of my good health, I have to be ready for my death any time because of my old age.

I never thought that I could be expelled by the authorities because I was fulfilling all my duties as a loyal citizen. It hurts very much; and even more, it hurts when I recall the actions of people exploiting their neighbors with impunity.

My stay in the nursing home from the middle of November until the end of that month last year was... (Richthofen, 1946).[171]

Unfortunately, the rest of the letter vanished. "Dear Julek" from Stanisław's letter was Juliusz, my grandmother's brother-in-law, and Marysieńka was Juliusz's daughter.

As Stanisław noted, the majority of women after the end of World War II, undertook professional work. For a short period of time, my grandmother taught Polish and French in a place called *Pomoc Dzieciom* [Help for Children] in Kraków, but it closed after a short time. Then, she found a job in the State Museum in Kraków, from which she retired in 1958. She did not have any practical training and education, and her questionable background (intelligentsia, the German maiden name) in Communist Poland did not serve when she applied for jobs. Her poor health, stamina, and self-confidence did not help. My grandmother simply was physically and emotionally burned out. For years, she rented one of her rooms to university students, which provided a small but stable income and the company of young scholars with whom she easily bonded.

Maria, who was ten years older than Grandmother Antonina, also rented one of her rooms to students, but being an excellent cook, she also provided them home cooked meals. It was additional income that supplemented her husband's salary and then his pension. I still remember her hints on how to cook the excellent Polish borscht and the German potato salad. I also remember our family gatherings, three generations sitting together in Maria's salon, decorated with her antique set of furniture and a grand piano in the center of the room. Maria served tea

---

[171] Ivona Tarko's archives: S. Richthofen to A. Strzelecka, Letter, 1946.

with rum in old German white china teacups decorated with gold and navy blur trim and Juliusz played piano.

The next Stanisław letter on October 15, 1947, brought more details about his life in Germany.

Germany 10a, Rathen.Kreis Pirna October 15, 1947
Diakonissenheim Felangrund

To my dear, all

I thank dear Julek for his letter of September 22nd, from Zakopane, which I received on September 29th. I guess he already came back to Kraków, relaxed, happy, and full of energy, so needed in his work for the benefit of his family.

I also received a postcard from Zakopane from dear Marylka, written on September 3rd, which I received on September 12th. You were worried unnecessarily that I would not receive your mail because it was underpaid. The post office was so accommodating that they did not ask me to make a payment. I sent a card to Niusia for her Name Day and I hope she got it on time.

I am concerned that Marylka felt tired. I hope that the stay in Zakopane strengthened her. The universal upheaval in which we live changed the situation of household duties for many women, who have to do chores to which they were not destined; also, many pensioners have to work again. And yet, it seems to me that humanity wants to fix the historical injustice of the last millennium and carry out the love of neighbor by ending the bloodthirsty wars of the 20th century.

The news about the death of our dear Dr. Ludwik Wilczyński caused me deep sorrow. Immediately after receiving this sad news, I wrote a condolence letter to his closest relative, but I am also sending you, my dear Julek, the words of my deepest sympathy because you have lost one of your oldest friends, a selfless man always ready to help.

I, who used to have a few good acquaintances in addition to my relatives, feel in my old age, already departed. My Kraków experience taught me to abstain from making confidential friends. Now I painfully experience the loss of such a good and selfless man, who so cordially hosted me like no other, not even a relative. He was also the last person to whom I said good-bye when I was expelled from Kraków. I believe he was one of the victims of the Nazis: arrested, barred from his own house, which was taken for military purpose; with no possibility to oppose, he suffered more when he witnessed the sad fate of his cousin and heir, General Malinowski. All together it was too much for his old heart. He passed away fairly wealthy, and I believe that if Malinowski could not be his heir, there will be relatives from the side of Mrs. [Mauthnerowa?] or from the side of Professor Krzyżanowski.

My thoughts are with you, my dear. I hope your dear grandson and his mother benefited from a visit in Gdów. I remember this town very well because it was one of which I and my late sister would be deporting.

How do you handle the high costs of living, especially Tolunia? I read in the local newspaper a few days ago that a part of the Polish treasure was returned from Romania, and I hope this will help to lower the prices.

The 16th of this month will be the second anniversary of my expulsion. Here, everybody is afraid of winter; we have neither fuel nor electricity. Besides this, I was deprived of my coat. At the end of May, I entrusted it to a representative of a large company from Dresden to dye it and I got a receipt. I was assured that I would have my coat back in six weeks. When this time passed, I was told that the firm did not have my coat so my request could not have been made and finally, on September 24th, I learned that there was no evidence of my coat in the firm, so I assume that it was stolen. I wrote a complaint letter and went with it to Pirna court on September 11th where I was promised that the case would be taken up shortly. I wear a borrowed coat.

I hug you all cordially. Sincerely yours, Uncle S. Richthofen (Richthofen, 1947).[172]

In his letter Stanisław mentioned Tadeusz Malinowski, General of the Second Polish Republic who fought against the German Nazis in Poland in September 1939. After the defeat of Poland, he left for France, and then Great Britain, where in London he lived until his death in 1980. The Communist government of Poland withdrew General Malinowski's Polish citizenship on September 24, 1946, which was restored in 1971 when Edward Gierek, the first Secretary of the Polish United Worker's Party, opened Communist Poland to Western influence.

Stanisław asked how Antonina was dealing with the high costs of living in Kraków; obviously, she did not do very well as the city office in spring 1948 issued her a certificate of poverty and gave her food stamps. Her daughters recollected that after the war, they received parcels with American food a few times sent by The United Nations Relief and Rehabilitation Administration (UNRRA); they remembered receiving American cheese, Spam, and grape jelly.

Stanisław always remembered the family members' Name Days that customarily were celebrated in Poland as more important than birthdays. I have a few postcards with the image of flowers and wishes he sent to my grandmother and her daughters. I learned from his correspondence that he was the resident of a nursing home managed by the Diakonie Pirna, a charitable organization affiliated with the Protestant church, which helped the poor and the elderly regardless of their religion and nationality. The third and last letter I have that was written by Stanisław Freiherr von Richthofen to my grandmother was on December 13, 1948.

---

[172] Ivona Tarko's archives: S. Richthofen to A. Strzelecka, Letter, 1947.

Germany 10a Rathen, Kreis Pirna December 13th, 1948
Diakonissenheim Felsengrund

Dear Tolunia,

Thank you and your dear daughters for wishes you sent for my Name Day, and the coming holidays: Christmas and New Year's Day. I received them on December 7th.

From the bottom of my heart, I wish you all, my dear, a nice Christmas surrounded by the family, and I hope that the New Year will bring you good health and radical improvement of your situation. You are one of many, among millions living in poverty, impoverished by the current times, which means that you must continue striving to get through this with hard work and diligence. We witnessed the greatest turning point in world history. The old time has passed irreversibly as did the old political system. Unless ill or old and unable to work, everyone has to work to put food on the table. My sad status of the state "rentrier"[173] is a painful situation for me because I thought that my honest work during my life would provide me with a good existence at my old age. In contrast to my hope, the opposite has happened.

I wrote to dear Julek that my situation would be better from the beginning of December because I would receive a modest pension of 90 German marks paid in advance and not at the end of month. I was disappointed when in December I was told that my payment for October would be 50 German marks, not 90, so I immediately protested. I do not write about it to you to complain, but to let you know that the family cannot count on my help. I barely make ends meet, denying myself almost everything. I already lost much, like all of us, during the monetary reform last summer.

I hope that Dear Alinka received my wishes for her Name Day. If not, it was lost somewhere at the post office.

Unfortunately, my thoughts and desire to come back to you all in Kraków is only a dream. If I receive an official approval to return,

---

[173] A pensioner.

I believe there are no other formal obstacles, but I would not be able to afford it financially. I am not even sure if any of my material possessions remain. What I want to say is that our parting is probably forever.

I am happy to know that you have nice tenants who pay rent and that you have some income from the institution *Pomoc Dzieciom* [The Help for Children], and that dear Olek helps you.

I do not have much to say about my stay here: perfect punctuality, neatness, and order are here. The Diakonisse, for whom the love of neighbor and philanthropy are a part of their vocation, are social, pleasant, and obliging. They are perfectionists and everything is done on time. There are no quarrels, screams, or cries, which makes the place very peaceful.

I could say the same about my companions (about 20) and auxiliary service (also about 20), who are young women ages 17 to 23. They first learn housekeeping and then maids are chosen from them to stay and work.

I have a good relationship with my entire group, but I am close to a professor emeritus, 82 years old, displaced from Tilsit, and a 71-year-old, almost blind, widow of a professor from Wrocław, and one completely paralyzed widow of an entrepreneur from Berlin, who was killed during the air attack.

Now, I send you, dear Tolunia, and your dear daughters warm hugs.

Sincerely yours,
loving Uncle S. Richthofen (Richthofen, 1948).[174]

At the end of 1948, Stanisław's nieces appealed to the Office of Liquidation asking for the annulment of the office decision depriving them of Stanisław Freiherr von Richthofen's assets. On August 11, 1949, Antonina and Maria received an official letter of the Kraków Regional Office of Liquidation with a note that the decision could not be changed

---

[174] Ivona Tarko's archives: S. Richthofen to A. Strzelecka, Letter, 1948.

because Stanisław Freiherr von Richthofen was deprived of his property in Poland as a German citizen.[175]

In the nursing home in Pirne, Stanisław met Gertrud Oertel, the opera singer, who was coming regularly to the nursing home to visit her relative. It is not clear how long they knew each other before they got married on February 6, 1951. Gertrud was forty-four years old and Stanisław was ninety-one. He moved to Gertrud's apartment in Berlin, in the Kopenick district, where she lived with her sister and mother. The next two years with Gertrud and her family was a happy period in Stanisław's life. He let his nieces know, that he was truly in love, for the first time in his life. He passed away at the age of 93 on November 28, 1953.

I asked Karl-Friedrich Freiherr von Richthofen to help me find Stanisław's tomb; and after engaging in the search a few other people, determined that Stanisław's last resting place was a cemetery in Berlin-Friedrich Hagen.

In 1953 Antonina and Maria lost "Uncle Staś," as they called him, who for 30 years was their substitute father and cared dearly about them, even from a distance. His nieces lived behind the Iron Curtain, and this fact explained why they were not able to correspond freely during his last years of life. The first couple years in Poland after the end of the war somewhat resembled life in the pre-war Polish Republic; but the 1947 election to the Diet and its forged results, brought total victory over the Communist party. In 1948, the Polish United Workers Party became the dominant political party and Poland, which since then was converted to the Communist state and became a satellite of the Soviet Union. The period 1947-1956 in Poland was called the Stalin era. In 1952, the Polish Parliament adopted a constitution modeled on the Soviet constitution from 1936, and the Polish state was named the People's Polish Republic. The Communists clashed with every opposition force and the repressed members of the Catholic Church, and the culminating event was the arrest of Polish Primate Stefan Wyszyński on September 26, 1953. Many

---

[175] Ivona Tarko's archives: Document L. Likw. -II-73/19/49.

citizens were sent to prison under even the slightest suspicion; one of my grandmother's tenants, Mrs. Janka, was denounced in her workplace because she said that money collected there for the Communist party event should be send to support the Warsaw orphans, the children who lost their parents in the 1944 Warsaw Uprising. She was accused of being an enemy of the People's Polish Republic, arrested, and sent to prison.

The Communist terror lessened in 1956 with the arrival of a new leader of the Polish United Workers Party, Władysław Gomułka; but my grandmother and her sister lived deprived of contact with Western Europe. The Communist authorities, despite the change of party leaders, had one overriding goal - to control and manipulate information to convince the Polish citizens that they lived in the best political system. Many younger citizens had a dilemma: to pursue their career with the support of the Communist party, struggle as an oppositionist, or stay as far away as possible from reality and be content with mediocre jobs. From that time, I remember the concept of "internal immigration." Antonina and Maria were not pressed to become members of the Communist party and party membership was not required in their careers; one of them was close to her retirement and did not hold a prominent position at her workplace and the other did not work outside her home. My grandmother and my grand aunt focused on the family which was growing through the marriages of their daughters and births of grandchildren.

I called my grandmother Babcia (Grandma). Since I had only one grandmother, I did not have to look for a special name for her. I never had a chance to meet my fraternal grandmother, who was raped and murdered by Soviet soldiers in Dorohusk, by the Bug River, at the end of 1944.

I remember Grandmother Antonina often immersed in reading. She liked to read memoirs and biographies mainly, but she appreciated good literature. I remember a conversation with her about a World War II book during which she asked me how it was possible that the nation which gave the world many magnificent composers and poets, produced also inhuman individuals who incited the war and its tragic toll.

In the mid-1960s Grandmother Antonina met historian Norman Davies, an acquaintance and then husband of Masia Zielińska, the student of medicine who rented a room in my grandmother's apartment. When he visited Masia, my grandmother, who did not speak English, had nice conversations with him in French. They both enjoyed the chats because my grandmother liked talking about history and literature and Norman Davies wanted to learn the Polish perspective on its past. Later, he wrote in one of his feuilletons that the only way to gain true knowledge of Polish history was through discussions with the Poles. The official textbooks were full of lies and omissions. The main source of his historical knowledge of Poland was a great man who later became his father-in-law (Davies, 2000).[176]

Grandmother Antonina was invited to the wedding of Maria (Masia) Zielińska and Norman Davies, which took place in Kraków on Christmas 1966. If I am not mistaken, the ceremony was held in the church of St. Mary in the Main Square. My grandmother stayed in touch with Masia for the next few years, even after she moved to Great Britain.

As it had for centuries, my family gathered at weddings and funerals. Maria née von Richthofen Gawrońska became a widow in 1967. I remember the funeral and reception for Juliusz Gawroński. He passed away on November 4, 1967, and we gathered a few days later at the cemetery and then in the Gawroński salon with Juliusz's grand piano in the center of the room, which seemed to me cold and silent as a burial chapel.

Both sisters, devout Catholics, were overwhelmed with joy when Karol Wojtyła became Pope John Paul II in the fall of 1978. A couple years later, we all raised our hopes for a better future with the birth of the Solidarity Movement in 1980.

---

[176] N. Davies, Boże Igrzysko, czyli Alicja w polskiej krainie czarów, Smok wawelski nad Tamizą, Kraków, 2000, p. 38.

My grandmother worried a great deal when martial law was announced in Poland on December 13, 1981. Her friend Basia Pióro, who lived in Gdańsk, wrote asking her to pray for the peace in their tortured homeland and to pray to her patron, St. Anthony, and offer her ailments.

> God usually hears the prayers of persons who are pious and suffer silently like you (Pióro, 1982).[177]

Maria née Freiin von Richthofen Gawrońska died at the age of 95 on August 23, 1983. She was laid to rest in the Gawroński family tomb at the Rakowicki cemetery in Kraków. The passing of Maria, her only sister, plunged Antonina into grief. Her health deteriorated, but mentally she was sharp and interested in events in her family and country.

Krystyna, composed this poem dedicated to her mother.

> Mother
> Her silver hair reminds me of white chrysanthemums
> And her calm smile sun in late autumn.
> Blue eyes, innocent, look at me as if they belong to a child
> Who does not know the world?
> Here, she is – my old mother.
>
> Her heart friendly to each person,
> To strangers and related,
> Does not hurt anybody and sows only kindness.
> She gives away everything
> That she possesses,
> Humbly does not want anything for herself.
>
> She forgives harm instantly.
> Why in her eyes other is somebody
> And she is nobody?
> Mother!
> You constantly forget
> You live on Earth not in Heaven
> And if angels exist
> They want to be like you (Strzelecka, 1979).[178]

---

[177] Ivona Tarko's archives: B. Pióro to A. Strzelecka, Postcard, 1982.
[178] Ivona Tarko's archives: K. Strzelecka, Matka, 1979.

Grandmother Antonina née Freiin von Richthofen Strzelecka passed away on September 29, 1984. As she instructed in her will, she was laid to eternal rest beside her parents Bolesław Freiherr von Richthofen and Bronisława née Sędzimir Freifrau von Richthofen in the Wielogłowski family tomb founded by her great-grandfather Walery.

I remember when my mother and I were putting together the obituary of Grandmother Antonina and my mother's moment of hesitation about whether or not to write down the baronial title by my grandmother's maiden name. I simply asked – why not? The argument that we lived in a Communist country and should not use aristocratic titles was no longer threatening to us.

With the death of Antonina Freiin von Richthofen, the surname of von Richthofen in Poland ended.

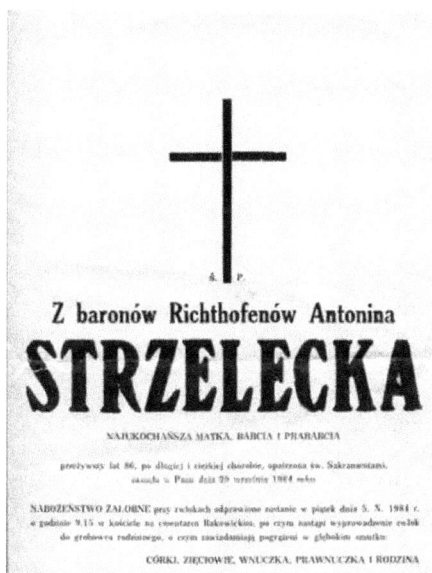

Left: The obituary of Antonina Freiin von Richthofen Strzelecka, beloved mother, grandmother, and great-grandmother. *Right:* Photo taken of Antonina a few years before her death for her ID in the People's Polish Republic.

The Wielogłowski family tomb in the Rakowice Cemetery in Kraków, Poland.[179]

---

[179] Ivona Tarko's archives.

Epilogue

My husband and I were driving from Frankfurt, Hesse, to Bamberg in Bavaria the last weekend of September 2014 as part of my first trip to Germany. During that drive I spotted a forest near the town of Hanau where the Grimm Brothers were born, and *Hansel and Gretel* immediately came to mind. In seconds, I was remembering my childhood and my warm pleasant feelings for Grandmother Antonina, the coming 30th anniversary of her death on September 29, and all the changes that have happened in my life, in Poland, and in Europe since she passed away.

Surprisingly, I had never visited Germany even though I grew up in neighboring Poland. I traveled from far away (the United States) for this initial visit in 2014. Germany was already united and Poland was free and democratic; and both countries were members of the European Union and NATO.

I regretted that my grandmother and mother did not live to see all these changes, but I knew that they would be excited to witness not only the political changes, but also the advancements in science and technology. Although they lived in an era without computers and the Internet, I could imagine how they would be happy to be connected to the world and to see on a computer screen the distant places they only talked about.

My research on Grandmother Antonina and her family prompted me to contact Dr. Karl-Friedrich Freiherr von Richthofen, the archivist of the von Richthofen family and an enthusiast of the family history, who shared his knowledge of our German ancestors with me. Karl-Friedrich's assistance was essential in my study of the Richthofen family's foundational generations. On the other hand, my work on the Polish line of von Richthofen brought to light the descendants of Wilhelm, forgotten or never known by the younger generations. The oldest of the von

Richthofen family trees was the fruit of Wilhelm's work; and the original handwritten and only printed copy of that tree were kept safe in Kraków by my grandmother.

One part of my first trip to Germany was to accomplish another first for me - attending the 28th von Richthofen family reunion on September 26, 2014 in the charming old town of Bamberg. I remember excitedly waiting in the reception hall of Welcome Hotel Residenzscholss to meet for the first time Karl-Friedrich Freiherr von Richthofen and his wife Sabine. The first member of the von Richthofen family I met that day was Andreas Freiherr von Richthofen, who organized the reunion. He is a resident of Bamberg and was the director of the von Richthofen family association board at that time. The family members soon started to arrive and introductions, greetings, and chats followed. Among my newly met relatives was Wolfgang Freiherr von Richthofen, who remembered the sister of Gertrude née Oertel Freifrau von Richthofen, Stanisław Freiherr von Richthofen's wife. Unfortunately, too much time had passed since Stanisław's death to expect to meet someone who could remember my great-grand-uncle.

I still have very vivid memories from Bamberg and the warmth and friendliness of Karl-Friedrich and Sabine von Richthofen and the many other members of the family who welcomed me, their newly discovered cousin, cordially. I sat among the von Richthofen family members and chatted about the past and present days, our ancestors, and our families. I will never forget the moment when Dieprand Freiherr von Richthofen approached me. His physical resemblance to my grandmother struck me at once and his heartfelt smile and hug made me truly feel like a part of the von Richthofen family.

In his speech at the family reunion, Dieprand said that we should be the masters of our memories. His words reassured me that we had the same mission: keep alive the memories of our ancestors and pass our stories to our children and grandchildren. Many of our mutual family members struggled with obstacles overcame tragedies, and adjusted to dramatic changes; and 70 years after World War II, there we were sitting together at the same table. After the Bamberg meeting, Karl-Friedrich helped me to locate the tomb of Stanisław Freiherr von Richthofen, my great-grand-uncle. I was longing to light a candle on Stanisław's grave, and I hoped to do it during the next family reunion in Berlin in 2016.

My long-awaited visit to the grave of my Great Grand Uncle Stanisław Freiherr von Richthofen at the Evangelischer Friedhof Friedrichshagen Cemetery in Berlin finally happened in September 2016. It was a beautiful, warm, and sunny day in Berlin and the cemetery looked like a park with its tall majestic trees, evergreen shrubs, and fresh flowers. Dieprand Freiherr von Richthofen, who was there with me, translated the German inscription on Stanisław's tomb: "At evening time there shall be light," which was taken from Zechariah 14:7: "And there shall be a unique day, which is known to the Lord, neither day nor night, but at evening time there shall be light."

After placing flowers on Stanisław's tomb and lighting a candle, I said a prayer that sprang from my long emotional discovery of his life story. I assured him that he would not be forgotten by his family even though I live so far away from his final resting place. This visit brought closure to me and was even more inspiring than I imagined it would be!

Dieprand and I sat on the bench by the grave for a while and talked about life and death, and of course Stanisław. Dieprand suggested we take a few minutes for silent meditation or prayer before we leave. As I prayed, I focused on the lampion on Stanisław's grave, which I had brought as a gift to Stanisław from my home; and in the stillness, I heard the faint vibration of warm air produced by the small flame above the tomb. Dieprand broke the silence by pointing to a butterfly which had landed on the path beside Stanisław's tomb and asked, "Do you know that a butterfly is a symbol of the soul in Christianity? "I tried to absorb this moment and knew it would be etched in my mind forever. I remember then hearing children's laughter coming from a distance and knew that life and miracles were happening all around us. A fascinating coincidence struck me that made this visit even more special. The day of my visit at Stanisław's grave – September 19 - was his birthday!

I wrote this book to preserve the memory of one Polish line of the German von Richthofen family and to keep alive the story of Grandmother Antonina, Great Grand Uncle Stanisław, Great Grandfather Bolesław, and his parents and grandparents. I deeply believe my family was a part of European society through many centuries; and families like mine who lived in different countries at times of war and peace shaped history and modern Europe. Writing this story was an emotional journey to the past for me, during which I discovered that the years that separated me from my ancestors is not an obstacle to understanding their decisions and feeling their love, joy, longing, sadness, and anxiety. Time cannot destroy this connection if the knowledge of them is preserved.

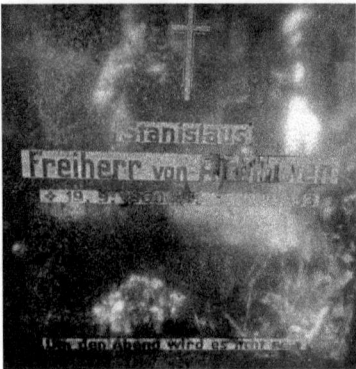

Dieprand Freiherr von Richthofen and I by the grave of my Great Grand Uncle Stanisław (Stanislaus Wilhelm Freiherr von Richthofen) at the Evangelischer Friedhof Friedrichshagen Cemetery in Berlin on September 19, 2016.

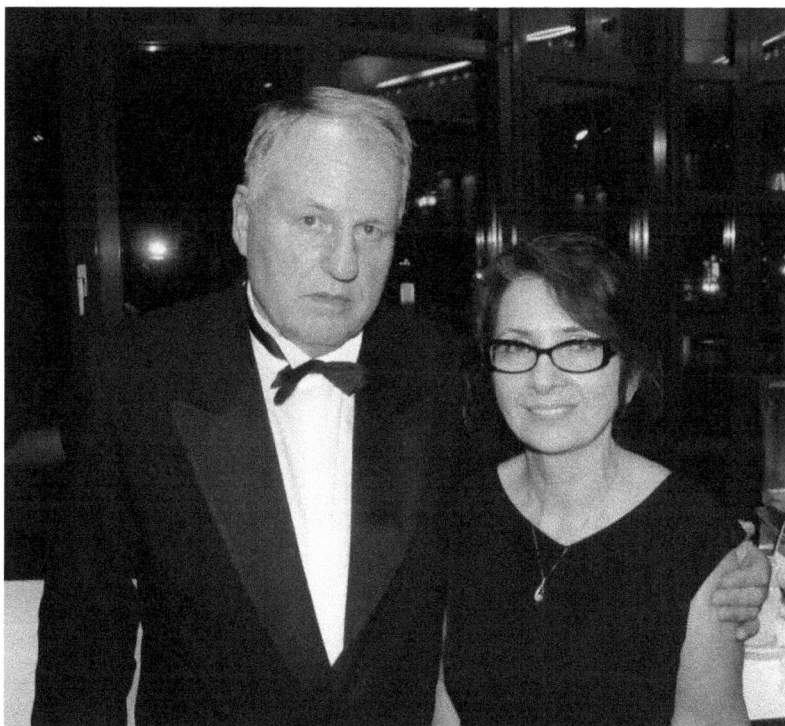

Karl-Friedrich Freiherr von Richthofen and I at the von Richthofen family reunion in Bamberg, on September 27, 2014.[180]

---

[180] Ivona Tarko's archives.

Index of Names